Pat & Carina —
this man has been
an inspiration to me.

LUKA JANTJIE

RESISTANCE HERO OF
THE SOUTH AFRICAN
FRONTIER

Kevin Shillington
16/12/u

LUKA JANTJIE

RESISTANCE HERO OF THE SOUTH AFRICAN FRONTIER

KEVIN SHILLINGTON

palgrave
macmillan

WITS UNIVERSITY PRESS

ALDRIDGE
PRESS

First published in United Kingdom by **Aldridge Press** in 2011
24 Thorney Hedge Road, London W4 5SD, United Kingdom
www.aldridgepress.co.uk enquiries@aldridgepress.co.uk

in association with

Wits University Press
University of the Witwatersrand, 1 Jan Smuts Avenue,
Johannesburg 2001, South Africa
www.witspress.co.za

Palgrave Macmillan
175 Fifth Avenue, New York, NY 10010, USA
www.palgrave.com

ISBN–13: 978–0–9520651–1–1: Aldridge Press paper edition, UK
ISBN–13: 978–0–9520651–2–8: Aldridge Press cased edition, UK
ISBN–13: 978–1–86814–549–2: Wits University Press paper edition, South Africa
ISBN–13: 978–0–230–33853–1: Palgrave Macmillan cased edition, USA
ISBN–13: 978–0–9520651–3–5: ebook edition when available, UK

For more information about Luka's story visit: www.aldridgepress.co.uk

A CIP catalogue record for this book is available from the British Library.

Prepared for publication by Aldridge Press
Design: John Aldridge
Cover design: Kevin Ancient
Maps: Kevin Shillington, Doug Hewitt and John Aldridge
Typeset in Giovanni 10/14pt

Distributed in UK by Gazelle Book Services
sales@gazellebooks.co.uk www.gazellebooks.co.uk

Printed and bound in China by WKT

DEDICATION

In memory of
Luka Jantjie Mothibi Molehabangwe

This book is dedicated
to his direct descendant
Kgosienewang II Jantjie and his family
and all the descendants of those Batlhaping and
Batlharo who fought alongside Luka
in the Langeberg in 1897.

REVIEWS OF 'LUKA' BEFORE PUBLICATION:
"Kevin Shillington … writes of his being long 'haunted' by the story of Luka's courageous defiance of the colonial authorities in a desperate and ultimately unsuccessful attempt to ward off land-grabbing colonists.

What is unique about Shillington's study is his ability to understand the impact of the discovery of diamonds through the eyes of a leader whose people were in the eye of the storm."

"…a pleasure to read… I am glad that this story will join the too-short list of biographies of nineteenth century Africans."

"History that smacks you between the eyes, revealing the subtleties and complexities of accommodation and resistance to colonialism."

PICTURE ACKNOWLEDGMENTS: The author and publishers wish to scknowledge, with thanks, the following photographic and illustration sources.
Within the text: Africana Library, Kimberley: 67, 145bcd, 151, 272; Africana, Johannesburg: 10, 18, 20; Aldridge Press collection: xi, 15, 17, 25, 31, 32, 35, 38, 43, 44, 45, 49, 54, 62, 64, 65, 66, 85, 86, 87, 90, 113, 122, 141, 156, 171, 182, 186, 188, 211, 213, 214, 215, 217 Woon, 219, 220b, 225, 227ac, 228 Dalgety, 236, 249, 250ab, 252a, 253, 254, 255, 266b, 288, 289; Author's collection: 3, 8 (Burchell, 1824), 4, 9, 10, 23, 24, 27, 68, 69, 109abc, 200, 206b, 216, 238; Botswana National Archive (Willoughby collection): 74, 116, 123, 174, 175, 178, 187; British Library: 145 (top, bottom 3), 177, 194, 209, 284b (The Graphic); Cullen Library, Johannesburg (Cape Times): 207b, 212, 220 insets, 222, 224, 227b, 223b, 243, 266a, 267, 268, 270, 274ab, 281, 282, 283ab, 284a; David Fayle/Siobhan Dawson: 257; Shula Marks: 12; McGregor Museum, Kimberley: 17, 25, 27, 41, 53, 56, 60, 71, 73, 75, 88, 95, 104, 112, 113, 114, 125, 127, 131, 135, 137, 138, 143, 144, 168, 170, 171, 176, 181, 185, 186, 195, 198, 199, 201abc, 202, 203, 205abc, 206a, 207ac, 220ac, 223, 237, 227def, 232-3 panorama (Fiona Barbour), 223a, 235, 240, 241, 247, 252b, 257, 258, 259ab, 260abcd, 261ab, 265, 269, 275ab, 276, 277; National Archives (Kew, UK): 72; Neil Parsons: 95; South African Public Library, Cape Town: iii; UCT Archive: 248. *The colour plate section (picture nos.):* Aldridge Press collection: 1, 2, 6, 7, 8, 9, 10ab, 11, 12, 13, 14, 15, 16, 17, 18, 20, 21, 22, 23, 24, 25, 27, 29, 30abcdef, 35; Author's collection: 26, 28; Cullen Library, Johannesberg (Cape Times): 19; The Jantjie family: 31, 32, 33, 34; McGregor Museum, Kimberley: 3; Judy Seidman: 5; South African Public Library, Cape Town: 4. *Cover illustrations:* South African Public Library, Cape Town: a; McGregor Museum, Kimberley: b.

The publishers have made every reasonable effort to trace the copyright holders, but if they have inadvertently overlooked or misclassified any, they will be pleased to make the necessary arrangements at the first opportunity.

CONTENTS

LIST OF MAPS AND FIGURES

NB *The 16-page colour plate section is between pages 146 and 147.*

NOTES ON TERMINOLOGY

Jantjie/Jantje (pronounced 'Yanki') For the spelling of Luka's surname (his father's name), I have used the modern spelling – 'Jantjie' – as used by his family today rather than the contemporary nineteenth-century spelling – 'Jantje'. Luka himself used the spelling 'Yañki'.

African linguistic prefixes When referring to the names of African peoples, academic discourse in English generally uses only the stem word – 'Tswana' or 'Tlhaping' – dropping the prefix used in African languages. In this book I prefer to retain the prefixes that Africans themselves use when speaking English in this part of southern Africa: thus 'Batswana' for the general group of people, 'Setswana' for their language, and 'Batlhaping' (singular: 'Motlhaping') for this particular group of Batswana – Luka Jantjie's people. Similarly, I use the modern spelling 'Basotho', except in quotations when the contemporary spelling 'Basuto' is used. The Xhosa and the Zulu, however, are so well known without their 'Ama-' prefix that I use the stem only, for the few occasions when they are mentioned.

Bechuana This was the contemporary spelling for 'Batswana', used by missionaries and other Europeans in the nineteenth and early twentieth centuries, hence the colonial term 'Bechuanaland'. British Bechuanaland was the name of the crown colony that the British established south of the Molopo River from 1885 until its absorption in 1895 into the Cape Colony, and thence into the modern Republic of South Africa. North of the Molopo River, the country that is today the Republic of Botswana was known by the British during the colonial period (1885–1966) as the 'Bechuanaland Protectorate'.

Dutch/Afrikaans Following the Dutch East India Company's establishment of a settlement at Cape Town in the seventeenth century, the early European colonists of South Africa came mostly from the Netherlands, but also from northern Germany and France. The language they spoke was a dialect of Dutch, modified by loan-words from African and other sources. It was not recognised as the distinct language of 'Afrikaans', and its speakers 'Afrikaners', until towards the end of the nineteenth century. Official nineteenth-century documents of the Boer republics were written in Dutch, usually by recent immigrants from Europe. It was not until 1925 that Afrikaans replaced Dutch as one of South Africa's two official languages, alongside English. In this book, concerned as it is with the nineteenth century, I refer to the language as Dutch/Afrikaans.

The **Khoesan**-speaking peoples (also spelt 'Khoisan') – of whom the Korana were a branch – were the indigenous population of the south-western region of South Africa until their displacement or absorption by European colonists and other African societies between the seventeenth and nineteenth centuries.

GLOSSARY

boer	literally 'farmer': rural European, Dutch/Afrikaans-speaking colonist (Dutch/Afrikaans)
bogadi	dowry or bridewealth (Setswana)
bogwera	male initiation ceremony (Setswana)
dikgosi	plural of *kgosi* (Setswana), see below
drift	river-ford, river crossing
kgosi	king or chief (Setswana)
kgotla	king's court or central meeting place (Setswana)
kloof	ravine or steep-sided valley (Dutch/Afrikaans)
kopje	small steep hill (Dutch/Afrikaans) – sometimes shortened to 'kop'
laager	a circle of wagons formed for defence (Dutch/Afrikaans)
lechoku	red ochre clay used as a cosmetic, smeared on the skin to protect it from heat and parasites (Setswana)
lekgowa	European, a white person (singular) (Setswana)
letsholo	large, centrally-organised, annual winter hunt (Setswana)
maburu	boers, as distinct from other white people (Setswana)
mafisa	a system of lending cattle to dependants (Setswana)
makgowa	Europeans, white people (plural), as distinct from *maburu* (boers) (Setswana)
mephato	age-regiments, formed after initiation (singular: *mophato*) (Setswana)
merafe	plural of *morafe* (Setswana), see below
Mokaapa	The Cape (Setswana)
morafe	state or kingdom, used for both a geographical area and/or the people who recognise the authority of a single *kgosi* (Setswana)
pitso	a general gathering of the people, usually called by the *kgosi* (Setswana)
schanze(s)	natural stone defences running along steep mountain contour lines (Dutch/Afrikaans)
sibilo	metallic ore, ground to a powder, mixed with *lechoku* clay and used as a cosmetic, most usually smeared onto close-cropped hair on the top of one's head (Setswana)
veld	field or open country, usually grassland (Dutch/Afrikaans)

Preface

In the darkness of the early hours of Friday 30 July 1897, a solitary man in his early sixties made his way down a steep-sided valley in the Langeberg – a mountain range in the remote western dry-lands of South Africa's Northern Cape Province. He wore a greatcoat to ward off the bitter cold of winter, for the temperature that night dropped to below freezing point. But no thick outer garment could disguise the ragged condition of the man's inner clothing, his dusty and unkempt hair or his emaciated body. Despite the poverty of his outward appearance, however, the man carried a Winchester repeating rifle, the most up-to-date weapon of the day.

The man's name was Luka Jantjie. He was a *kgosi*, a leader of his people, and he normally took great care with his appearance. His present unkempt condition was the result of the five months of siege that he and his people had suffered, trapped in the confines of these mountains. And with every breath that they inhaled, their nostrils were assailed by the sickening stench of rotting carcasses – cattle that had been felled by the deadly plague of rinder-pest. The disease had been brought to the Langeberg three months previously by the transport oxen of the besieging colonial army; and the ground was too hard to bury the carcasses. The cattle lay where they had died, depriving the people of food, and polluting the few natural springs of fresh water that normally enabled survival in the valleys of the Langeberg.

The upper reaches of this particular valley were crowded with people, possibly as many as two thousand – mostly women and children and elderly or infirm men. They were refugees from a colonial onslaught that had destroyed their crops and villages and driven them to this refuge, to seek the protection of their *kgosi*. Despite the numbers seeking his protection, by the end of July 1897 Luka Jantjie could command no more than five hundred men who were fit enough to defend the valley. Some had rifles, but most were armed with muzzle-loading hunting guns. A few were left to guard the upper valley, but most had been deployed a couple of kilometres away upon a rocky promontory that guarded the entrance to the valley; and that was where Luka Jantjie was now going, to rejoin his men in their forward defensive positions for he expected an attack at first light.

He walked slowly down the valley for the ground beneath his feet was rocky and uneven and the soles of his shoes were worn thin. And he walked with a heavy heart for he had just taken leave of his wife and family whom he had left at the head of the valley in the care of his eldest son.

He made his way through the protective barricade of ox-wagons, rock-reinforced trenches and thorn scrub that had been thrown across the upper reaches of the valley and then he carried on down the broadening valley to meet his destiny. He could not know if he would ever see his family again for he doubted that his weakened people could hold off another colonial assault for long; and he had vowed that he would seek an honourable death in battle rather than suffer the indignities of surrender. But he would never have guessed the true horrors that awaited him.

Who exactly was Luka Jantjie? We know that he was a *kgosi* of the Phuduhutŝwana branch of the Batlhaping, the southernmost of the Setswana-speaking peoples of southern Africa, the Batswana.

But how had it come to this, that he and his people should be holed up in the remote fastness of the northern Langeberg, standing alone against certain attack by a vastly superior colonial force that was heavily armed with repeating rifles, machine guns and artillery?

These are some of the questions that this book sets out to answer. In doing so it follows the story of Luka Jantjie, from the putative year of his birth in

1835 to his final showdown with colonialism in 1897. His lifespan covers that critical period in South African history when the various forces of colonial rule expanded from the British-ruled Cape Colony to invade and subdue the whole of the African-ruled interior that is today the modern Republic of South Africa.

Luka Jantjie was not a natural hero, who flaunted heroic deeds or indulged in heroic rhetoric. Rather he had heroism thrust upon him. In his middle years, at a time when he was assuming much of the political authority of his ageing father, Luka found himself unwittingly at the interface between pre-colonial African independence and a new level of aggressive colonialism that was sparked off by the discovery of diamonds on the borders of his people's territory.

Present at the start of that seismic event – the birth of South Africa's mineral revolution – Luka Jantjie was the first independent African political authority to be faced with the consequences of the diamond discoveries.

Thus at the heart of this story is Luka's confrontation with colonialism: how he struggled to maintain his own authority and to safeguard his people's rights to their ancestral lands and to their personal freedom and dignity.

Throughout his life Luka had not been opposed to change. The son of a devout Christian convert, he had been brought up as a literate Christian and, as far as he was able, he sought to follow the Christian missionaries' message of peace and the avoidance of war.

With every passing decade from 1870, however, colonial encroachment was ratcheted up. Luka did his best to avoid open conflict – not always successfully – and to live peaceably within the ever-expanding colonial state. The colonists, however, were determined to force his people into the role of second-class citizens in the land of their birth. On this point Luka would not compromise. There was a line in the sand beyond which he would not be pushed; and that line was drawn at the Langeberg in 1897.

I first came across the name of Luka Jantjie in the late 1970s when researching the history of the southern Batswana during the period of their colonisation in the late nineteenth century.[1] As I researched the colonial record, the name Luka kept cropping up, invariably linked with some derogatory epithet: 'the greatest living scoundrel', because he flogged a white man for murdering his servant; 'a mischievous and cunning fellow', because his actions threatened

[1] Kevin Shillington, *The Colonisation of the Southern Tswana, 1870–1900* (1985).

to undermine British plans to seize his people's land; and 'a wild fellow who hates the English', because he exposed British legal hypocrisy. My interest was immediately aroused. In my mind the very adjectives used referred to a potentially heroic figure. Here was somebody who challenged the aggression of colonialism, a man who refused to accept the colonists' idea of his proper subservient place in their colonial state.

I was determined to find out more, both about the man himself and why he was so little celebrated in the annals of southern African history, so whenever I came across a mention of his name in some dusty archive, I made a note of it and slipped it into a large brown envelope marked 'LUKA'. And ever since I finished my general history of the region in the early 1980s, I have kept my envelope of Luka references as an 'open file', to be added to whenever possible. Thus for more than two decades I have in effect been haunted by Luka Jantjie's story. And the more I have found out about him, the more I have been determined to rescue his life from undeserved obscurity and to bring his remarkable story to a wider audience.

It has been a long and at times emotional journey, with numerous visits to the region: to the place of his birth and early life, and to many of the significant places of his adult life. I have climbed the steep and rugged slopes of the Langeberg and looked down into that steep-sided valley in which he built his final home. And, most movingly, one moonless night in early January, I slept under the stars of an unpolluted sky in the valley of his death, in the shadow of the Langeberg.

KEVIN SHILLINGTON
London and Dorset, England
May 2011

CHAPTER ONE

Prologue

The year 1835, the probable year of Luka Jantjie's birth, dawned hot and dry on the north bank of the lower Vaal River. The summer rains had so far failed to arrive, as had happened so often in the past decade and it was a worrying time for Luka's grandfather, *Kgosi* Mothibi of the main, Phuduhutŝwana, branch of the Batlhaping.[1] There had been no early rain to soften the sun-baked soil, so no sorghum had been sown in November or December and no pumpkins or beans had been planted. In this dry savannah land that is today the Northern Cape Province of South Africa, however, the Batlhaping were well-used to a short and unreliable summer rainy season and they placed little dependence upon cultivated crops. Cattle were the mainstay of their

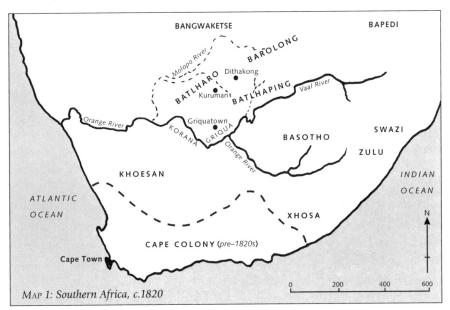

MAP 1: *Southern Africa, c.1820*

---

[1] The Batlhaping are a branch of the Batswana, the Setswana-speaking peoples of southern Africa. The modern Republic of Botswana is home to only about a third of the Setswana-speaking peoples. The rest live in what is now South Africa. In the nineteenth century the southern Batswana, of whom Luka's Batlhaping were the southernmost, lived south of the modern Botswana border, between the Molopo River and the Vaal.

livelihood, though even the cattle were losing their normal good condition as the tough natural grassland of the region became parched and worn.[2] But there was far more to concern Mothibi than the damaging effects of drought.

Mothibi's family proudly traced its ancestry to Phuduhutŝwe who was believed to have founded the *morafe* (state or kingdom) of the Batlhaping sometime in the seventeenth century. According to Batlhaping oral tradition, Mothibi was the ninth successive *kgosi* in direct line of descent from Phuduhutŝwe.[3] Now, from his small hilltop village of Mosesberg near the north bank of the Vaal in the mid-1830s, it is likely that Mothibi looked back with some regret to the early years of his reign when as *kgosi* of the Batlhaping he ruled over a powerful and united *morafe*.

In those days the Batlhaping had been famous for their huge herds of cattle that were mostly kept at distant cattle-posts – grazing lands with nearby springs, wells or streams. The cattle were tended by herdsmen and young boys while the bulk of the population lived in a large central town that was the capital of the Batlhaping. At the heart of that town was the royal ward of *Kgosi* Mothibi; and in the centre of the royal ward was the *kgotla*, the public meeting place where Mothibi held court. Here, judicial cases were heard and public affairs were discussed. The individual wards that made up the capital consisted of groups of related families who recognised a male head of household as their local headman, and he represented their interests at the meetings of the *kgotla*. The system allowed for a level of democratic accountability; and as the saying went: 'The *kgosi* is only *kgosi* through the will of his people'.

Mothibi certainly had come down in the world and he must have wondered in 1835 how widely he was still recognised as *kgosi*. Gone was the huge central town and the distant cattle-posts. Mothibi now lived in what was in effect little more than the royal ward, consisting of some two hundred traditional circular houses packed together on a hilltop.

When at the age of about forty in April 1812 *Kgosi* Mothibi had inherited the leadership of the Batlhaping from his father Molehabangwe, his capital had been at Dithakong on the northern edge of the Ghaap plateau. That had been a town of up to 10,000 people – an enormous size for a pre-industrial society, almost on a par with Cape Town at the time (*see opposite*, Burchell's painting of it in 1812). Although for environmental reasons the Batlhaping moved their capital to different sites about once every ten years, they kept

---

[2] For environmental conditions in the region in January 1835: P R Kirby, *The Diary of Andrew Smith, 1834–36* (Van Riebeeck Society edition, 1939), Vol. I, pp220–247.
[3] P-L Breutz, *The Tribes of Kuruman and Postmasburg* (1963)

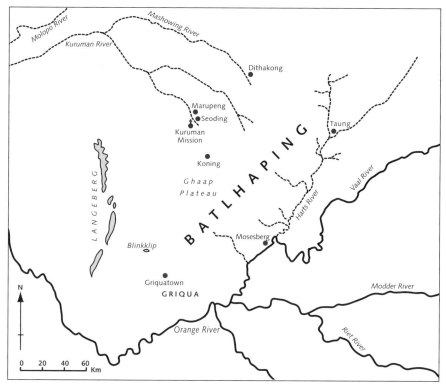

MAP 2: *Batlhaping country, 1820–1835. nb dotted lines indicate seasonal rivers.*

coming back to Dithakong as it was an historic centre of some significance. Its name, 'place of stone walls' in Setswana, referred to the ancient dry-stone walls that covered a ridge overlooking the town. They were remnants of older, pre-Batlhaping animal enclosures, possibly fifteenth century, and for this reason the site seems to have had special spiritual meaning to the cattle-owning Batlhaping.

From this historic town the Batlhaping had dominated the plateau region north of the Vaal River. And yet, within two decades of his accession, Mothibi's *morafe* had been split asunder and his people scattered across the region as several smaller, separate *merafe*.[4] Mothibi must have dwelled on how this had

---

[4] *Merafe*: 'states' or 'kingdoms' (plural form of *morafe*).

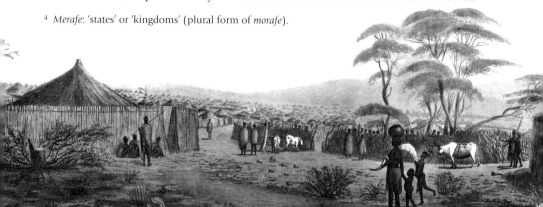

come to pass. The local autonomy of the wards and the level of democratic freedom implicit in the ward and *kgotla* system may have made the breakup possible. But he was not an unpopular ruler, nor was he dictatorial; he ruled through the consensus of his people. If indeed, from his hilltop refuge in the mid-1830s Mothibi did look back over the previous two decades, he is likely to have blamed the disintegration of the great united *morafe* on external factors, and in particular, the intrusion of newcomers from the south.

Modern photo showing the stone-walled enclosures at Dithakong on the northern edge of the Ghaap plateau, where Kgosi Molehabangwe had his capital of up to ten thousand people.

Ultimately, the trouble emanated from *Mokaapa* ('the Cape'), that colony of *makgowa* (white people) who lived far to the south. The Batlhaping had known about *Mokaapa* for several generations, having first learned about it from the Korana. These were a group of Khoesan[5] refugees who had settled in the valley of the lower Orange River, below its confluence with the Vaal, early in the eighteenth century. The Korana would have brought with them stories of the violence of firearms and slavery that characterised the colony founded by the Dutch East India Company in the mid-seventeenth century. The main trouble for the Khoesan people was that the European settlers of the colony, known as Boers (from the Dutch for 'farmer'), regarded the

---

[5] The Khoesan (also spelt Khoisan)-speaking peoples were the indigenous population of the southwestern part of southern Africa. They were the people whom the European settlers of the Dutch East India Company found in residence when they first settled the Cape in the seventeenth century. The white settlers referred to the Khoesan by the derogatory terms 'Hottentots' and 'Bushmen'.

4

indefinite hinterland as theirs for the taking; and in the dry interior, that was suitable only for hunting and low-density herding, they plundered the sparsely settled indigenous Khoesan population, killing or enslaving them or driving them to seek refuge beyond the constantly shifting boundary of the colony.

The Korana of the lower Orange had brought with them some of the cultural trappings of the colony that they had left behind, including some local Dutch names and words, a few items of European-style clothing and a small number of muzzle-loading guns. The Korana were highly regarded by the Batlhaping and there developed a strong tradition of Phuduhutŝwana royals marrying Korana women. Mothibi's mother was Korana, as was one of Mothibi's own wives, Kegogile, who was to become the grandmother of Luka Jantjie.

A particular group of outcasts from *Mokaapa*, about whom the Batlhaping were more ambivalent, were the Griqua. Known in the colony as 'Basters', they were people of mixed-race origin, the product of liaisons between white male colonists and imported slave or Khoesan women. They spoke the local dialect of Dutch that was in due course to become Afrikaans and they wore European-style clothing. To all outward appearances they were dark-skinned versions of the colonists themselves. Rejected on racial grounds by colonial society, they were hunting well north of the Orange River by the 1790s; and in 1807 Mothibi's father, *Kgosi* Molehabangwe, had allowed a group of Griqua families to establish a base at a spring that they called Klaarwater, some fifty kilometres north of the Orange River.

The Batlhaping referred to the Griqua as *Masetedi*, a name thought to derive from *Baster*.[6] Molehabangwe probably regarded them as a useful trading connection with the colony. It soon became clear to the Batlhaping, however, that with the advantage of horses, guns and wagons, this particular group of newcomers were serious hunting rivals and some of them were dangerous cattle-raiders. These developments had occurred in the final years of Molehabangwe's long reign and although he paid host to white people from the Cape Colony on two occasions[7], he did not see the need to press them for guns.

Molehabangwe's son and successor Mothibi, on the other hand, regarded the acquisition of guns as a high priority, not merely to match the Griqua

---

[6] *Baster* (Bastura) = *Basetedi* / *Masetedi*; the prefix *Ma-* used for outsiders, *Ba-* for insiders.

[7] In 1801, the Truter and Somerville expedition, sent officially by the Cape government to buy cattle from the Batlhaping (see J Barrow, *A Voyage to Cochin China*, 1806); and 1805, the visit of the German adventurer, W H C Lichtenstein (*Travels in Southern Africa*, 1814).

in the hunting field, but also for personal defence. For a number of years Mothibi's Batlhaping had been experiencing the ravages of raiders from the south: outcasts from the Cape Colony who had been settling in the valley of the Orange and in the mountains to the north and south. Their leaders included individuals of European and mixed-race origin, often fugitives from colonial justice, who were attracted by the profits to be gained from raiding north of the Orange River. They gathered around themselves gangs of Khoesan, Korana and Griqua and lived a life of banditry. They sought not only cattle, ivory and animal skins, but also, ominously, children for sale into slavery in the Cape. Children were preferred because, isolated on remote farms in the colony, they could more readily be cowed through violence into acceptance of their fate.

Within weeks of his accession as *kgosi* in April 1812, Mothibi had heard that a single *lekgowa* (European), with attending Khoesan servants, was approaching from *Mokaapa* and intending to visit the new *kgosi* of the Batlhaping at Dithakong. It was too good an opportunity to miss. The Griqua were unwilling to sell them guns, but Mothibi was confident that from this man he would get a gun.

The visitor from the Cape Colony, under British control since 1806, was a thirty-two-year-old English botanist named William Burchell. He had arrived in Cape Town in December 1810 after several years as a government naturalist on the Atlantic island of St Helena. Determined to follow the route of the previous two expeditions to the Batlhaping, Burchell had an ox-wagon specially built and fitted out for the journey. It was to become his home for the next four years. He bought a second wagon, hired some Khoesan servants and accompanied two missionaries as far as the Griqua village of Klaarwater, which they reached in September 1811. Burchell then spent many months on a long diversionary trek, collecting more Khoesan servants and hunters, before setting off from Klaarwater for the Batlhaping capital in June 1812. Accompanied by a Motlhaping trader named Muchunka, who agreed to act as the Englishman's guide and interpreter, Burchell finally reached Dithakong on 13 July 1812.[8]

Burchell was a short, lightly built and quietly spoken man who appears to have created an immediately favourable impression among the Batlhaping by his politeness and the respect that he showed to his hosts. Burchell himself found Mothibi a mild-mannered man, not given to boasting, loud talk or laughter like his brother, Moleme. There were two other brothers besides:

[8] For Burchell's visit to Dithakong, see *Travels*, Schapera edition (1953), II, pp362–84.

Molale, and the youngest, Mahura, whom Burchell estimated to be aged about twenty and whom he described as 'remarkably handsome' and of 'fine proportions'. Burchell sketched a portrait of Mahura (*see p10*), whose future daughter is believed to have become the wife of Mothibi's son Jantjie, and thus the mother of Luka Jantjie.

After the first public meeting with Burchell in the *kgotla*, *Kgosi* Mothibi and his older brothers climbed into their visitor's wagon and got straight down to business. They needed a gun, and if Burchell was truly their friend as he claimed, then he would give them one. Burchell was somewhat taken aback by the abruptness of the demand, but Mothibi pressed his case. The bandit, Jager Afrikaner, and his brothers had been attacking his people and supplying guns to other bandits in the region. The Batlhaping would not feel safe until they too had acquired guns. Burchell had no intention of supplying them with guns, even a single one, arguing privately in his journal that it might in future be used against some other white man like himself. The argument that he used with Mothibi, however, was that he only had enough guns to supply each of his own Khoesan servants and hunters and that it would be too dangerous for any of them to travel through the country unarmed. It was not an argument that impressed Mothibi; even Burchell admitted in his journal that it was a pretty feeble excuse and one that implied that he distrusted his hosts. It also made Mothibi's own point: guns were needed for personal security.

Mothibi raised the issue of the gun again the next day. This time Burchell argued that the Batlhaping had no use for a gun because they had no gunpowder or shot. That was easily resolved, Mothibi replied: Burchell who was their professed friend would give them powder and shot and would teach them how to use the gun. It must have been clear to Mothibi that Burchell was casting around for any excuse and really he had no sound argument for his refusal to sell them a gun. The Batlhaping *kgosi* could see that with persistent pressure he could wear down this *lekgowa*'s resistance.

On the third day Burchell thought he had devised a suitable stratagem to defuse the tension. When, as expected, Mothibi asked again for a gun, Burchell agreed in principle to sell him one, but said that he would only hand it over after he had arrived safely back in Klaarwater. Mothibi parted from this meeting well satisfied: the *lekgowa* had agreed in principle to the sale of a gun. It only remained to settle the timing and manner of the handover. For the moment he reassured Burchell that when the time came he would send his brothers Moleme and Molale to collect the gun from Klaarwater as proposed.

The next day Mothibi called Burchell into the *kgotla* and in front of a large public gathering he handed over two oxen, in payment for a gun. Burchell had been hoping to avoid such a firm commitment to a deal and he declined the offer. Mothibi added two huge elephant tusks, but Burchell protested that he had no use for ivory. So Mothibi replaced them with two more oxen, remarking that he knew that this was more than the Klaarwater Griqua paid for guns from the Colony. The meeting broke up without agreement, but Burchell knew that he was on the road to defeat. His Khoesan servants were getting nervous and pressed him to agree to any price; otherwise, they feared, they might not get out of Dithakong alive.

Burchell's painting shows the kind of muzzle-loading gun Mothibi acquired.

The following morning the offer was increased to six oxen and Burchell felt that he could do nothing but agree, still assuming that the weapon would be handed over after his return to Klaarwater. Mothibi then asked to see a demonstration of the gun's capability. Burchell led them to the edge of the town and got some of his Khoesan hunters to discharge their weapons. One of the weapons had not been properly loaded and it failed to fire. This gave Mothibi his opportunity. Clearly not all the guns functioned properly and he thus reasonably insisted that his brother Molale be allowed to fire one. A good gun that belonged to one of the Khoesan hunters was duly loaded and handed over to Molale who successfully discharged it. No sooner had this been done than Mothibi told his brother to take the gun home. So far as he was concerned, the deal had been done: Burchell had been outwitted, and the Batlhaping had their first gun.

Within months of William Burchell's departure in August 1812 and before the Batlhaping had managed to acquire any more firearms, their relations with the Griqua were complicated by the arrival at Klaarwater of Christian missionaries from the London Missionary Society (LMS).

In 1813 Revd John Campbell, on special mission from London, persuaded the 'Basters' to change their name to the more indigenous-sounding *Griqua*[9] and thus Klaarwater became 'Griquatown'. Campbell devised a written Griqua constitution which he said would gain them official recognition by the Cape government as an independent state, a recognition that was in fact granted within a decade. This greatly transformed the political security of the Griqua, who had hitherto only been in the region by the kind permission of the Batlhaping *kgosi*. The LMS too now had a secure base from which to extend their mission activities northwards to the Batlhaping and beyond.

In 1817 Mothibi agreed to allow two LMS missionaries from the Griquatown mission to settle at the Batlhaping capital.[10] At the time Mothibi was in the process of moving his capital sixty kilometres southwest to Marupeng in the Kuruman valley, and he probably felt his security would be strengthened if he had his own resident white people. They could then provide a direct trading link with the Cape Colony, which he knew was the ultimate source of guns. One of the two men, the lay missionary James Read, proved only too willing to trade guns in exchange for ivory and other hunting produce, including the expertly sewn fur karosses for which the Batlhaping were widely renowned. The LMS, however, disapproved of such blatant profiteering and in 1820 Read was replaced by the more evangelistic Revd Robert Moffat (*below right*) and his wife, Mary.

In due course the Moffats were to exert a strong influence upon certain of the Batlhaping, although there remained some within Mothibi's family who distrusted the missionaries from the start. In particular they suspected that the Moffats were agents of the Griqua. Until he learned Setswana, the language of the Batlhaping, Robert Moffat was dependent upon Griqua assistants who, in their poor Setswana, acted as interpreters. Furthermore, whenever the Batlhaping capital was threatened by raiders, the Moffats and their colleagues, the Hamiltons, retired to the protection of Griquatown.

[9] The name was derived from some of their Khoesan ancestors from the Cha-guriqua clan.

[10] The LMS missionaries referred to Dithakong by its singular form, *lethako*, which they mispronounced and spelt *Lattakoo*. When the Batlhaping capital moved to the new site of Marupeng on the Kuruman River, they referred to it as *New Lattakoo*.

The LMS mission house in Griquatown, now the Mary Moffat Museum.

It took Moffat seven years to master Setswana, during which time he failed to make a single convert to Christianity. But he did make a number of significant enemies among some of the leading Batlhaping who resented his regular criticisms and denigration of their customs. For instance, in the drought-stricken month of December 1822 Moffat had made a dramatic intervention in the *kgotla* when he challenged the consensus of the meeting that a failed Mongwaketse[11] rainmaker should be put to death. Mothibi's younger brother, probably Mahura, shook a spear in Moffat's face and threatened him with death for daring to defy the *kgotla*. The white missionary, he declared, had brought nothing but drought to the Batlhaping. Moffat replied that he would rather die than face expulsion from the country, pleading only that the women and children of the mission be spared. The courage and passion with which he spoke, albeit in very imperfect Setswana, greatly impressed *Kgosi* Mothibi and probably saved the missionary's life and that of his whole Christian mission. The rainmaker was banished, the missionaries were spared and a gentle sprinkling of *pula* ('rain') relieved the tension of the moment.

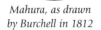

Mahura, as drawn by Burchell in 1812

Subsequently, the missionaries' reputation was enhanced by Moffat's contribution to the battle of Dithakong in 1823. In June of that year a group of many thousands of Basotho,[12] displaced by

---

[11] The Bangwaketse (singular, Mongwaketse) were a more northerly Batswana people with whom the Batlhaping regularly traded. The capital of their *morafe* was at Kanye – now in Botswana.

[12] Sesotho-speaking peoples who in the early nineteenth century generally lived southeast of the

10

warfare south of the Vaal, had converged on the former Batlhaping capital of Dithakong. Part-army, part-civilian refugees in search of food, they were attracted to the region by news of the Batlhaping's huge herds of cattle.[13] Mothibi had immediately ordered his cattle to be driven to the relative safety of the Langeberg mountain range, far to the west. As the Batlhaping prepared to abandon Marupeng and follow their cattle westwards, Moffat hastened to Griquatown where he persuaded the Griqua to come to the aid of the Batlhaping.

Thus on Thursday 26 June 1823 fewer than two hundred Griqua horsemen armed with guns faced the massed ranks of the Basotho armed with spears and cowhide shields. The Batlhaping age-regiments, similarly armed with spears and shields, were held in reserve as the Griqua launched their attack. A group of Griqua rode up to just short of spear-throwing range, fired a volley and then withdrew to reload while another group rode forward. The Basotho stood no chance; they suffered terrible casualties; but they stood their ground through seven hours of this one-sided battle before the Batlhaping were sent in to finish the job. There was not one Griqua casualty throughout the day, though it was reported that in excess of five hundred Basotho lost their lives.[14]

For the Batlhaping, the battle of Dithakong demonstrated beyond all doubt the crucial importance of firearms in modern warfare, quite apart from their usefulness for long-distance hunting. From that day onwards the acquisition of guns, horses and ox-wagons became a major priority for the leading men of the Batlhaping.

Over the following years, however, Mothibi's authority suffered a series of blows. In 1824 and again in 1825 a renegade band of Griqua attacked villages and cattle-posts along the Kuruman valley. This led a number of Batlhaping to question the loyalty of Robert Moffat who was supposed to be the friend of the Griqua. Why was he not preventing them from attacking the Batlhaping? Some went so far as to question the wisdom of *Kgosi* Mothibi's agreeing in 1824 to grant the missionaries a long-term lease on a site further up the Kuruman River. Here the missionaries had better access to the waters of the spring (or 'Eye') of the Kuruman to irrigate their fruit and vegetable gardens. This, combined with the fact that the site was separate from the Batlhaping

Vaal. Estimates of numbers vary greatly. Contemporary witnesses referred to them as 'a horde',

13 The Batlhaping referred to them as *Mantatees*, a misnomer based upon the name Mma-Ntatisi, queen regent of the Batlokwa kingdom in the western Drakensberg. Her military prowess was such that the Batlhaping assumed that any invading Basotho must be led by her. In fact neither she nor the Batlokwa were anywhere near Dithakong in 1823.

14 R Moffat *Apprenticeship at Kuruman* pp73–111; Thompson *Travels and Adventures in Southern Africa* (1827) pp174–85 for eye-witness account of John Melvill, Cape agent at Griquatown.

capital, allowed the mission, now known as 'Kuruman', to act more or less independently of the *kgosi*'s authority.

Furthermore, the presence of the mission was eroding some of the Batlhaping's traditional cultural practices. Increasing numbers of people were imitating the material culture of the missionaries; wearing hats, jackets and trousers – sewn from leather – in the European style, and abandoning the use of *lechoku* and *sibilo*, the traditional cosmetics

Kgosi Molehabangwe (1745–1812) wearing a sibilo cap; portrait by Samuel Daniel.

of the Batlhaping. *Lechoku* was a red-ochre clay that was smeared over the body as a protection from the sun and parasites. *Sibilo* was a metallic ore that when ground to a powder was mixed with *lechoku* and smeared thickly on the head to form a glistening cosmetic 'cap'. The only known source of *sibilo* was a mine at Blinkklip, a small hill east of the Langeberg, near the modern mining town of Postmasburg. The Batlhaping were the sole producers of this valuable mineral which they traded northwards to the Bangwaketse in exchange for iron and copper that they fashioned into knives and ornaments.

The missionaries believed that they would only succeed with their religious mission if they could change the symbolic practices of the Batlhaping. And recognising that the cosmetics of *sibilo* and *lechoku* were important symbols of Setswana culture, the missionaries went out of their way to erode their use. They declared that the wearing, mining and trading of *sibilo* and *lechoku* were evil, 'heathen' practices, and they took every opportunity to promote the virtues of 'cleanliness' and the wearing of European-style clothing.

At the same time the missionaries discouraged people from attending the highly symbolic initiation ceremonies which were held every few years. These entailed several weeks of schooling teenage boys and girls in the historical culture, religion, morals and mores of the Batlhaping. The ceremonies, which culminated in circumcision for the boys, marked their formal passing into adulthood. The initiates, drawn from right across the *morafe*, were then formed into male and female age-regiments that could be called upon to perform important national tasks, including defence and warfare. The regiments, usually led by an initiate from the royal family, thus strengthened

12

both the traditional culture of the Batlhaping and the political power of the *kgosi*. The missionaries regarded the initiations as a major barrier to the type of Christian conversion for which they were aiming and they took every opportunity to roundly condemn them.

Mothibi's apparently tolerant attitude towards the Moffats in the face of these cultural criticisms, led many within the *morafe* to begin to question his authority as *kgosi* of the Batlhaping. And it was at this very time of crisis in Mothibi's leadership, in March 1825, that Petlhu, his twenty-year-old son and heir, died suddenly of a fever.

The unexpected loss of their *kgosi's* heir strengthened the feeling within the capital that allowing the white missionaries to live among them had brought nothing but bad fortune to the Batlhaping. Mothibi himself appears to have gone into deep mourning and for a year he moved away with his immediate family, settling at Koning some fifty kilometres to the south. In their *kgosi's* absence many people began to look to his younger brother Mahura for stronger leadership.

When Mothibi returned to the Kuruman valley the following year he found that Mahura had moved the Batlhaping capital upstream to Seoding, a site directly across the river from the mission at Kuruman. It is unclear whether this move was made entirely for environmental reasons, or was born of a desire to keep close to the missionaries, either for their material advantages or to prevent them from asserting too much independence. It is unlikely to have been for religious reasons, as Mahura was a traditionalist, and was clearly distrustful of the missionaries. Mothibi, on the other hand, was less clear in his attitude. On a personal level he had great respect for both Robert and Mary Moffat; but he was ambivalent about the cultural challenges that they offered. He did nothing either to discourage or embrace the changes that were taking place; and for a few years the leadership of the *morafe* seems to have been divided between the two brothers.

Meanwhile, the threat from armed raiders steadily increased, mostly coming from the desert margins of the northwest. The raids were prompted perhaps by the supply of gunpowder that Moffat kept at the mission for his own hunting use. By January 1828 the increased insecurity and the continuing drought had helped develop a consensus among the Batlhaping that it was time to move their capital away from the Kuruman region. And it was at this point that divisions between Mothibi and Mahura came to a head. Mahura was the one to take the initiative and he led about half the *morafe*, at least five thousand people, back to the historic site of Dithakong. There he enhanced his reputation by successfully waylaying a band of Korana raiders, killing eighteen out of twenty-seven.

Following the departure of Mahura, Mothibi had moved south, leaving behind several thousand people in villages around Kuruman. Initially he took the remaining members of the *morafe* to a site on the south bank of the lower Vaal; but a few years later, in 1831, he moved back to the north bank of the river to build his much-reduced town on the flat top of Mosesberg. Even here, however, Mothibi could not escape the influence of the missionaries and the divisions this provoked within his own immediate family. Familial tensions were intensified in the early 1830s when one of his own sons was formally baptised a Christian.

The turning point had come at Kuruman in 1827. In July of that year Robert Moffat returned to the mission after several months of intensive language study in a remote village among the Barolong.[15] That Sunday, for the first time, he preached to the people in fluent Setswana. The church was packed and according to the Moffats the impact was electrifying.[16] Now at last the people could begin to comprehend the spiritual message that the missionaries had for so long been trying to convey. For their part the Batlhaping were also perhaps amazed and a little flattered that this *lekgowa* should speak their language, and so well.

Among those who now showed particular interest in learning more of the Christian message was Jantjie,[17] one of the sons of *Kgosi* Mothibi and the future father of Luka, the subject of our story. Jantjie was in fact Mothibi's eldest son, but by a junior, Korana wife, Kegogile. His name was thus drawn from his mother's heritage, being the Dutch/Afrikaans for 'Little John'.

Jantjie was born in about 1797 so he would have been about twenty-five in 1822 when the young Robert Moffat, of similar age, had challenged the decision of the *kgotla* over the Mongwaketse rainmaker. That example of a man prepared to risk his own life in order to save another may well have impressed the young Jantjie. The following year he would have witnessed and perhaps taken part in the battle of Dithakong. It is possible that the slaughter witnessed in that battle instilled in him a lifelong aversion to warfare. Whatever the pointers towards his Christian conversion, Jantjie in later life

---

[15] Northern neighbours of the Batlhaping. Moffat believed that the Barolong spoke a 'purer' form of Setswana, the Batlhaping's own Setswana being 'corrupted' by Korana dialect.

[16] Mora Dickson, *Beloved Partner: Mary Moffat of Kuruman* p84.

[17] Pronounced 'Yanki', contemporary spelling 'Jantje'. See page ix for explanation.

was to demonstrate that he valued truth and peace above all else.

By the time that Jantjie accompanied his father south from Kuruman in January 1828, he had probably already learned a considerable amount from the now Setswana-speaking Moffat about the Christian message of peace. The LMS, however, did not lightly grant baptism and it was to be another eighteen months, July 1829, before Moffat baptised his first Christian convert, a Khoesan servant from the colony. But the Moffats made this, their first convert baptism, into a huge religious event, coinciding as it did with

Moffat's printing press in Kuruman today.

the baptism of their own third infant daughter, Helen. People interested in the Christian message came from far and wide and it is very likely that Jantjie travelled north from the Vaal to attend the ceremony.

Moffat had already begun his great Christian project, the translation of the Bible into Setswana; and towards the end of 1830 he returned from a trip to Cape Town armed with printed copies of his Setswana translation of the Gospel according to St Luke. He also brought back a printing press which he immediately put into service printing his translations of Christian tracts and hymns. The latter proved very popular in attracting people into the Church, particularly as the missionaries had banned the singing of traditional Setswana songs. Religious conversions and baptisms at Kuruman followed regularly through the early 1830s.

Despite their distance from Kuruman, the same trend reached Mothibi's people at Mosesberg. They had become the responsibility of Revd Isaac Hughes, the LMS missionary at Griquatown, which was about eighty kilometres west of Mosesberg, much nearer than Kuruman. Hughes would have focussed particular attention on Jantjie, for the conversion of a son of the *kgosi* would have had great influence among the Batlhaping. And a key part of Hughes' work became the teaching of reading, so that potential converts could read the 'Word of God'. Thus in the early 1830s Jantjie learned to read St Luke's Gospel in Setswana. However, neither Hughes nor Moffat saw much point in teaching any broader literacy beyond the ability to read the Bible,

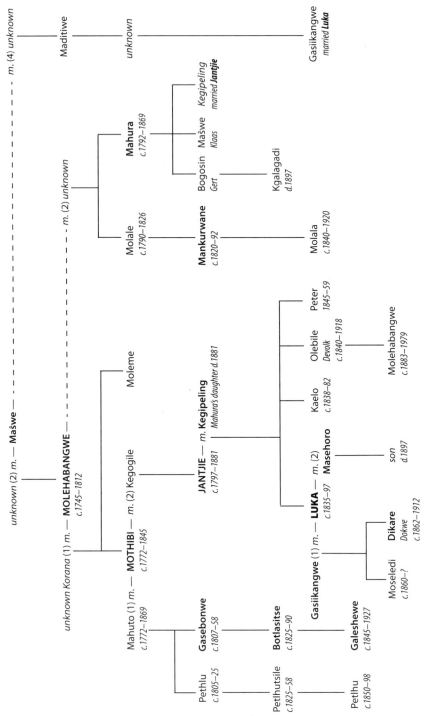

Batlhaping family tree, showing descent from Kgosi Molehabangwe.

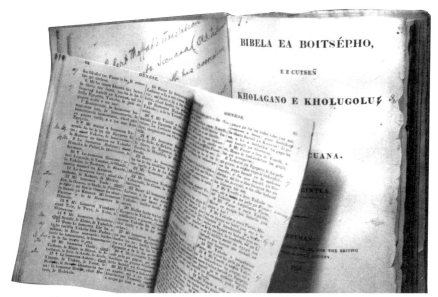

Robert Moffat translated this Old Testament into Setswana and printed it in Kuruman in 1853.
Luka and his father would have read this. It is annotated with Moffat's handwritten corrections.

so little attention was paid to writing. Thus Jantjie learned to sign his name, 'Jantje Mothibi',[18] but that appears to have been the extent of his writing skills. His learning of the new faith, however, was clearly enough to impress the missionaries, and sometime in the early 1830s he was formally baptised.

By then Jantjie was probably already married, although there is no suggestion that his wife became a Christian. She was reputed to be a daughter of Mahura, Mothibi's younger half-brother, which would have meant she was Jantjie's first cousin. It was not unusual for Batlhaping royals to marry first cousins. In this way the dowry or bridewealth (*bogadi*) that was paid to the woman's family was kept within the extended family. In the early nineteenth century *bogadi* for a high-status bride such as Mahura's daughter comprised up to ten head of cattle. The bride's name, Kegipeling, suggests Korana heritage so it seems that Mahura, like his elder brother Mothibi, had probably also chosen a Korana woman for one of his wives. Thus Luka, the first-born child of Jantjie and Kegipeling, inherited mixed Batlhaping-Korana ancestry from both his father and his mother.

In early January 1835 Mothibi was visited by an ostensibly scientific expedition from the Cape Colony led by Dr Andrew Smith (*see overleaf*). However, Smith was under secret instructions from the Cape Governor to assess the strength of African polities north of the Orange River and the suitability of

[18] He used the contemporary spelling 'Jantje'. 'Jantjie' is used by his descendants today.

Dr Andrew Smith meets Kgosi Mothibi in 1835, on a secret mission to spy out the land north of the Vaal River for the Cape colonial government.

the region for future European colonisation. Mothibi, unaware of this secret agenda, welcomed the visit as a strengthening of direct trading links with the Colony. So far bandit raids and cultural challenges may have weakened the Batlhaping *morafe*, but they had not directly threatened its territorial integrity: Mothibi and Mahura had been free to move their settlements within what they perceived to be the Batlhaping's ancestral land. The year 1835, however, marked a change in this respect, and before the year was out, white settlers from the east of the Cape Colony had begun their invasion of the highveld north of the Orange that was to become known, in their historiography, as 'The Great Trek'.

CHAPTER TWO

Birth and early life
1835–58

Luka himself did not know the exact year of his birth. All he knew, as he stated to a Land Commission in 1886, was that he was born while his family was living at Mosesberg. That was between 1831 and 1839. Judging by estimates of his age at various times during his life, it is reasonable to assume that Luka was born in the middle of that period, that is, in about that fateful year of 1835.[1]

Initially his father had given him the Setswana name, Mpolokweng, but as a new convert to Christianity, he wanted his son to be brought up as a Christian from birth. That meant an infant christening and the selection of a Christian name. Jantjie had probably witnessed the christening of Robert Moffat's infant daughter, Helen, in 1829. The obvious name that came to mind was that of the man who had written the *Efangeleo* (Gospel) according to *Luka*, the Setswana form of Luke. Thus when Mpolokweng, son of Jantjie, was christened, he was named Luka Jantjie.

During the first few years of Luka's childhood, his father remained in close contact with the missionaries at Griquatown and at Kuruman, and the small Christian community of Mosesberg received periodic visits from Isaac Hughes of Griquatown. By the mid-1830s the LMS had enough local converts to be able to employ some of them as deacons at many of the larger villages, and at some stage one was appointed to Mothibi's people. The role of the local deacon was to conduct Sunday services, mainly through reading and explaining passages from the Gospel, to encourage new expressions of interest, and to report any 'backsliders' to the overseeing missionary when he made his occasional visits. The deacon at Mosesberg would have appreciated Jantjie's useful support. His attempts to preach to the people, however, would not have been appreciated by Jantjie's non-Christian siblings.

Tension within the family reached crisis point in 1839 when the decision was taken to abandon Mosesberg. After eight years of poor rainfall, the

[1] LMS correspondence, Africa South, Bechuanaland; Shillington, *Colonisation*, pp12–21.

19

pasture of the region would have become worn and the nearby fire-wood scarce. But there was more to the decision to move than concern about the environment. Unhappiness at Christianity's erosion of cultural values and what was perceived to be the intrusion of the Griquatown missionaries appears to have provoked a split within Mothibi's family.

Gasebonwe, Mothibi's eldest surviving son by his senior wife Mahuto (*right*), had no time for Christianity and distrusted all *makgowa* and *masetedi* (Griqua). Aged in his early thirties at the time, Gasebonwe had considerable support within the reduced *morafe* and he led away about a thousand people (more than half the Mosesberg settlement) to establish a new town separate from the Christians. He took with him his mother, Mahuto, and the other children of her senior line. Among Gasebonwe's following was Petlhutsile, the young teenage son of his late elder brother Petlhu. Born in or around the year of his father's death in 1825, Petlhutsile had been entrusted to the care of his uncle, Gasebonwe. In due course Gasebonwe established his town up the Harts valley at a place called Borigelong.

Mothibi, aged nearly seventy at the time, was unsure what to do. Initially he moved with Jantjie to Dikgatlhong ('where rivers meet'), between the confluence of the Harts and Vaal, but in 1841 he went to join Mahuto, Gasebonwe and other members of the senior line at Borigelong. He remained there until his death in 1845.

Jantjie had declined to accompany his father. If he had followed Mothibi to Borigelong, Jantjie might have expected no more status and authority than that of a councillor to a senior half-brother who would have inherited the authority of *kgosi* from his father. But more important than his political status within the family, Jantjie probably saw Mothibi's departure as an opportunity to break free from the disapproval of his 'traditionalist' senior siblings and to pursue his own vision of a Christian life. By remaining at Dikgatlhong Jantjie was able to take charge of his own nominally Christian community. In doing so he became a *kgosi* in his own right, even if this 'modern' *morafe* that he presided over was small. The number of confirmed Christians at Dikgatlhong was little more than fifty out of a population of about five hundred.

The non-Christian members of the Dikgatlhong population who stayed with Jantjie would have done so either because they were happy with the cultural changes associated with Christianity or because they were tied to him by the social obligations of *mafisa* debt. Under the *mafisa* system,

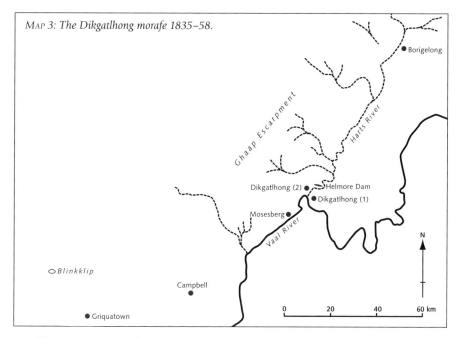

MAP 3: *The Dikgatlhong morafe 1835–58.*

wealthier members of the community loaned out cattle to the poor in return for cattle-herding services. The borrowers had use of the cattle for their staple diet – soured milk – and sometimes they were allowed to keep some of the progeny, but the original cattle remained the property of the lender. While the relationship was beneficial to both sides, it ensured that a Batlhaping royal such as Jantjie had a built-in body of dependants who were obliged to stay with him.

Jantjie accepted that European culture in general was a form of modernity that should be embraced and guided by the moral and spiritual precepts of the Gospel. This was basically the message of the missionaries: for most of his life as *kgosi* of this branch of the Batlhaping, Jantjie was to remain strongly swayed by the advice of the missionaries. And it was in this atmosphere of modernity that his son Luka grew to maturity.[2]

Luka Jantjie was assisted in his education and social development by Revd Holloway and Anne Helmore, a young missionary couple fresh from England. The Helmores had arrived at Griquatown in November 1839 and had visited Dikgatlhong shortly afterwards.[3] At the time the town was in a state of flux, only half-built and with *Kgosi* Mothibi as yet undecided whether he should move on and join Gasebonwe, the Helmores decided to wait in

[2] Shillington, *Colonisation*, pp12–16.
[3] *LMS*, Bechuanaland, Helmore's correspondence: Griquatown 1839–40, Dikgatlhong 1841–55.

Griquatown until the settlement was firmly established. In the meantime the couple practised their Setswana, and Holloway explored the region. He felt that the north bank of the Harts, a few kilometres above its confluence with the Vaal was a far better site for a long-term settlement. Here, on the rising ground overlooking the valley, the people would have access to the springs of the Ghaap escarpment, as well as the good grazing, water and thatching reeds of the Harts valley itself. Helmore's chance to join the Batlhaping settlement came in 1841 when the Christian *Kgosi* Jantjie was left in charge at Dikgatlhong. According to Helmore it was he who persuaded Jantjie to move to the north bank of the Harts; but Jantjie moved so promptly that it is likely that he himself had already identified the new site as preferable for a long-term settlement.

Luka would have been about six years of age at this stage, old enough to retain firm memories of the move. He would still have been under the super-vision of his mother and was probably given minor tasks such as carrying thatching reeds to keep him occupied. He would have been fascinated by the Helmores. They were both fluent in Setswana and they employed local Batlhaping to help them build a rectangular house. It was constructed of mud-brick, a material new to the Batlhaping, who used wattle and daub between frameworks of poles for their circular houses. Besides his regular preaching duties, Helmore, ever the practical man, would have been fully involved in the physical task of making mud-bricks. His wife, Anne, as dedicated to the mission concept as her husband, was to make her mission role that of educa-tion, and in due course a second rectangular building was constructed to act as church, meeting house and school.

From about the age of nine or ten Luka, like other boys of his age, would have been required to learn the important skills of cattle-herding. For this they were sent out to the cattle-posts, to live in crude shelters for months at a time, where they came under the supervision of older youths. The cattle-posts of Dikgatlhong were either across the Harts and between that river and the Vaal, or around springs in the nearby Ghaap escarpment and on the Ghaap plateau. As the son of the *kgosi*, Luka would have been given some calves to rear and these and their progeny would in due course have become the basis of his own herd of cattle. For the Batlhaping, cattle were important not only for their milk and as an accumulation of wealth and influence, but for certain social obligations, the most important of which was the payment of *bogadi* (bridewealth or dowry) at the time of marriage. Without owning or borrowing cattle, a man could not get married.

Cattle graze in the valley below Dikgatlhong in the 1970s; shows the landscape Luka grew up in.

Schooling at the cattle-post would normally last for several years. Jantjie, however, regarded a knowledge of Christianity as just as important as traditional cattle-keeping skills for the new 'modern' culture that was developing at Dikgatlhong. Thus Luka would have spent a short while at his father's cattle-post, learning important life skills, before being brought back to Dikgatlhong and enrolled in Anne Helmore's school. Luka would have been one of the few boys in the mission school, for most were away with the cattle and the school was largely attended by girls. In due course he would have been joined by his younger brothers Kaelo and Olebile (also known as Devolk), born in about 1838 and 1840 respectively, although they would have been quite junior to him.

The main subjects on the school curriculum were literacy and the Christian faith. Anne Helmore believed that the general skill of writing was just as important as reading: complete literacy was a life-skill, not just a route to Christianity. Perhaps, having been brought up within the gender strictures of early nineteenth-century England, Anne appreciated more than her male colleagues the value of well-founded literacy as a route to self-fulfilment.

As the eldest son of the *kgosi*, Luka was bound to have had particular attention paid to him by Anne Helmore and it was under her guidance that he first learned to read and write in Setswana. Coming straight from England, Anne was unfamiliar with the local dialect of Dutch/Afrikaans that was the language of the Griqua and the Boers, and so, when teaching Luka to write his name, she spelt his surname as she heard it pronounced: 'Yañki', rather than following the contemporary Dutch spelling of 'Jantje'. And throughout his life Luka retained 'Yañki' as his own unique spelling of his surname:[4]

Luka Yañki Mothibi Molehabañue

---

[4] The spelling 'Jantjie' is used by Luka's descendants, although some prefer the older spelling 'Jantje'. Luka's unique spelling of 'Yañki' is only used here when he himself is directly quoted.

The tree at the Helmore's mission school at Dikgatlhong where Luka learned to read and write.

Luka was to regard literacy as a very important skill. It demystified the world of the *makgowa*, enabling him to read documents and formal communications for himself. His ability to write added authenticity to messages sent between *dikgosi*[5] and in due course it enabled him to communicate in writing with colonial officials. Despite his literacy, however, he operated predominately in an oral culture: as far as is known he wrote no personal letters or recollections.

Luka learned much more from Anne and Holloway Helmore than literacy and Christianity. Although it is not mentioned in any of the mission correspondence, Anne would also have taught basic numeracy as well as a range of general knowledge. Certainly in adult life Luka had a full understanding of cash transactions and had his own bank account. It is likely that much of his early knowledge in this respect was learned at Anne Helmore's school. Luka would have spent only a few years at the school, but beyond his academic accomplishments he would have learned a lot from the way that the Helmores related to the people among whom they lived. Coming straight from England with no experience of life in the Cape Colony, the Helmores were not contaminated by the racism that was inherent in colonial society, and thus a genuine friendship and mutual respect seems to have developed between Luka and his mentors. They treated him with the respect due to a social equal and this appears to have left a lasting impression on the young man. It was perhaps why he was later to find the racism of colonialism so frustrating and in his view so unnecessary.

As a good Christian, Jantjie had suspended *bogwera* (initiation) at Dikgatlhong and the equivalent symbol of adulthood for Luka and his brothers in this modernising world would have been learning to use a gun. By the 1840s a number of the leading men at Dikgatlhong had purchased muzzle-loading guns, ox-wagons and horses, and hunting for trade rather than just for food and fur karosses was becoming an important part of economic life for the

[5] The plural form of '*kgosi*'

24

Traditional Batswana techniques of hunting prior to the widespread use of guns, driving eland, wildebeests and zebra into a long ditch and fence.

better off. Sometime in his teens, probably after he left school, Luka would have learned to load and fire a gun and he would have acquired at least one gun of his own. He probably also learned to ride a horse. He was soon to have ample opportunity to practise these newly-acquired skills.

From 1848 through to late 1851 the Dikgatlhong region was struck by the perennial problem of drought. As the health and fertility of their cattle suffered from the decline in good grazing, men turned increasingly to hunting to make up the deficit in cattle, food and tradable goods. Hunting now took men away from the town for weeks and sometimes months at a time as they travelled northwards with their ox-wagons into present-day Botswana. They shot antelope which they dried for meat, jackals for their fur to sew into cloaks (karosses) and elephants for their ivory tusks. The latter in particular could be exchanged for guns, horses and wagons from the colony. It was probably on one of these long-distance hunting expeditions that Luka, then in his mid- to late teens, gained his first experience of hunting big game. In due course he was to gain a reputation as a hunter of some renown.

Meanwhile the Helmores lamented the general dispersal of the Dikgatlhong community. Girls were taken out of school to go with their mothers in search of wild food – roots and berries – while boys were removed to tend the cattle-posts and search for fresh pasture that had not already been overgrazed. At first the missionaries feared their loss of religious influence over the

A Bakwena kaross maker in the early 1920s.

dispersed community, but then in

1850 Helmore noticed what he considered to be a positive cultural change. Men were beginning to take over the role of cultivation. Hitherto this had been the work of women, who tilled the soil with a hand-held hoe and grew sorghum or beans on a small scale to supplement the basic diet of soured milk and goat or game meat. With the mission introduction of the ox-drawn plough, however, the men now saw a role for themselves in cultivation: handling oxen, after all, was traditionally men's work. Helmore reported approvingly that some of the men had 'purchased or borrowed ploughs and taken the management of the corn fields upon themselves.'[6] In doing so they considerably enlarged the scale and significance of cultivation. They began to open up the water courses at the cattle-posts, particularly in the Ghaap escarpment behind Dikgatlhong, and to dig channels for irrigation.

This development was the spark that fired Helmore's imagination and led him to devise a major plan that would bring the community back to Dikgatlhong and provide for the town's long-term future and economic stability. He would build a dam across the dry riverbed of the Harts so that when the rain returned and the river began to flow, the water would be saved. He estimated that this would provide irrigation to grow enough crops to feed the whole population of six hundred people on a regular and stable basis. Helmore's plan, however, overlooked two important factors: the historic importance of cattle in this marginal environment; and the point that the people of Dikgatlhong had already moved beyond the centrality of communal development prefering that very individualism that the missionaries promoted, as evidenced by the family-centred cultivation at the former cattle-posts.

Helmore was so convinced of the merits of his plan, however, that he allowed nothing to stand in his way. He surveyed the area and chose a site about four kilometres upstream from Dikgatlhong. The dam was to be six metres wide at the base, six metres high and about three hundred metres long across the valley. He felt sure this would create a large enough reservoir to provide irrigation water from one rainy season to the next. He enthused so much about it to Jantjie and the leading men of the town that for most of 1851 they provided their labour free for the project.[7]

There is no mention of the direct involvement of Luka, then aged about sixteen, in either the discussion or the work on the dam itself, but

---

[6] LMS, Helmore, 'Likatlong', 1 January 1851.

[7] LMS, Helmore's correspondence, 1851–55; K Shillington, 'Irrigation, Agriculture and the State: The Harts Valley in Historical Perspective', in Beinart et al (eds), *Putting a Plough to the Ground*.

A recent photograph of the dam that Holloway Helmore had recommended as a way of improving farming and Luka's people built in the early 1850s – indicating the scale of the enterprise.

he probably played a role in some capacity. Work began in the scorching heat of January 1851. With Helmore fully involved in the physical labour, he and the Batlhaping volunteers dug a six-metre-wide trench across the valley down to what appeared to be the bedrock. Their only tools were spades and wheelbarrows bought from Helmore's own meagre funds. By the end of the year the work was almost finished, but as soon as the first rains began to fall at the beginning of December the Batlhaping dispersed to the cattle-posts to plough and cultivate on their own account. As it happened, it was the heaviest rainfall for a decade and by the end of December the reservoir was so full that it weakened the foundations at the eastern end of the dam.

The damage merely added to the Batlhaping's growing scepticism about the value of the dam, and in the following year Helmore found it hard to persuade them to provide any more free labour, either to repair the damage and to complete the dam. Despite Jantjie's willingness to follow the lead of his missionary, the *kgosi's* ability to command communal labour

1920s photo showing a Tswana house and domestic life similar in many ways to Luka's time. Note the traditional women's thatched roof and the thatched granary bin (left) in the background.

had been seriously weakened by the very individuality that the missionaries themselves encouraged. It was a contradiction that was to frustrate the missionaries throughout the pre-colonial period. It took Helmore a further three years to get the dam strengthened and completed. But the people were not committed to the project, and after the Helmores went on long leave to England in December 1855, they failed to maintain the dam. In the heavy flooding of late 1856 the river simply re-routed itself around the eastern edge of the dam wall.[8]

In the meantime Luka had other matters on his mind. In the early 1850s, when he was about eighteen, his family arranged his marriage. Although Luka would have had his own small herd of cattle by then, it is likely that his father would have paid the *bogadi* cattle to the family of the bride. In this way the son remained obligated towards the father.

In 1853 or 1854 Luka Jantjie married Gasiikangwe, a third cousin descended from Maditiwe, half-brother to Luka's great-grandfather Kgosi Molehabangwe. On his marriage, Luka would have moved out of the house that he shared with his younger brothers, Kaelo and Olebile, and the youngest, Peter (born in 1846), and he and Gasiikangwe would have moved into a newly-built house, though still within the royal ward. The early years of their marriage, however, were to be overshadowed by a series of failed pregnancies and infant deaths.

During this time Luka and other members of Jantjie's family began to cultivate regularly at Manyeding on the Ghaap plateau, about twenty-five kilometres east of Kuruman. There was a reliable spring there, and although the local grazing was not the best quality for raising cattle, the land fed by the spring was suitable for irrigated cultivation. Luka and Gasiikangwe established a house there although they retained a home in Dikgatlhong. Manyeding was to become a regular sub-village for the royal ward of Dikgatlhong.

Luka might at this point have been expected to settle down to some form of regular domestic life, accumulating cattle, the principal aim of most Batswana men. He was, however, the eldest son of a *kgosi* of the Batlhaping, and as such he had additional responsibilities. So from about the age of twenty-three, Luka began to take an active advisory role in his sixty-year-old father's decisions as *kgosi* of the Dikgatlhong *morafe*. Indeed, the year 1858 was to mark a turning point in Luka Jantjie's life. Although he was already in his early twenties and a married man of four or five years' standing, 1858 was the year that Luka Jantjie came of age.

[8] *LMS*, Ross, Likatlong, 28 April 1856; *TVL*, A551/2, Moffat to Helmore, Kuruman, Feb. 1857.

CHAPTER THREE

Adult responsibilities
1858–1867

The year 1858 began with the return of drought, coupled this time with the endemic cattle disease, 'lungsickness' (*bovine pleuro-pneumonia*), which cut a swathe through the Batlhaping herds. The people grew desperate; they could survive without cultivated crops, but not without cattle that provided for their daily consumption of soured milk.

Within the Christian community at Dikgatlhong many became disillusioned with the new religion. Dikgatlhong by this time had a population of about a thousand, of whom 340 were registered Christians. Revd William Ross had taken over as resident missionary from the Helmores in 1856 and he reported that there were debates within the Christian community as to whether the Christian or the 'heathen' God was to blame for the drought and the return of lungsickness in the cattle.

Jantjie, a convert to Christianity, was always loath to question the wisdom of the missionaries. Luka, on the other hand, had been born to the religion and felt no such debt of gratitude. Without questioning the religious aspects of Christianity, Luka challenged some of the cultural restrictions imposed by Ross and his colleagues. Why, for instance, should the missionaries ban the trade in *lechoku* and *sibilo*? They were not condemned in the Bible. Luka saw a revival of the trade in traditional cosmetics as a means of replenishing his family's herds of cattle, and he was not going to be put off by the petty restrictions of an outsider with very different cultural assumptions. He persuaded his father to go along with him in defying Ross's ban: quite an achievement considering his father's great reluctance ever to defy the missionaries.

In what was probably a deliberate snub to Ross, Luka chose a Sunday in April, the Sabbath, to lead a party of wagons out of Dikgatlhong bound for Blinkklip. Jantjie went with him: perhaps he preferred not to remain behind and face the wrath of Ross. The missionary had already publicly upbraided them for bringing 'great sorrow on the community'.[1] Ross, however, did not

[1] *LMS*, Ross, Likatlong, 29 April 1858.

29

dare expel the *kgosi* or his son from the Church as he might have done to lesser Church members. At Blinkklip the party mined the *sibilo* ore and dug the *lechoku* clay and then carried these valuable cosmetics to the northern, non-Christian Batswana, who still valued them and who still had healthy cattle to sell in exchange.

Luka and Jantjie were away for a couple of months, returning in June with their newly-acquired cattle to find themselves being drawn into a conflict that was far more dangerous than the vagaries of drought and cattle disease or the cultural intrusion of Christianity. Together with his father Jantjie, the young Luka was about to be initiated into the high politics of colonial warfare. It was not a conflict of their making; but rather that of their cousins up the Harts valley, the Batlhaping of Borigelong and Taung, although even they could not entirely be blamed for the horrific consequences of their actions.

The roots of the conflict were to be found in an earlier large-scale invasion of the highveld north of the Orange River by Boers from the eastern Cape Colony. Known in Afrikaans historiography as 'The Great Trek', this had begun in the 1830s. Emigrant Boers had come in large, well-armed groups with their wagons, horses, cattle and guns, and their slaves and bonded servants. Attacking any Africans who impeded their progress, they had established themselves on the highveld north and south of the upper Vaal. Then, laying claim to this vast territory 'by right of conquest', they had proclaimed the 'republics' of the Orange Free State south of the Vaal and the South African Republic north of the Vaal (the 'Transvaal'). Their huge pastural farms were widely scattered and largely dependent upon the forced labour of the local African population. And whenever their security was threatened or their labour demands challenged, they would form a local mounted commando to enforce their will.

Although to some extent the Batlhaping of Taung and Borigelong had brought their new troubles upon themselves, in reality it was only a matter of time before the Boers would attempt to impose their writ further down the Vaal and the valley of the Harts, even as far as Dikgatlhong. It was not even the Batlhaping who lit the first spark of open warfare. This was done by a Khoesan leader named Kousop, who was based on the north bank of the Vaal near the modern town of Christiana.

In May 1858, while most of the male Free State Boers were in the south of the country engaged in war with Moshoeshoe's Basotho kingdom, Kousop led a raiding party deep into the Free State. They attacked Boer homesteads in the Boshof district, killing the inmates and making off back across the

Vaal with what William Ashton, a missionary at Kuruman, described as an 'immense quantity of stock.' Mounted on Boer horses and wearing Boer clothes, Kousop's triumphant men paraded their booty at the Batlhaping town of Borigelong.[2]

Kgosi Gasebonwe, impressed by the booty and the apparent easy success of the raid, allowed his nephew, Petlhutsile, to gather a band of young men and go raiding on his own account. Petlhutsile was joined by Gasebonwe's younger brother, Boyung. They raided two Boer settlements on the north bank of the Vaal, killed up to fifteen people and returned with horses and ox-wagons piled high with all manner of looted goods. The Bamaidi Batlhaping who lived at Manthe near Taung joined in the raids. By this time the Boers on both sides of the Vaal were on the alert and they ambushed one group of raiders, killing about a dozen of them and capturing their horses and guns.

All this had happened while *Kgosi* Jantjie and his son Luka were away on their *sibilo*-trading trip to the north. By the time they returned to Dikgatlhong in June, the leader of the South African Republic, M W Pretorius (*see left*), had already formed a commando of five hundred armed and mounted men and moved them down the north bank of the Vaal to threaten the Batlhaping. Meanwhile the Free State Boers had assembled a similar commando on the south bank of the river, opposite Kousop's village.

Kgosi Mahura of Taung hurried to Kuruman with his sons, Maŝwe and Bogosin, to buy ammunition from Moffat's son, Robert, who had set up a trading store there. Moffat senior was away in Cape Town and William Ashton had been left in charge of the mission. Ashton urged Mahura to send a message to Jantjie at Dikgatlhong asking him to intervene on his and Gasebonwe's behalf to try and prevent a Boer attack. Jantjie had a wide reputation as a Christian man of peace, even among the Boers.

Despite his general distrust of missionaries, on this occasion Mahura followed Ashton's advice. His willingness to involve Jantjie illustrates the range of political authority within the wider Batlhaping *morafe*. The two sons of Mothibi, Jantjie and Gasebonwe, each had their own claim to respect from the others. Jantjie was the elder of the two in years, even if by a junior wife, while Gasebonwe was technically the senior, being son of the principal wife,

---

[2] For accounts of the war of 1858: *LMS* correspondence: Ashton, Kuruman, 5, 25 July, 7 September 1858; Ross, Lekatlong, 24 August, 1 November 1858.

Contemporary engraving (probably by Baines in the 1860s) showing a Batswana kgotla meeting.

Mahuto. Mahura on the other hand was their uncle, a younger half-brother to Mothibi. He was in fact only a few years older than Jantjie, but he was the last surviving son of Molehabangwe, even if by a junior wife, and this would have given him a degree of authority over his nephews (*see family tree p16*). Mahura had the largest following – at least five thousand lived at Taung – and he was in practice the more powerful. On an issue such as this, however, where blame was likely to be involved, he was careful to involve the others. When it suited them, both Mahura and Gasebonwe were keen to defer to the authority of Jantjie as the eldest son of Mothibi, especially if there was a chance that he might get them out of trouble.

Jantjie agreed to make the two-day journey upriver to Pretorius's camp near the present town of Bloemhof. He was accompanied by Luka, who was to act as his secretary. According to Ashton, Jantjie's peace mission travelled with several ox-wagons as they took a considerable retinue of advisers and servants with them, as well as supplies for the whole party for at least a week. It is tempting to imagine that they travelled in the same wagon and that the father used the two long days of slow travel to impress upon his young son the need for caution when dealing with *maburu*.

The meeting with Pretorius was Luka's first experience of coming face to face with a white political leader. Jantjie may well have spoken the Griqua or Korana dialect of Cape Dutch, the latter learned from his mother Kegogile, so he was probably able to converse directly with Pretorius. Luka too almost certainly spoke the language of the Griqua and the Boers, having had plenty of trading contact with the former at Griquatown.

One thing that Luka would have learned from the meeting was the dogged intransigence of a man like Pretorius, who had the confidence of power on his side. In the end Jantjie recognised that the Boer leader's demand for the

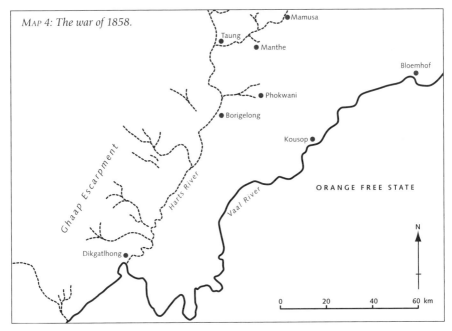

MAP 4: *The war of 1858.*

return of all looted goods as well as heavy compensation would be too much for Mahura or Gasebonwe, and he and his son came away from their meeting with Pretorius with no agreement in sight. They got back to Dikgatlhong to read the June edition of Ashton's monthly mission newspaper *Mokaeri oa Becuana* (The Instructor) in which Ashton warned that those who live by the sword must expect to die by the sword.[3]

The Free State Boers launched an attack on Kousop's village on 6 July, killing Kousop himself and many of his people in their first volley, fired from across the river. They then crossed the Vaal and a party of twenty-eight went in search of those who had fled. They were not interested in attacking the Batlhaping, who had confined their raids to the north bank of the Vaal. Petlhutsile, however, together with his uncle Boyung and Botlasitse, Gasebonwe's eldest son, had gathered a couple of regiments of mounted men. They were armed with guns and were looking for a fight. When they saw the relatively small size of the Boer searching party, they attacked it. But as the Boers took up a defensive position, one of their number escaped to warn the main Boer force, who quickly came to their aid.

[3] *Mokaeri oa Becuana* was a Setswana-language paper, printed on the Kuruman press and published monthly from 1857 to 1864 when Ashton was transferred to Dikgatlhong. It was an important tool for stimulating literacy among the Batlhaping. It contained letters from readers as well as mission news, births, marriages and deaths, and some preaching and moral advice from the editor, William Ashton. Some copies are in the South African Library, Cape Town.

In the battle that followed, the Boers showed their greater experience of fighting with guns. The inexperienced Batlhaping, used only to hunting wild animals with their muzzle-loading guns, had to dismount in order to load and fire their weapons while the Boers were able to load and fire from the saddle. As soon as the Batlhaping dismounted, the Boers fired at their horses, driving them off and leaving their riders on the ground and vulnerable. As the Batlhaping tried to escape, the Boers rode them down, killing many as they fled towards the river. Petlhutsile was shot and although he escaped the scene of the battle on foot, he died before he reached home. Boyung was lucky to escape on horseback with no more than a bullet through his hat. Botlasitse had part of his saddle shot off, but he also made it safely back to Borigelong.

Meanwhile, with Mahura still in Kuruman, Pretorius moved his camp up to the outskirts of Taung where Gasebonwe and the Bamaidi *kgosi* Motlhabane were believed to have taken refuge. Several weeks passed with no sign of a settlement, and in the first few days of August Jantjie and Luka travelled up to Taung once more, to attempt another peace mission. But their efforts were in vain. The Boers were determined to attack Gasebonwe and Motlhabane and all who stayed with them. Jantjie had parked his party's wagons in Taung, but now, convinced that a Boer attack was imminent, he and Luka beat a hasty retreat to Dikgatlhong, presumably on horseback, leaving their wagons and oxen behind. Mahura, who was on his way home from Kuruman, halted at an outlying village well away from the impending conflict that he wanted no part of.

Pretorius's commando launched its attack on Taung on Tuesday 10 August. Mahura's younger brother Sakoe was killed early in the fight, as was a brother of Motlhabane. An unnamed son of Mahura was also killed. The Boer attack was headed by their Korana and Khoesan servants, who took many casualties. Four Boers were killed and many were wounded. By the end of the day the Batlhaping defenders had been driven out of Taung leaving behind about thirty dead.

The Boers spent the following day sacking the town. They vented their fury on the missionaries, whom they blamed for arming the Batlhaping. They destroyed the church and school buildings, tore up school books and took the church bell. Throughout Thursday there was skirmishing in the hills as the Boers sought out Gasebonwe. They made their way to a hastily-deserted Borigelong which they looted and largely destroyed before returning to their camp outside Taung. Through Friday a stillness descended over Taung and there was no fighting that day.

A contemporary engraving of a Boer raid on a Korana village on the Vaal River, probably in 1885. It illustrates the type of brutal treatment meted out in the late 1850s to the Batlhaping who lived near the Korana of Mamusa (Schweizer-Reneke today) pictured here.

On the Saturday morning the Boers captured an unnamed Motlhaping woman, gave her a white flag and a heavy sack to carry on her back and sent her to the Batlhaping with an invitation to peace talks at the Boer camp. Knowing what the sack contained, the woman refused the mission on the grounds that she would surely be killed; but the Boers held her young child as a hostage and threatened to kill the child if she did not go. The woman made her way to the Bamaidi capital Manthe, not daring to take the load she was carrying to Gasebonwe's people. She sought out the Manthe mission teacher, Gasiboriwe. She put the sack down at his feet and out rolled the head of Gasebonwe.

The teacher hastily buried Gasebonwe's head near the church and raised a pile of stones over the burial site. He promised the woman that he would protect her from Batlhaping vengeance and sent word to Motlhabane, explaining what had happened and that the Boers wanted peace.

As word spread of Gasebonwe's fate there was consternation in the Batlhaping camps, many declaring that they would kill the woman who had brought their *kgosi*'s head. On the pleading of the teacher, however, Motlhabane ensured her protection. In the absence of Mahura, his sons Bogosin and Maŝwe agreed with Motlhabane that they should enter peace talks with the *maburu*. Motlhabane sent the woman back with a message that they would meet the Boers to discuss peace the following day, Sunday. The woman, who considered she had been lucky to have escaped with her life, took the message back to the Boer camp and successfully reclaimed her child.

After many hours of tense negotiations that Sunday a treaty was duly signed, Bogosin and Maŝwe signing on behalf of Mahura. Among the articles that the Batlhaping signed up to was an undertaking to pay the Boers for 'war expenses'. Without specifying what these expenses were, the Boers departed with 115 captive children, many wagons, including those of Jantjie and Luka – neutral interlocutors in the conflict – and more than a thousand head of cattle. In all, more than fifty Batlhaping had been killed in the fighting, including six of the prominent men of the *morafe*. What hurt the Batlhaping most, however, was the theft of their children. It was common practice among the Boer commandos to seize as many children as they could when raiding their African neighbours. They claimed that these were 'orphans', but if they ever were, it was only because the Boers had just shot their parents. These children were then forced into 'apprenticeships' that amounted to slavery in all but name. The lure of human loot was a strong motivating force for the frequency of Boer commando raids. For the Batlhaping, the theft of their children was a major reason for their refusal to co-operate with any further demands from Pretorius for 'war expenses.'

The first such demand came towards the end of 1858. According to Pretorius, Mahura was to hand over, within three months, 8,000 cattle, 300 horses and 500 guns. The prodigious numbers involved was clearly an attempt by Pretorius to totally impoverish the Batlhaping and destroy them as an independent entity. Besides this, Pretorius demanded the surrender of ten named men whom he claimed were responsible for the raids on Boer farms. These were not Mahura's people, but Gasebonwe's, and they had initially been demanded of Gasebonwe himself before the attack on Taung. Since Gasebonwe had refused to hand them over at that time, he had suffered the ultimate penalty, as had fifty other Batlhaping who had died in the attack. Mahura thus saw no reason why he should be held responsible now for their surrender.

Mahura got his sons to write to Pretorius, protesting that neither he nor his sons, who had signed the treaty, had ever agreed to the payment of any such sum. When they had signed the treaty they thought that their only obligation was to return to the Boers any of their livestock that they might come across. They thought the large number of wagons already taken by the Boers was more than enough to pay for the war. Furthermore, his people would give up no more cattle, horses or guns, seeing that not only had they been impoverished by the sacking of their towns and villages, but the Boers had also stolen and enslaved their children. Mahura received no response to this letter. The three-month deadline passed and nothing happened.

Over the following years the Boer demand was periodically renewed and Mahura was told that he would forfeit his country if he did not pay the 'fine'.

But the Batlhaping children were not returned and Mahura continued to ignore Pretorius's demands.

Ostensibly the dispute between Mahura and Pretorius had nothing to do with Jantjie and Luka; they were merely innocent and neutral victims who had lost their wagons and trek-oxen. But it was an issue that would not go away and ultimately it would compromise the integrity of the whole *morafe* of the Batlhaping, with disastrous consequences for Jantjie, Luka and the people of Dikgatlhong.

In the meantime, Luka would have learned many lessons from the war of 1858. He and other Batlhaping had been using firearms for hunting game for many years; but the recent war had vividly demonstrated the importance of firearms as weapons for personal defence. Details of the fighting were widely related throughout the Batlhaping *morafe* and from what he learned Luka would have appreciated the need to be able to reload a gun quickly and to master the skills of loading and firing from the saddle. Beyond that, aside from the horrors of war itself, he would have learned of the ruthlessness of the *maburu* and their disregard for African life when they wielded superior military power. The Boer retaliation had been out of all proportion to the offences committed against them. Fairness and justice mattered naught to them when indigenous Africans stood in their way. In particular, the beheading of Gasebonwe had deeply shocked the Batlhaping. It was an image that would have made a deep impression upon Luka, even though he was not present at the time. It may even have influenced his determination not to surrender when he himself was confronted by armed colonists later in his life.

By 1859 Luka was in his mid-twenties and was an experienced hunter with firearms. The number of guns imported into the *morafe* from the Colony increased enormously in the years following the war of 1858, and learning how to use the weapons became an important priority for the men of Dikgatlhong. Luka had probably already taught his brothers Kaelo and Olebile the intricate skills of loading and firing a muzzle-loading gun (*see similar gun overleaf*). No matter what the skill of the handler, however, these guns were dangerous implements, and in September 1859 an accident occurred with one of them that had a profound effect upon the entire Jantjie family. Exactly how the accident occurred is not known as the Dikgatlhong missionary, William Ross, merely reported the event, not the details.

Luka was apparently working with his gun, loading it or cleaning it. His thirteen-year-old youngest brother Peter was with him, presumably eager to learn about guns. Perhaps Luka was teaching him how to handle the gun. All we know is that the gun went off accidentally, and Peter was shot dead.

Death was never far away in the Batlhaping *morafe* of the mid-nineteenth century. The rate of infant death was high: Luka himself had lost his fifth child only a few weeks earlier, and William Ashton's wife had died in child-birth at Kuruman in February that year. Deaths such as these were accepted as part of normal life. Even the deaths that occurred in warfare were accepted as part of the risk of going to war. But the death of Peter Jantjie in September 1859 was so violent, sudden and unexpected that it must have had a profound effect upon the whole family.

Jantjie was devastated, not least because his youngest son Peter was, in the words of William Ross, 'a great favourite'. We can only surmise how Luka felt. Within days of the accident, he packed up his wagon and, in defiance of missionary strictures, went off to Blinkklip to mine *sibilo* and *lechoku*. He went with the blessing of his father and was away for several months. Returning in early December, he did not stay long in Dikgatlhong. By the end of the month he had loaded up his wagons again and gone off on a long-distance hunting trip, this time accompanied by his father. It was the only recorded occasion on which Jantjie accompanied his son Luka on a long-distance hunting trip. Normally Luka would have been accompanied by just a few companions and some servants, and so it is fair to speculate that the fact that his father went with him on this occasion was probably related to their joint grief over the death of Peter.

Further shocking bereavements were to follow. Towards the end of 1860 news filtered south to Dikgatlhong of the disastrous fate that had befallen the Helmores who had been on a special mission to the Kololo in the extreme north of present-day Botswana. The mission had been the brainchild of David Livingstone, who had visited the Kololo on his exploratory travels a few years previously. Before their departure for the north in 1859, Anne Helmore had spent six months at Dikgatlhong with her four young children while her husband was preparing for their mission, travelling regularly between Kuruman, Dikgatlhong and the Cape Colony. Holloway and Anne had both been popular at Dikgatlhong, not least with Luka himself who had grown up with them and had learned much at Anne's school. On this occasion the Christians of the town had begged them to remain at Dikgatlhong; and once

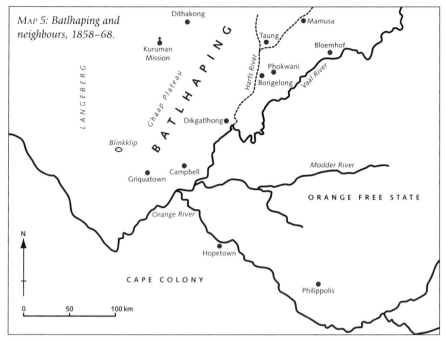

MAP 5: *Batlhaping and neighbours, 1858–68.*

it became clear that the couple were committed to their new mission posting, a considerable number of Batlhaping from the town – deacons, assistants and servants – volunteered to go with them. Now, the news that reached Dikgatlhong was that the Helmore mission had arrived at their destination in February 1860; they had not been welcomed by the Kololo who had been expecting David Livingstone; and within three months most of them were dead from fever. Among the dead were both Helmores, two of their four children, the wife and child of another missionary, Roger Price, and at least three of their Batlhaping companions.

In May 1861, the Batlhaping survivors of that disastrous mission returned to Dikgatlhong and the town went into deep mourning. The survivors brought back tales of how they had been poisoned by the Kololo leader, Sekeletu, and had all their goods seized. The poisoning story was later discounted by Roger Price, the surviving missionary of the expedition, and malaria seems to have been the most likely culprit. William Ross reported that, in memory of the Helmores and their Batlhaping companions, both Luka and Jantjie contributed generously to the expense of rebuilding the school at Dikgatlhong. The school at the time had more than a hundred regular students.[4]

The people of Dikgatlhong had barely had time to come to terms with

[4] *LMS*, Ross, Likatlong, 14 June 1861.

39

these tragedies when the district was struck by an outbreak of smallpox. For several weeks the infection spread through the *morafe*, leaving forty people dead in Dikgatlhong.

It was just at this moment in June 1861 that an itinerant Griqua trader named A W Greef laid claim to the property title to the 'farm' of Dikgatlhong. This included the town and all its land, from the Harts River to the Ghaap escarpment. Greef claimed to have bought the title from a fellow-Griqua named Kars, resident of Campbell, east of Griquatown. Kars' ownership had apparently been approved by Adam Kok III of Philippolis who had formerly been Griqua chief at Campbell. Kars had previously tried to sell this title to Jantjie in 1857, but Jantjie had turned him down flat. The land had belonged to the Batlhaping for generations by historic right of occupation and Jantjie pointed out that it had been his grandfather Molehabangwe who had granted the Griqua permission to dwell within the Batlhaping *morafe* in the first place. Molehabangwe had granted no right of ownership, only a right of usage.[5]

Nevertheless, Greef persisted with his claim, announcing that he intended to build a house for himself at Dikgatlhong and set up a permanent trading store in the town. He also wanted to take over at least one of the springs that flowed from the Ghaap escarpment and grow food there to sell within the town. Greef claimed that he had been offered £1,000 for the title by a colonial speculator based in Hopetown, the northernmost administrative town of the Cape Colony, which by this time had extended its boundary all the way to the Orange River.

Luka urged his father to stand firm against any Griqua claims to Dikgatlhong. Jantjie, as usual, turned to his missionary for advice. Ross explained the significance and meaning of written title deeds, presumably pointing out that Boers on both sides of the Vaal were expanding their settlements ever closer, and that their land claims were backed by title deeds. Whether or not Ross actually *advised* them on what action to take, towards the end of 1861 Jantjie, Luka and the leading men of Dikgatlhong decided, much against their instincts, that they had no option in this rapidly changing world but to offer to buy the title themselves. Greef agreed to the sale and said that sixty oxen would settle it. The Batlhaping presented him with fifty-six oxen and fifty-three sheep and goats. Greef accepted the stock, but he then drew up conditions, not previously mentioned. These included the demand that Jantjie should protect him, Greef, as the sole legal trader in Dikgatlhong and its district. Greef was also to have sole control of a spring, the land around it

---

[5] *LMS*, Ross, Likatlong, 14 June 1861, and 12 March 1862

and a site for a second house in Dikgatlhong as well as the new trading store that the resident trader van Blerk was currently building.

Luka was outraged at these conditions. Against his advice, an agreement had been reached and a sale had been made. Now Greef expected to be able to retain many of the benefits of ownership after he had sold the title deeds. As a man well used to trading in valuable hunting commodities with the traders of Kuruman and Griquatown, Luka knew how a deal, once made, should be respected, and so far as he could see this man was trying to cheat his father. He turned on Greef and angrily seized the title deeds from his hands. The two men almost came to blows. According to Ross, it was Jantjie who calmed the atmosphere at the time, by suggesting that they take the case to Nicholas Waterboer, the Griqua leader at Griquatown. Luka reluctantly agreed, but it was the beginning of a distrust and animosity between him and Greef that was to persist in the decades to come.

They met with Waterboer (*left*) and his councillors at Campbell in December 1861. Waterboer acknowledged that the Griqua had no right to sell Batlhaping land which had never been sold to them in the first place; but since Greef would not accept the payment without the conditions attached, Waterboer told Jantjie to take the livestock home and to keep the deeds.

For the time being the Batlhaping rights to Dikgatlhong seemed to have been settled. Not only did they have the land by historic right of occupation, but they also now had a 'title deed'. The only problem with possessing this deed was that it implied Batlhaping acceptance of the Griqua right to issue such a deed. It was a legal point that was to store up trouble in the future.

And trouble was hastened to the land of the Batlhaping by the discovery of a large diamond, weighing in at twenty carats, that was picked up on the south bank of the Orange River in 1867. With its discovery and that of others in subsequent months along the lower Vaal, the land of the Dikgatlhong *morafe* became the epicentre of events that were to prove one of the major turning points in southern African history, with disastrous consequences for Luka and the Batlhaping of Dikgatlhong.

41

CHAPTER FOUR

The defence of the diamond fields

1867–1871

It was the itinerant colonial trader John O'Reilly who brought the first diamond into Hopetown in 1867. That initial gem, named 'the Eureka', was treated with a certain degree of scepticism in colonial circles. It was not widely known at the time how diamonds were formed or that there could be any such thing as a diamond mine: it was assumed that this was a chance find, unlikely to be repeated.

For a number of years itinerant colonial traders had been working among the Batlhaping, buying grain, livestock and general hunting produce in exchange for goods such as ammunition, clothing, domestic utensils, iron cooking pots, tea, coffee, sugar and cheap Cape brandy. The latter, distilled from a liquor brewed from the waste of the wine industry (skins, pips and stalks), was made specifically for the 'African market' – part-payment for labour in the Colony or to ease trading transactions beyond the border. Now O'Reilly and others like him spread the word across the lower Vaal region that they were offering 'generous prices' in livestock, consumer goods and brandy for any diamonds discovered lying on the ground.

The Batlhaping, Korana and Griqua of the region responded accordingly and during the first half of 1868 a steady number of small diamonds filtered down to the colony. Even then Cape merchants still regarded diamonds as merely a minor addition to the general 'interior trade' that was still domi-nated by ivory and ostrich feathers. It is likely that initially Luka also took this view of the earliest diamond discoveries.

During the 1860s a major traffic in arms and ammunition in exchange for ivory and ostrich feathers had developed between the Cape Colony and the Griqua, Batlhaping and other peoples north of the colony. Kuruman became an important hunting terminus,[1] with at least one secure ammunition

---

[1] Shillington, *Colonisation*, pp21–25.

A contemporary engraving showing an early white prospector in Batswana territory checking the weight of the diamonds he has discovered. Many more were to follow his example, and pose a threat to the well-being of many Batlhaping communities in the area.

magazine and two permanent trading stores. Luka himself had become a prominent member of the long-distance hunting fraternity and by the mid-1860s he was journeying as far as the valley of the Shashe river on the present border of northeast Botswana and southwest Zimbabwe. The region lay between the northern Batswana *morafe* of the Bangwato and the Ndebele kingdom of Mzilikazi and was reputed to be heavily populated with elephants. In this period of the 1860s the southern Batswana hunters such as Luka, with their ox-wagons, horses and guns, had a clear hunting advantage over the local Bangwato and Ndebele hunters, who did not yet have regular access to firearms.

Luka appears to have accumulated considerable wealth through the hunting trade, much of it invested in cattle. But he would also have bought new guns, wagons, horses, clothing and other consumer goods for himself and his family. It is hardly surprising that he did not immediately react to the discovery of a few small stones that appeared to be so highly valued by the white people. Even the Cape merchants were slow to react, though by the middle of 1868 the colonial merchants of Hopetown recognised that diamonds were more than just an occasional addition to the 'interior' trade.

There were two rival merchant partnerships in Hopetown: Lilienfeld Brothers, and Phillipson & Wykeham; during the course of 1868 they each established their own resident trading agent north of the colonial border. The Lilienfelds' agent was Stafford Parker who set up a thriving business exchanging Cape brandy for diamonds at Jan Bloem III's Korana village of Pniel on the south bank of the Vaal. Phillipson & Wykeham had their own agent on the other side of the river, an American diamond dealer named

David Bebell, who set up his store in Dikgatlhong.[2] In accordance with mission strictures, *Kgosi* Jantjie, who was himself a teeto-taller, had banned the sale of brandy in Dikgatlhong; but Parker faced no such restrictions in Pniel, and as a result he seems to have got the better diamond-dealing opportunity in the region.

A simple shop typical of the area at this time.

It is probable that sometime during the course of 1868 Luka began to take an interest in the diamond trade and to organise searching parties along the north bank of the lower Vaal where most of the gemstones were being found. Parker extended his business across the river to deal directly with the Batlhaping and it is possibly at this point that Luka sold Parker some diamonds in exchange for Cape brandy. There is no suggestion in the mission record that he had previously consumed colonial liquor, though he had almost certainly drunk the traditional home-brewed sorghum beer. He was certainly on at least one occasion consuming Cape brandy in 1869.

By the end of 1868 the pace and scale of diamond searching had increased dramatically though it was still in the hands of local Africans who sold the gems to colonial traders. J B Robinson, later to become a major diamond and gold-mining capitalist, established himself at Hebron on the north bank of the Vaal and claimed to have bought £10,000 worth of diamonds in his first six weeks of business. Batlhaping and Korana of the Vaal River region quickly realised the high value that the traders placed upon diamonds and began asking 'exorbitant prices' for them, which ate into the traders' hitherto exorbitant profits. By the early months of 1869 the search for diamonds had become a major arm of the Batlhaping economy. Along the north bank of the Vaal, between Hebron and the river's junction with the Harts:

> [They] would form themselves into long lines, joined hand in hand, and walk slowly over the ground and look for diamonds, especially after rain; and if they found one they would take it to a trader.[3]

Whatever Luka's involvement in the diamond trade during 1868, in the early months of 1869 he had other matters on his mind.

---

[2] Shillington, *Colonisation,* pp35–38; Phillipson & Wykeham Letter Books, De Beers Archives, .
[3] J L Babe, *The South African Diamond Fields* (1872), p19.

Engraving of a 'Bechuana Chief' by Thomas Baines (1867). Although the face-profile does not resemble Luka's later portrait, the riding boots, breeches, coat, jaunty hat and tusks represent the wealth, stature and hunting prowess that would have been Luka Jantjie in his mid-thirties.

In February 1869 the South African Republic (Transvaal) renewed its demand for payment from Mahura for war expenses due from 1858. President Pretorius himself came to a Transvaal farm on the north bank of the Vaal not far from Taung, probably near the present town of Christiana. From there he sent letters to Mahura and to Jantjie, as well as to Motlhabane and Botlasitse, although it was clear that he considered the former two the most important. They were all invited to meet him at Christiana.

Jantjie showed his copy of the letter to William Ashton who had been resident missionary at Dikgatlhong since 1864, following the death of Ross the previous year. According to Ashton, Pretorius's letter claimed that he wanted to meet the Batlhaping *dikgosi* in order 'to consult together for the good of the people & country, & to take away the hinderance to peace & prosperity.' It is unlikely that Jantjie or Luka trusted Pretorius's sincerity where peace and prosperity was concerned, but they probably also distrusted the wisdom of Mahura and the other *dikgosi* whose rash actions in 1858 had got them into this dispute in the first place. Under the circumstances they knew it would be unwise to ignore the President's invitation, and so father and son loaded up their wagons, and accompanied by councillors and attendants, they made the two-day journey to Christiana.[4]

Pretorius opened the meeting by supplying the assembled *dikgosi* with copious amounts of Cape brandy. Jantjie refused the liquor on principle. If Luka drank any on this occasion, he did not drink to excess. According to Ashton, however, who had the story from Jantjie, Mahura and probably also

[4] *LMS*, Ashton, Likatlong, 6 July 1869.

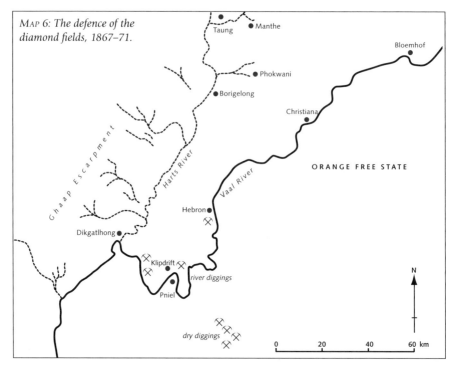

MAP 6: The defence of the
diamond fields, 1867–71.

Botlasitse, drank so much that they were incapable of discussing anything that first day of the conference.

In the ensuing days the Boers plied Mahura with less brandy, but it was said by Ashton that he was so eager to get the liquor that he would have agreed to sign anything. Under the circumstances, it was probably left to Jantjie and Luka to argue the Batlhaping case against the 'fine' demanded by Pretorius and his men. The upshot of the meeting, which lasted several days, was that the original demand for 8,000 cattle, 300 horses and 500 guns was whittled down to 3,000 head of cattle in settlement of all claims. Pretorius drew up a document in Dutch[5] to this effect, adding that the cattle should be delivered within three months. He presented it for all the *dikgosi* to sign.

It is likely that Luka was able to read enough of the Dutch document to understand its central thrust and he was concerned about the extent to which his father was being drawn into this dispute. Jantjie, ever the peacemaker, said that although he had taken no part in the war of 1858, a point acknowledged by Pretorius, he would help the other *dikgosi* by collecting some of the cattle from his own people, rather than see the country forfeited to the

[5] In the Boer republics Dutch still remained the official language of government. The dialect of Afrikaans, the language of Boer and Griqua, had not yet been transcribed into writing.

South African Republic. On Luka's advice, however, Jantjie refused to put his own name to the agreement on the grounds that the original dispute had been nothing to do with them. Pretorius apparently responded by saying: 'But surely you will sign your own words, you say they must pay cattle rather than give up the land, & you have promised to assist them to do so.' One can imagine Jantjie in turmoil over this, torn between his son's advice – 'Don't sign' – and the persuasiveness of Pretorius. In the end he concluded that if he did not sign he would look deceitful, and the one thing that Jantjie valued more than anything in negotiation was his own honesty and integrity. So, reluctantly, he concluded that he had no option but to add his signature to the crosses marked by Mahura, Botlasitse and Motlhabane.

As soon as Jantjie and Luka got home they called a general meeting to explain the situation, and then they sent people out around the villages and cattle-posts to collect their share of the 'fine'. Some weeks later a large body of people set off from Dikgatlhong with 300 cattle – ten percent of the total – that they had collected. According to Ashton they travelled in a party of fifty wagons, which clearly entailed a large number of the people of Dikgatlhong, determined to see that their contribution to the total was not wasted.

They arrived at Taung to find that the other *dikgosi* had so far contributed nothing. When Jantjie remonstrated, Mahura replied: 'Where are our children?' referring to those taken by the Boers in 1858. Jantjie apparently conceded the point, for he and Mahura then drafted a letter to Pretorius. It is probable that Luka in fact drafted the letter, which Mahura would have marked with his cross and Jantjie would have signed. The letter explained that they would not give up any cattle until their children had been returned.[6]

Jantjie and his people returned with their cattle to Dikgatlhong to await a response to the letter. The answer came from Commandant Jan Viljoen and Mr Best, landdrost[7] of Bloemhof. They came first to Dikgatlhong and insisted that Jantjie accompany them to Taung. They clearly considered that if anyone could talk the Taung people into accepting a deal of some sort, it was Jantjie. When the deputation arrived at Taung, Mahura was asked what he intended to do. After consultation with his councillors, the answer came back:

Nothing! You took our waggons & oxen, cows & goats, you killed our people, & enslaved our children, & we will give you nothing.

The Boer deputation returned to their government, leaving the people of

---

[6] *LMS*, Ashton, 6 July 1869.
[7] Landdrost: magistrate, responsible for land matters.

Taung and district seriously worried about the possibility of attack from another Boer commando. Jantjie returned to Dikgatlhong concerned about how his signature on the recent agreement might involve him in a conflict that was not of his making. It is not known whether Luka had accompanied his father to Taung on this occasion: possibly not, as back home in Dikgatlhong more immediate matters were taking a dangerous turn.

At what was now known as the 'diamond fields', along the north bank of the Vaal, Luka was attempting to keep control of events. He had begun regular patrols along the river bank, doing some diamond searching on his own account. Parker periodically crossed the river from Pniel and Luka sold some diamonds to him. Part of these transactions involved brandy. It was round about this time that Ashton expelled Luka from membership of the Church for drunkenness.[8] It is not clear how excessive or frequent Luka's drinking was, and it is possible that Ashton, the pious missionary, may have exaggerated its extent. He may have felt that Luka, unlike his father, was too defiant of the missionary's authority. What is certain is that at the same time that he was reputedly drinking, Luka was quite soberly asserting his father's authority over the diamond fields. He was charging fees from any 'foreigner', especially the Korana and any Africans or *makgowa* from the Free State or the Cape Colony. For that fee he issued a permit to search for diamonds within the Dikgatlhong *morafe*. This was defined as anywhere within the Harts–Vaal territory north of the Vaal River.[9]

By the beginning of the post-harvest dry season in May 1869 the number of prospectors crossing the river was getting beyond Luka's control. Some *makgowa* from the colonies set up camp and began digging into the ground, convinced that there must be some central point of origin for the precious gems. Appreciating the power of the written word in *makgowa* society, Luka advised his father to issue a proclamation banning any person from using a pick or shovel and digging for diamonds within the *morafe*. Ashton supported the idea and had the proclamation printed at Kuruman. Luka distributed copies to all potential diamond seekers within the territory of Dikgatlhong.

Still more prospectors, traders and speculators from the Boer republics and the British colonies of Natal and the Cape came to the diamond fields. Most, for the moment, accepted Luka's assertion of Batlhaping political authority along the north bank of the river; but the pace of business was rapidly accelerating. 'Horses, wagons, cows, sheep, cash, goods etc. [were

[8] *LMS*, Ashton, 6 July 1869.
[9] Shillington, *Colonisation*, pp39–43.

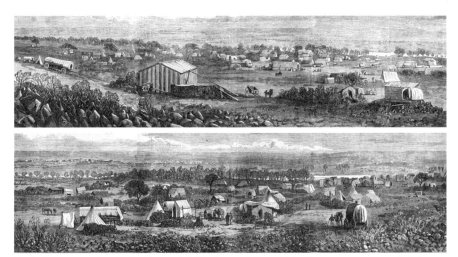

Early days prospecting in the diamond fields; hot and dusty, living in wagons, tents and tin houses – it was not nearly as idyllic as it appears in these contemporary engravings.

being exchanged for diamonds] at a deuce of a pace."[10] Luka and his father began to worry that the integrity of the *morafe* itself was under threat.

In July 1869 the Lilienfelds of Hopetown offered to pay Jantjie for the exclusive mineral rights to diamonds found in his country. Jantjie rejected the offer on the grounds that neither he nor his son could prevent their own people from picking up and selling diamonds to whomever they wanted, let alone the outsiders who were now flooding into the country.

Acting on what was probably the advice of William Ashton, Jantjie wrote to the Governor of the Cape Colony, Sir Philip Wodehouse, asking for the British government to take his country under British 'protection'. The letter was written in Ashton's handwriting and signed by Jantjie, so it appears that Luka played no part in this. If he had been consulted, he might not have approved of such a surrender of ultimate authority to the whim of the regional 'superpower'. He had learned much about the dangers of dealing with a more powerful state in his negotiations with the Boer leader Pretorius; but at the same time he would have deferred to his father's authority.

The missionaries of the LMS on the other hand believed in the benevolence and ultimate good that would result from any extension of British authority. And it would not have been difficult for Ashton to persuade Jantjie of the benefit of British protection. It was widely known that in the previous year Wodehouse had saved Moshoeshoe's Basotho kingdom from military annihilation at the hands of the Free State Boers by declaring a British

---

[10] *Colesburg Advertiser*, 7 September 1869.

'protectorate' over the remnants of Basutoland. Moshoeshoe had been left with local power over his own people and the Basotho had been guaranteed the protection of their remaining land from white occupation. This was the kind of protection that Jantjie's letter sought. Ashton travelled to Hopetown to deliver the letter into the hands of the local Civil Commissioner, for forwarding to the Governor. He attached to Jantjie's letter an English translation and his own covering letter, dated 2 August, explaining the background to the case. Ashton was careful to emphasise the potential threat from Pretorius and the South African Republic.[11] Ashton and the LMS in general were very averse to any extension of Boer power.

The Hopetown merchants were also concerned about the potential Boer threat to their free access to the 'interior trade' that was of such value to the economy of the Cape Colony. At their urging, the Port Elizabeth wholesale merchants petitioned the Cape Colonial Secretary, Richard Southey, arguing the case for British annexation of Griqua and Batlhaping territory before it fell into Boer hands. Meanwhile the Hopetown merchants were busy acquiring rival mineral as well as land 'concessions' from Mahura and from Waterboer.

An insolvent colonial trader named Theodore Doms produced a document, which he claimed had been signed by Mahura, that granted the holder the sole concession to dig for diamonds within Batlhaping territory. Doms had ostensibly acquired this 'Mahura Concession' on behalf of Phillipson & Co to whom he was deeply in debt, but he then double-crossed his financial backers by secretly selling the document to a Transvaal consortium headed by President Pretorius. If *Kgosi* Mahura, within months of his own death, had indeed marked his cross on Doms's 'concession', it was presumably in exchange for brandy. But whatever the circumstances of its signing, Mahura had no such primary authority over the Batlhaping that entitled him to sign such a document. When news of the document reached Hopetown in early August, Ashton, acting on his own initiative, sent an official notification in the name of Jantjie Mothibi to the newspapers of the Cape Colony. The notice repudiated the so-called 'Mahura Concession' as well as any action taken by Theodore Doms.

This was one of the last acts performed by William Ashton on behalf of the Batlhaping before he went on long leave to England. His departure at this critical time for the Dikgatlhong *morafe* left *Kgosi* Jantjie ever more dependent upon the initiative and advice of his eldest son, Luka.

$\sim$ $\sim$ $\sim$

---

[11] *LMS*, Ashton, 6 July 1869.

Two deaths in 1869 marked the final passing of a generation of Batlhaping leaders. In April 1869 Mahuto, the senior widow of Mothibi, finally passed away aged just a few years short of a hundred. Seven months later Mahura died at Taung (*see family tree, p16*).

In his late seventies at the time of his death, Mahura had been the last surviving son of Molehabangwe, whose rule stretched well back into the eighteenth century. Mahura's place at the head of the Taung *morafe* was taken by his nephew, Mankurwane, the son of Mahura's older brother Molale who had died in 1826. Mahura had acted as Mankurwane's regent ever since, despite the fact that Mankurwane was almost fifty years old at the time of Mahura's death. New challenges now lay ahead, which the new *kgosi* would struggle to deal with.

Occurring when it did in November 1869, Mahura's death symbolised the passing of an era. It also marked a turning point in the fortunes of the diamond fields.

In the month of Mahura's death a party of white men from the British colony of Natal began digging for diamonds at Hebron, on the Vaal River. Theirs was the first large group of white prospectors to openly defy the authority of Jantjie and Luka. One of the party was Herbert Rhodes, the elder brother of the future diamond magnate, Cecil Rhodes. The problem was compounded by the Korana chief, Jan Bloem, who began selling diamond-digging concessions which could not be his to sell as they were across the river in Batlhaping territory.

Luka drafted a complaint to the Cape authorities which Jantjie signed and sent to the Cape's Civil Commissioner at Hopetown, but the latter simply forwarded the letter to Cape Town through official channels. With no immediate response from Hopetown, Luka assembled a military force of five hundred men, most of whom were armed with guns; they were supported by thirty wagons carrying ammunition and supplies. Accompanied by his father, Luka led the Batlhaping army along the valley of the Vaal to the 'drift' or river-ford opposite Pniel where Bloem had been operating. The effect was immediate. White traders, prospectors and Korana fled across the river, leaving a terminally-ill Bloem alone to face the army.

Jantjie did not want a confrontation, and on his advice the Batlhaping forces withdrew without proceeding to Hebron, where the Natal group carried on quietly digging, though without much success. Within days Bloem was dead and Parker returned to the north bank to continue with his brandy trading. Meanwhile, most of the white traders and prospectors who had fled across the river turned their attention elsewhere.

The interest of the colonial traders, prospectors and speculators now shifted to a fairly barren region forty kilometres southeast of the river where, within two years, the modern city of Kimberley was to mushroom into existence. The previous month, in October 1869, some diamonds had been found there, well away from the river. The land of these 'dry diggings' was under Free State title and the farms Bultfontein and Du Toit's Pan were quickly purchased by the Hopetown traders, Lilienfeld Brothers, in November 1869. With excitement now focussed on the dry diggings, the pressure was eased slightly along the Vaal.

Nevertheless, Luka stressed to his father the need to build up the Batlhaping armed forces. The show of military strength in November had worked on that occasion and not a shot had been fired, but Luka appears to have believed that it was only through threat of force that the Batlhaping could hope to maintain their territorial integrity. In January 1870 Luka and his father travelled to Hopetown to see if the Civil Commissioner had acted on their complaint. Receiving no help from that quarter they went to Phillipson's store and ordered two cannon, the type and size of which is unspecified in the surviving record. They also ordered 2,000 pounds of ammunition. Luka clearly meant business. On the official permit request signed by Jantjie the cannon were declared to be for his 'own protection and that of his people.' The cannon arrived in Hopetown in March, but Phillipson did nothing to inform Jantjie and Luka of their arrival. He did not appear to consider it a matter of any urgency.

Early the following month, a colonial prospector was sifting through the debris that his servants had dug out near the drift across the river from Pniel when he found several diamonds. For months prospectors had been speculating that there must be some source, a 'mine' from which the diamonds along the banks of the river bed had originated. Now, in April 1870, they believed that they had found it. There was an immediate rush of 'diggers' and speculators from the Cape Colony and Natal as hundreds abandoned the dry diggings and rushed to the new river-digging site which they named Klipdrift.[12]

In the absence of William Ashton, Jantjie was now increasingly following the lead of his son Luka, who by this time had come round to the idea of asking

---

[12] Shillington, *Colonisation*, pp39–60.

The Vaal in the 1890s; looking much the same as in the 1870s. Note the tent on the river bank.

the British for some sort of protection from this invasion by British subjects. Father and son proceeded immediately to Hopetown, where on 19 April 1870 Jantjie lodged a formal protest, demanding, in the words of the local Cape Civil Commissioner, 'protection against British subjects who defy his authority in the country which he claims as his own.'[13] Unbeknown to Luka and Jantjie, however, their request was badly timed: Governor Wodehouse was about to depart from the Colony on the conclusion of his term of office and he was not prepared to make any such decision. Accordingly, in a letter from the Attorney-General dated 12 May 1870, Jantjie's request for protection was turned down.

In the meantime, while in Hopetown, Jantjie and Luka went to Phillipson's store to purchase some supplies and they saw their two cannon there waiting for collection. They were possibly old ship's cannon for they were unmounted and of unknown dimensions. The Batlhaping *kgosi* and his son demanded to be given immediate possession of their artillery and guaranteed to deliver '150 head of first class oxen for each cannon within a week.' Phillipson, however, refused to let them have the cannon, preferring to deal through his own agents in the field, David Bebell, who was resident at Dikgatlhong. So Jantjie and Luka returned home with neither British protection nor their cannon.

As part of the deal for taking delivery of their cannon, Jantjie was eventually persuaded in May 1870 to grant to Bebell, for the price of £750, the right to issue diamond-prospecting licences in Jantjie's name throughout Batlhaping territory from Dikgatlhong to Hebron. The cannon were duly delivered to Dikgatlhong at the end of May. Ironically, many months later Phillipson complained that they had still not received payment from Bebell.

---

[13] *CA*, CO 3168, Civil Commissioner, Hopetown, 19 April 1870.

By this time the white diggers of Klipdrift had organised themselves into a Diggers' Mutual Protection Association, under the chairmanship of Stafford Parker. Parker's initiative in forming the Association was probably at the behest of his Hopetown backers, the Lilienfeld Brothers, who hoped to gain a trading monopoly in the supply of diamonds from Klipdrift. The official object of the Association was to provide some sort of order to the claims that were being marked out by individual prospectors. The Association also provided 'mutual protection' for its members to establish a prospecting monopoly at Klipdrift in defiance of Jantjie's authority. And despite his connection to the Lilienfeld Brothers, Parker managed to persuade his fellow diggers that the Association would also protect them from the designs of speculative merchants and capitalist companies.

Although they called themselves 'diggers', the white prospectors on the diamond fields did very little actual digging themselves. This was done by their African servants. The diggers, so-called, sat on benches, supervising the digging, sieving and washing of the debris. Their work entailed sifting through the stones that were laid out on 'sorting tables' (*diamond washing filter, left*).

By early July there were eight hundred white prospectors at Klipdrift and Parker's committee had divided the area up into individual claims of 30 square feet (about eight square metres) each. Jantjie tried demanding £5 per claim, but mostly his efforts were in vain. They just refused to pay. Klipdrift itself was already becoming overcrowded and white prospectors began spreading out upstream towards Hebron and downstream towards the Harts, to Keiskama and Gong-Gong. Away from Klipdrift, Jantjie was able to collect ten shillings (50 pence) per sifting 'cradle', usually supervised by several white men, or a quarter of that per individual white man. Africans – Batlhaping or others – were not charged. Bebell was collecting fees at Keiskama, while Luka was collecting fees, as well as digging, at Hebron.

With fortunes riding on a chance find, and white prospectors assuming the racist superiority of colonists, violence was never far from the surface in the early diamond fields. The colonial newspapers had reported a particularly sickening story as early as August 1869. It was alleged that a white man had accused his African servant of concealing a diamond by swallowing it. When the servant failed to produce the diamond, the white man cut open his stomach to retrieve it. The newspaper did not report whether the assailant found the diamond, merely that the victim had since died. Whatever the truth of this particular story, it represented the atmosphere of violence that could easily be expected during that early scrabble for diamonds along the Vaal River valley.

A more closely recorded story of violence occurred in late July 1870, while Luka was prospecting for diamonds near Hebron. A German colonist named Schwab shot his African servant dead, apparently for allowing his cattle to stray. Luka was the accepted authority in the area and two Boers who were also prospecting nearby had no hesitation in helping Luka to arrest the man. Together they tied Schwab to his wagon, flogged him and confiscated his goods, to an estimated value of £70.

Parker was incensed: that a black man should flog a white man – even if that black man was widely recognised as the legitimate authority in the area, undisputedly so at Hebron itself. Eager to prove that no black man should exercise authority over the white prospectors of the diamond fields, Parker displayed all the racist contempt of a seasoned colonist. Gathering together a group of like-minded men from Klipdrift, he proceeded to Hebron and 'arrested' Luka. The Batlhaping *kgosi* and the two Boers were marched to Klipdrift under armed guard and confined to a tent.

Jantjie, the great peacemaker, now prepared for war. He summoned together as many armed men as he could and, with his two cannon mounted on a wagon, he moved his army across the Harts. As had happened the previous November, most of the white prospectors, including many in Klipdrift, fled across the river and waited to see what would happen. It was unclear what Parker intended to do with Luka, whom he described as 'the greatest scoundrel living.' Seeing the approach of Jantjie's army, however, a group of prospectors who were uncomfortable with Parker's high-handed action, took charge of the situation. They decided to put Luka and the two Boers on trial.

Luka's trial, so-called, took place in a large tent before a jury of nine white diggers. The former double-crossing, bankrupt speculator Theodore Doms declared himself to be acting as Luka's legal representative. This was the man who had twice sold (to Phillipson and to Pretorius) the dubious 'Mahura concession' which claimed that Mahura was the sole Batlhaping authority north of the Vaal. Under the circumstances, it is highly unlikely that Luka would have willingly hired such a man. There is no record of what evidence or arguments were used in the trial, only that it ruled that Luka and the two

Contemporary photo of river diggings (prospecting for diamonds) at Christiana in the Transvaal.

Boers were to be released. They were to return the goods that they had seized from Schwab, who was fined a mere £25 for the murder of his servant, a fine that was later remitted.

It appears that the 'respectable' prospectors of Klipdrift wanted to avoid any sort of confrontation that would interfere with the diamond-hunting business. By quickly releasing Luka they ensured that Jantjie's army was called off and the white people of Klipdrift were able to get back to 'digging' as quickly as possible. At the same time, by the mere fact of holding some sort of trial, they had asserted the white man's claim to make rulings over any case involving one of their own.

For his rash behaviour Parker lost his chairmanship of the Diggers' Mutual Protection Association, which was formally dissolved and reformed as the Diggers' Executive Committee under the leadership of a local medical doctor, J R Robertson. Parker was not finished, however, and his actions soon became even more high-handed.

Following Luka's release, Doms' motives began to become clearer. Claiming to possess Luka's power of attorney, Doms began selling to white speculators titles to 6,000 acre plots of Batlhaping land within the Harts–Vaal territory. Despite Doms' claims, it is extremely unlikely that Luka would have authorised any such power. Indeed, at the Arbitration Commission that the British were to set up at Bloemhof in 1871, Jantjie denied that he or any of his family had ever given any legal authority to Doms at any time. Although a few at Klipdrift showed some interest in Doms' titles, very few paid him any money, and certainly no money was ever passed on to the Batlhaping, in whose name Doms claimed to be acting. It was, however, one more complication in the morass of claims and counter-claims, that Luka and Jantjie could have done without.

The leaders of the two Boer republics had observed the drama of Luka's arrest and trial and they chose to interpret it as ambiguity over legal authority in the region, an ambiguity which they moved swiftly to correct. Aware that the Cape government was already being petitioned by colonial merchants to annex the diamond-bearing ground, the two republican governments asserted their own claims to the region. In August 1870 the Orange Free State established a magistrate south of the river at Pniel while the following month the South African Republic established one on the north bank at Hebron. The Cape government, awaiting the arrival of a new Governor, was slow to respond and their magistrate, John Campbell, did not arrive at Klipdrift until December 1870.

By October 1870 there were five thousand white prospectors at the river diggings, most of them clustered around Klipdrift. It appeared by November that the claims were becoming exhausted as fewer and fewer diamonds were being found. With the return of the rains that month, the majority of the white prospectors rushed back to the 'dry diggings' of Bultfontein and Dutoitspan where they were soon to discover diamonds on another neighbouring farm, owned by the Boer, Nicholas De Beer.[14]

As the number of prospectors at Klipdrift declined, Parker seized control of the Diggers' Executive Committee and declared himself President with one of his henchmen, Roderick Barker, as a committee member. A colonial newspaper wit named them 'Parker and Barker, the Barker and Bitor [sic].' Parker renamed Klipdrift 'Parkerton' and began selling off commercial plots for the new township. Few seem to have accepted the change of name, and in December Parker joined up with Doms, who had by this time given up any pretence of acting for Luka. The two of them ran their land scam, selling titles to riverside plots to disillusioned white prospectors of Klipdrift. At the same time Parker and his henchmen set aside two days a week for clearing the riverside region of Batlhaping cattle and impounding them. The animals were slaughtered for the growing meat market at the dry diggings.

With the arrival of a British magistrate at Klipdrift in December 1870, Doms and Barker decided they would be better able to effect their land scams if the Transvaal authorities were expelled from the region. With this in mind the two men came to Dikgatlhong to try and borrow Jantjie's cannon. Luka

---

[14] The mine on this farm was in due course to become the original home of the De Beer's Mining Company, founded by Cecil Rhodes in 1880.

was not present at the time and Jantjie turned them down flat. There was, however, a Morolong at Dikgatlhong called Jacob Nakentsi. He claimed to be the Barolong diamond fields' representative of *Kgosi* Moroka of Thaba 'Nchu in the Orange Free State. He was also involved in diamond prospecting along the Vaal between Gong-Gong and Klipdrift. Nakentsi favoured military action against the Boer republic and he persuaded Jantjie to let him take the cannon to his river-digging claim and have them properly mounted. Then if Doms and Barker took them from there, Jantjie could deny all responsibility.

Had Luka been present, it is very unlikely that Jantjie would have approved of such a flimsy subterfuge. Luka would have sympathised with Nakentsi's sentiments, but after the experience of 1858, he would almost certainly have disallowed their cannon, even indirectly, from becoming involved in so reckless a venture, especially one that entrusted them to such scoundrels as Doms, Barker and Parker.

In the first week of January 1871 Nakentsi brought the two mounted cannon to Klipdrift. Doms and Parker, reassured by the presence of the artillery and a 'native representative', Nakentsi of the Barolong, issued a proclamation ordering the South African Republic to withdraw its magistrate from Hebron. The ultimatum threatened that if republican officials failed to withdraw completely from the Harts–Vaal territory within two weeks they would be driven out by the 'armed forces' of 'the Barolong and Batlapin Tribes' under the command of their 'Commander-in Chief', Roderick Barker.

John Campbell, the British magistrate at Klipdrift, was quick to react. He issued a proclamation forbidding any British subject from taking up arms against the South African Republic. A few days later Doms withdrew his ultimatum; he had just heard that a new British Governor, Sir Henry Barkly, was arriving at the Cape with authorisation to annex the diamond fields.

Campbell reported to the Cape Colonial Secretary, Richard Southey, who was acting for the Governor until the new man's arrival later that month. Campbell explained the action that he had taken in order to maintain the peace and security of the diamond fields and he urged a quick British resolution of the crisis. At the same time Campbell linked Jantjie, and the Batlhaping of Dikgatlhong with the dubious activities of Parker, Doms, Barker and their 'body of roughs'.

Thus Jantjie, Luka and the Batlhaping entered the territorial dispute that was to follow, with their case dangerously flawed by the activities of those who claimed fraudulently to act in their name, and with the British already turned against them.

CHAPTER FIVE

The loss of the diamond fields
1871–1876

In January 1871 Sir Henry Barkly arrived in Cape Town to take up his new post as Governor of the Cape Colony and High Commissioner for South Africa. The latter title gave him powers to represent British interests beyond the Cape Colony, and that of course included the diamond fields. He wasted no time in hurrying north to see the area for himself and to work out the best way to ensure that this potentially wealthy region could be acquired for Britain. Barkly arrived in Klipdrift in February 1871, to be greeted by an enthusiastic crowd of colonists, who declared their loyalty to Britain and proposed to change the name of Klipdrift to Barkly. With British colonists in a small town in the Eastern Cape showing equal enthusiasm for the new name, this one soon became Barkly West.

Kgosi Jantjie had gone to Klipdrift to try and see High Commissioner Barkly and to press his case for the protection of his people's land. It is likely that he took Luka with him as they would have been expecting to write or sign some agreement with the British representative. Unfortunately for them, William Ashton was still away on leave until July and so at this crucial moment in the shaping of British policy towards their territory, Jantjie and Luka lacked a sympathetic champion who could get them an audience with the High Commissioner. As it was, the local British official, the magistrate John Campbell, simply refused to allow them access to Sir Henry Barkly.

Even if they had managed to speak to the High Commissioner, however, it is unlikely that they would have gained anything by it, for Barkly had already pre-judged the issue. Briefed in Cape Town by Colonial Secretary Richard Southey and in Klipdrift by Magistrate Campbell, Barkly had decided that British acquisition of the diamond fields was to be based upon the Griqua chief Nicholas Waterboer's claims to the region, as developed by his lawyer David Arnot. Arnot based Griqua claims to the whole of the Dikgatlhong *morafe* and beyond upon a treaty of friendship concluded between Waterboer's father, Andries Waterboer, and *Kgosi* Mahura of Taung in 1842.

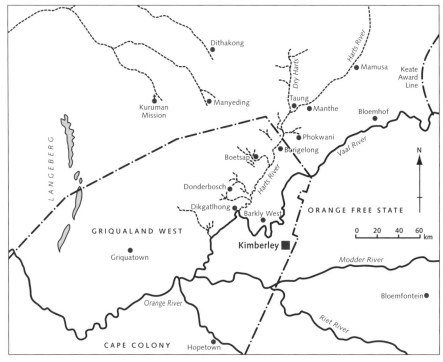

So far as Mahura had been concerned, this had been a treaty of friendship and one that conveyed no territorial concession whatsoever. Now that Mahura was dead, however, Arnot (*left*) used this treaty to make two false claims: first that it had indeed been a territorial agreement, and second that Mahura was the senior *kgosi* of the Batlhaping and that he therefore had the authority to make such an agreement. According to Arnot, this meant that everything south of Mankurwane's immediate authority, including Borigelong and Dikgatlhong, belonged to the Griqua (*see map below*).

MAP 7: *The loss of the diamond fields, 1871–76.*

Arnot had already intimated to Southey shortly before Barkly's arrival that in the event of Griqua claims being accepted, Waterboer would ask for British 'protection': in other words, he would surrender his authority to the British. In order to retain the appearance of impartiality, however, Barkly announced at Klipdrift that the whole question of who had authority to rule the region would be decided by a special commission. This would start hearing evidence within a month at Bloemhof on the middle Vaal, one of the westernmost settlements of the South African Republic. But Barkly's professed impartiality was a sham. He had already decided that Jantjie would not be allowed to put forward any territorial claims at Bloemhof. To have allowed Jantjie to present a case against the Griqua would have undermined the whole legal basis for British annexation of the diamond fields. The Bloemhof Commission was, in essence, an elaborate rubber stamp, designed to give the gloss of legality to British ambitions in the region.[1]

The Orange Free State refused to submit to the Bloemhof Commission, arguing that there was no case to be made against their right to all of the land between the Vaal and the Orange, which contained the dry diggings of Bultfontein, Dutoitspan and De Beers. The British decided they would have to find a way to placate the Free State. In the meantime, the cases submitted for arbitration were those of the South African Republic, Mankurwane's and Motlhabane's Batlhaping, Moroka's Barolong and Waterboer's Griqua.

Jantjie and Luka made their way to Bloemhof where the Commission heard evidence between March and June 1871. They were accompanied by the leading men of the outlying villages of the Dikgatlhong *morafe*, in particular those of the river-digging region along the north bank of the Vaal. Jantjie had already been told by the Klipdrift magistrate John Campbell, who happened to be one of the two commissioners at Bloemhof, that he would not be allowed to present a claim. However, he was determined that his people's case would be heard.

Theodore Doms was also present at Bloemhof, but Jantjie refused to allow him to act for the Batlhaping. Instead he turned to the Revd Ludorf, Wesleyan missionary to Moroka's Barolong at Thaba 'Nchu in the Orange Free State. Ludorf was there to present Moroka's ambitious claims to most of the territory between the middle Vaal and the Molopo River, modern Botswana's southern border.[2] Ludorf agreed to act for Jantjie. He persuaded Commissioner Campbell to allow Jantjie and the headmen of his villages to give evidence of where they lived and for how long. Although this evidence was heard, and it showed widespread Batlhaping occupation of the whole of the Harts–Vaal territory, it was not allowed to be presented as a Batlhaping claim to any authority in the region.[3]

[1] Shillington *Colonisation*, pp43–55

[2] Moroka's Barolong had lived in this region until the 1820s when they were forced by raids to retreat to Thaba 'Nchu near the emerging Basotho kingdom of Moshoeshoe. Now that his Barolong had been encircled by the Orange Free State, Moroka saw this as his opportunity to reclaim the lands of his ancestors.

[3] *Evidence taken at Bloemhof . . .*, known as the Bloemhof Blue Book (Cape Town 1871).

It is interesting to note that Luka was not allowed to give evidence at Bloemhof. Perhaps Campbell felt that Luka's presence may have given some credence to Doms. The latter's actions towards the end of 1870 had threatened to endanger British interests by stirring up war with the South African Republic. On the other hand, Campbell may have rightly felt that Jantjie could readily be persuaded into acquiescing with the British 'legal process', whereas the more outspoken Luka, whom Campbell described as 'a mischievous and cunning fellow', would have been more difficult to cow into submission.

The Commission received a formal letter from John Smith Moffat, the son of Revd Robert Moffat who had returned to England in final retirement the previous year. J S Moffat's letter was presented in the form of a petition arguing the case of the Batlhaping, but Campbell refused to allow even this to be submitted for arbitration. After the Commission had finished hearing evidence in June 1871, Luka wrote to Moffat on behalf of his father complaining that they had not been allowed to present the Batlhaping case at Bloemhof. And yet despite this, complained Luka's letter, Jantjie and the other *dikgosi* had been informed by Campbell that they would have to pay 'their share' of the expenses of the arbitration.

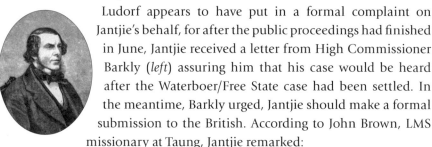

Ludorf appears to have put in a formal complaint on Jantjie's behalf, for after the public proceedings had finished in June, Jantjie received a letter from High Commissioner Barkly (*left*) assuring him that his case would be heard after the Waterboer/Free State case had been settled. In the meantime, Barkly urged, Jantjie should make a formal submission to the British. According to John Brown, LMS missionary at Taung, Jantjie remarked:

> I don't understand the English. They tell a man one day that they [*sic*] have no country, and the next day wish him to give that country over.[4]

Barkly's promise of a hearing of the Dikgatlhong case, however, never materialised. It was a point that caused great resentment within the Batlhaping leadership and helped to confirm Luka's deep distrust of the British and most *makgowa* besides.

The issue that Jantjie, Luka, Botlasitse and their fellow Batlhaping *dikgosi* found most humiliating, however, was the fact that the Arbitration Commission recognised just one 'Paramount', as 'Chief of all the Batlhaping',

---

[4] *Diamond News*, 15 December 1874.

and that was Mankurwane of Taung. According to Campbell, the Batlhaping of Botlasitse and Jantjie were subjects of Waterboer, which left Mankurwane as the only independent Batlhaping chief. In the view of Jantjie and Botlasitse, however, Mankurwane was merely the son of a younger brother of Mothibi, and born by a junior wife of Molehabangwe. Mankurwane's acceptance of the paramount role was not only a falsehood; it was a betrayal of the rest of the Batlhaping *morafe*, for it abandoned them to British colonisation. Campbell's promotion of Mankurwane and the latter's acceptance of it provoked great resentment among the families of Jantjie and Botlasitse. Some years later William Ashton was to remark:

> This act has done more to set the … chiefs and their people against our Government than almost any other; they always speak of *this act* with scorn and contempt.

Meanwhile, the Bloemhof papers were referred to the British Lieutenant-Governor of Natal, Robert Keate, for final arbitration and he gave his ruling in October 1871. Keate tried to pin back the boundary of the South African Republic by awarding to the Barolong most of their claims. The Keate Award Line placed the South African Republic well to the east of effective Boer settlement, indeed well to the east of Bloemhof itself. In reality, however, the British did nothing to enforce the line, and the Boers of the Bloemhof district simply ignored it.

So far as the diamond fields were concerned, Keate, as expected, awarded all of Waterboer's claims. Within days High Commissioner Barkly announced the acceptance of Waterboer's request for British 'protection' and the annexa-tion of the whole of Arnot's 'Griqualand' as the British 'Crown Colony of Griqualand West'. This included most of Jantjie's Dikgatlhong *morafe*, though it left Manyeding and other Ghaap plateau springs beyond the northern boundary. It also split Botlasitse's *morafe*, enclosing Borigelong, but leaving his main town of Phokwani beyond the border (*see map 7, page 60*).

In the meantime a fabulously wealthy new diamond mine, known as 'New Rush', had been found at the dry diggings. In sheer size and wealth of diamonds it eclipsed all the others and following British annexation, the mine and the township that was mushrooming around it were re-named 'Kimberley', after the name of the British Secretary of State for the Colonies. Ironically, when the boundary that Arnot had claimed between the Griqua and the Free State was measured accurately it was found to run directly through the centre of Kimberley mine, leaving the whole of De Beers, Dutoitspan and

The Big Hole, Kimberley, in December 1873; showing how rapidly the mine got deeper in the early years, and the tangle of hoist ropes from hundreds of separate claims.

Bultfontein mines within the Orange Free State. The British hastily adjusted the boundary to ensure that the whole of the township of Kimberley and all of the dry-digging mines fell within the new Crown Colony. It was to be 1876 before the Free State finally conceded defeat on this issue and accepted £90,000 in compensation. No compensation, however, was ever considered remotely liable to the Batlhaping for their lost territory.

Jantjie reacted to the British takeover by ordering all Griqua to leave Batlhaping territory immediately. It was a futile gesture, however, as the British had already decided that the Dikgatlhong *morafe* as such had ceased to exist. Henceforth entitlement to land within the new Crown Colony would be determined by individual title deeds. The only land deeds that Jantjie possessed was the old Griqua deed to Dikgatlhong itself and its immediate environs, and A W Greef revived his old claim to this. There was, however, such a multiplicity of speculative land claims and counter-claims within the new colony that for the time being the Batlhaping remained in uninterrupted occupation of most of the territory of the old *morafe*.

In July 1872 the new British administration issued a proclamation banning any 'natives' from holding diamond-mining claims. Designed primarily for the Kimberley mines, it was also applied to the river-digging region. Although seldom enforced at the time, it made African trading in diamonds increasingly difficult. Luka had been among those Batlhaping who had taken up diamond prospecting more or less as a full-time occupation. In later years he was photographed in a smart check suit, wearing a diamond pin in his necktie and a diamond ring on his forefinger. These were both probably acquired at this time. What wealth Luka may have acquired from diamond prospecting on the early diamond fields was probably mostly invested in cattle, along with the purchase of ox-wagons and guns for hunting. At some stage he opened a bank account, possibly with the Standard Bank which opened a branch in Barkly West in 1871. This would probably have been for ease of trading rather than as a way of accumulating savings, which he would have more naturally invested in cattle. Once the restrictions on African diamond trading had been imposed in 1872, however, Luka appears to have abandoned diamond prospecting and returned to long-distance hunting, making on average one trip a year to northern Botswana.

Ox-wagons on the road north, showing what Luka would have invested in for his expeditions.

Expeditions such as these required considerable capital to invest in wagons, horses, arms and ammunition. This level of investment was not normally available to Batlhaping commoners and most of those who were now pushed out of the diamond business turned instead to the provisioning trade, for which the burgeoning city of Kimberley provided a ready market. Over the next few years, before colonial settlement took effect, the Batlhaping of the Harts–Vaal region provided large quantities of grain, meat and fire-wood for the Kimberley market. By 1874 Kimberley's labour recruiters were complaining that no Batlhaping were prepared to sign labour contracts for the mines as they were 'becoming wealthy' from the provisioning trade. By then, however, there were already signs of the trouble to come.

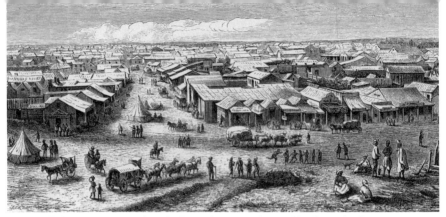
The rapidly burgeoning town of Kimberley in the 1870s, financed by the profits from mining.

In June 1873 a Motlhaping[5] at Boetsap, a spring in the escarpment up the Harts valley from Dikgatlhong, had a dispute with two local Griqua over a grain crop which the Griqua had harvested. He drove them out of Boetsap and they went to Barkly West to complain to the colonial magistrate. On their return towards Boetsap, the two Griqua were arrested by Matsemane, a half-brother of Jantjie. He took them to Dikgatlhong, but Jantjie, who was still unsure about his legal status in the colony, ordered Matsemane to release the men.

Luka was not so hesitant as his father. He had already been ordering individual Griqua woodcutters to cease their indiscriminate cutting of fresh firewood for the Kimberley market and he backed up his orders with a threat of force. His attitude seems to have been an acceptance of the fact of British overrule, for which he probably blamed Mankurwane as much as the Griqua; but he expected the individual and collective rights of the Batlhaping to be fully respected within the new state. And he saw it as his duty to protect those rights. For years the missionaries, from the Helmores through to Ashton, had been preaching the merits of British justice, and now was his chance to call that to account.

In this respect, Luka's assumptions were soon to be tested. A colonial trader-cum-lawyer and 'inveterate land-jobber' or speculator named John G Donovan laid claim to the 'farm' Donderbosch, the land around an important spring within the Ghaap escarpment just behind Dikgatlhong. Piet Boromelo and four other Batlhaping had worked the land at Donderbosch with Jantjie's permission since 1847. Donovan told the magistrate at Barkly West that he had 'purchased [the farm] from a native'. As Donovan passed through Dikgatlhong on his way to take possession of Donderbosch, he was stopped by Luka who ordered him off Batlhaping land and sent him back to Barkly West.[6]

[5] singular form of Batlhaping.
[6] *British Bechuanaland Land Commission*, (BBLC/8,9) Evidence of 'Luka Jantjie', March 1886

Donovan, however, would not give up that easily. In September 1873, while Luka was away, probably on a hunting expedition, Donovan employed two white men, Tighe and Hunter, to establish occupancy of Donderbosch. Following Luka's lead, Boromelo and the other Batlhaping at the spring 'arrested' Donovan's men before they could put plough to soil and expelled them from the area. Donovan responded by getting the Barkly West magistrate, W C Palgrave, to issue a warrant for the arrest of four Batlhaping for the 'assault' of Tighe and Hunter. Palgrave's police arrested the four men and imprisoned them in Barkly gaol.

The following month, Sir Richard Southey, Lieutenant-Governor of Griqualand West since January 1873, sent a letter to Jantjie warning him that he no longer had the power to take legal action against any white person within the colony. And as if to add insult to injury, Southey appointed A W Greef to be field-cornet[7] at Dikgatlhong. This was the man who had laid claim to the land title to Dikgatlhong and with whom Luka had subsequently nearly come to blows. It was thus no doubt with a sense of great satisfaction that Greef delivered Southey's letter to Jantjie.

Sir Richard Southey's executive council in Griqualand West: Southey (seated centre), David Arnot, law agent (standing, far left), Francis Thompson of Cornforth Hill (fourth from left).

Boromelo and his three companions spent several months in prison without formal charge or trial, before being fined £5 each and then released. William Ashton, back from leave since July 1871 and currently based in Kuruman, seemed to think that they would have had their fines remitted if they had admitted that they were in the wrong. That they chose not to

(*Land Commission*); GLW 166, *Land Court Evidence*, p86, evidence Piet Boromelo and others.
[7] A local government official, modelled on Dutch and Boer usage.

admit fault, and preferred the payment of a fine as a way to get out of prison, can be taken to signify that they upheld their right to defend their land at Donderbosch. In hearing and accepting only one side of the story, with no fair trial of the evidence, the new colonial authority had given an early indication of its racial bias. Under the circumstances, Luka would have approved of this act of defiance by Boromelo and his three companions.

During the course of 1873, government surveyors had been marking out the land on both sides of the Harts and up into the Ghaap escarpment, making it clear to all that the colony was to be divided into separate farms. In the wake of the surveyors, potential white settlers began moving onto the land, but in several instances they were driven off by the local Batlhaping who were determined to maintain their prior occupancy.

It was probably at about this time that Luka began building his stone house at Manyeding, the up-country village beyond the colonial border, which he and his wife had already established as the family's arable and grazing land since before the war of 1858.[8] The stone foundations of the house are all that remain in modern times, but close to it is a similar one still standing that was built by his brother, Olebile. The house was of rectangular design, probably modelled on those built by the missionaries. The front door opened into a central living room, with a bedroom at each end, left and right. A back door, opposite the front, led to a small kitchen attached to the back of the house.

This is Olebile Jantjie's house in 1978; Luka's stone house was next door and also looked like this.

[8] *Land Commission,* Luka evidence.

In the foreground the foundations of Luka's stone house in Manyeding in 1978.

The house was a statement of modernity and prestige, for at the time those two houses were the only two like it in the village of Manyeding. The building of the house was perhaps an indication by Luka of his disillusionment with the situation at Dikgatlhong. Nevertheless, he still considered Dikgatlhong to be the home of his father, and he still maintained his traditional-style circular house there.

Jantjie meanwhile was in his late seventies and was probably looking forward to a peaceful retirement under the protection of his son. At the end of 1873 he sent notice to Mankurwane and Botlasitse that he was considering moving from Dikgatlhong to join Luka at Manyeding. But he seems to have been undecided as to whether he would permanently migrate from the colony or keep a presence at Dikgatlhong. The move was probably on the advice of Luka, but this did not imply any abandonment of the family's claims to the old *morafe* within the colony. On the contrary, Luka may simply have seen it as an attempt to establish firmer hold of Manyeding and the northern half of the *morafe* in anticipation of any future British attempt to extend the colony.

In January 1874 Jantjie paid a visit to Kuruman to seek the advice of the missionaries, and Ashton wrote to Southey on his behalf asking that the Batlhaping rights to their land be settled one way or another. With Greef a field-cornet at Dikgatlhong, government surveyors marking out boundaries and farms, and Donovan still laying claim to Donderbosch, the Batlhaping, argued Ashton, felt very insecure within their own country. Southey simply replied that they would be much better off coming back into the colony where they would be under British protection, rather than staying beyond the colonial boundary where they might be taken over by the Boers of the Transvaal.

This latter point was a reference to Botlasitse who, it was alleged, had given himself over to Transvaal 'protection' so as not to lose his land to the British as Jantjie had done. That alleged agreement had been organised by the irrepressible Theodore Doms, now resident in the Transvaal. Botlasitse later denied that he had ever submitted to the Boers. In the meantime Botlasitse ordered his people to knock down any stone markers that were put up to mark out colonial farms in the Borigelong region, which fell within the Griqualand West colony.

That May of 1874 Jantjie and Luka returned to Dikgatlhong to harvest their crops on the farm, only to find that Greef had already harvested much of the grain crop. Greef clearly felt that as the recently appointed field-cornet for Dikgatlhong, he was above the law and could do as he liked. The arrogance of the man clearly riled Luka who, for the second time in his life, threatened Greef with violence.[9] He tried to physically expel Greef from the town, but Jantjie once again intervened, preferring to lodge a complaint with Southey.[10] On this occasion Jantjie's diplomacy over Luka's physicality appeared to pay off, though not for the reason that the old *kgosi* would have hoped – that the Batlhaping were in the right. The Lieutenant-Governor was hoping to sell off most of the land between the Harts and the Ghaap plateau for white settlement. The last thing he wanted was trouble between men like Greef and the local Batlhaping. Hoping to bring round the Batlhaping to an acceptance of the new colonial reality, Southey dismissed Greef as field-cornet in July 1874 and ordered him to quit Dikgatlhong.[11]

Sacking Greef, however, was an easy sacrifice for the Lieutenant-Governor. It did not mean that he had changed his land policy. And Southey confirmed the fears of the Batlhaping leadership in December 1874 when he announced a grand auction of farms northwest of the Harts. The government surveyor John H Ford had divided the land up into two parallel rows of 6,000 acre farms,[12] one row fronting onto the river and the other enclosing all the springs of the escarpment. In effect, Southey's proposed land sale took in much of the most valuable grazing and arable land of the Dikgatlhong *morafe*. The only 'farm' reserved for the Batlhaping was the town and environs of Dikgatlhong itself, which Southey informally set aside as belonging to Jantjie. Even this excluded the springs of the escarpment, rendering the land of very little real value (*see map 7, p60*).

[9] The previous time, as we saw, had been over the title deeds to Dikgatlhong in 1861.
[10] CA, GLW 19, Jantjie to Southey, 5 June 1874.
[11] GLW 65, CC Barkly West, 13 July 1874.
[12] Approximately 2,500 hectares, the standard size of a South African 'farm' at that time.

Selling wood in Kimberley market. The demand from the mines was huge, and prices rose rapidly.

Shortly before the auction Jantjie summoned a large national gathering, a *pitso*, of the Dikgatlhong *morafe* to discuss the land crisis. If Luka and Jantjie had been hoping for strong support for firm opposition to colonial land policies, however, they were to be disappointed. The consensus of the gathering at Dikgatlhong in December 1874 was to stay put for the time being and take no rash action. After all, people were doing quite well out of the Kimberley market and most people still had access to their land. Even in the previous few years when rainfall had been poor, there was still a market for meat, milk, thatching reeds and firewood. And now this year rain had fallen early, the land was softened and people were eager to get away to 'the lands' and tend their sorghum crops. Conditions promised a good harvest and prices were high on the Kimberley market.[13]

At the same time firewood was becoming a major commodity at Kimberley market. When the young Cecil Rhodes won the contract for pumping water out of the flooded Kimberley mine in 1874, he introduced industrial steam machinery to the diamond-mining business. And local timber, especially the hardwood of the camel thorn (*acacia erioloba*), was the ideal firewood for industrial steam machinery. The market price of firewood rose from £6 a wagon-load in 1875 to £12 by 1877. The region south of the Vaal was rapidly denuded of trees, and firewood in Batlhaping territory north of the Vaal became a prime commodity. The illicit felling of trees and 'wood-riding' the

---

[13] Earlier in the year the colonial trader R Spalding had set up shop at Spitskop, up the Harts valley from Dikgatlhong, and he reported a brisk trade in ox-drawn ploughs. He sold 100 that first year and a further 500 during 1875 and '76.

Lt Governor Southey (left) addressing regional leaders probably in Barkly West in 1874; Arnot stands on Southey's left; Waterboer (waving staff) and Mankurwane sit in front of church.

firewood to Kimberley became a major occupation for both Batlhaping and white colonist alike, with no regard to ownership or environmental impact.

Under these circumstances, William Ashton believed that on the matter of Batlhaping political authority the *dikgosi* were out of step with their subjects. He was pleased to report that the latter seemed contented with the new dispensation. The numerous small villages into which the old *morafe* had now divided were showing signs of individual prosperity and an increasing number were turning to the Church, attending Sunday services and learning to read and write. Very few people in the Harts valley region now adorned their bodies with the greasy clay of *lechoku* or wore the glittering *sibilo* in their hair. Most wore some European-style clothing. Many of the outlying villages had their own small chapel and a local deacon to conduct Sunday worship.

It was, Ashton believed, only the formerly privileged class of the *dikgosi* who resented the loss of their political authority and the fact that their rights to some of the best springs such as Donderbosch and Boetsap were being challenged by individual colonists like Donovan. The irony was that the Jantjie family had accepted the social changes associated with Christianity and European-style clothing that Ashton was promoting, way back in the 1830s. They were now finding that the colonists of this 'modern world' were not living up to their rhetoric of 'civilised justice'.

There may have been some truth in Ashton's interpretation, but he had a partial viewpoint. He did his best to champion the rights of the Batlhaping and he was scathing in his comments on the Griqualand West government's disregard of Jantjie's land claims and its interpretation of British justice. But in general terms he was in favour of the extension of what he saw as British civilisation in the region, as he believed that it would in the long term lead to the extension of Christianity. That, after all, was his primary objective. In decades past the LMS had seen the religious conversion of a *kgosi* like Jantjie as a key to the extension of Christianity; but now Ashton, like many other missionaries of the period, viewed the weakening of chiefly authority as the new key to the spread of Christianity. And he saw the gradual – 'and fair'

– extension of colonial rule as one way to achieve that.

Luka, on the other hand, clearly had a different perspective. In just a few short years he had witnessed the hypocrisy of colonialism in which he saw the denial of all the precepts of fairness and justice that the Helmores may have taught him. The British refusal to even hear evidence of Jantjie's political authority at Bloemhof in 1871 had exposed the Batlhaping of Dikgatlhong to the whim of colonial land speculators. It must have been clear to Luka that the reservation of Dikgatlhong itself as the personal property of Jantjie was little more than a crumb from the colonial table. It was probably this kind of treatment that fuelled Luka's decision to cut his losses in the new colony and shift more or less permanently beyond the reach of the colonial authorities.

Although henceforth both Jantjie and Luka were to consider Manyeding as their main place of residence, they still regarded the Batlhaping within the colony as their subjects and they still maintained a presence at Dikgatlhong, returning there from time to time. One such visit was for the happy occasion of Luka's second marriage, in April 1875.

As a professing Christian, accepted back into the Church in 1872 after his three-year suspension for drinking brandy,[14] Luka would not have married polygamously, so one can only assume that his first wife, Gasiikangwe, had died. His second bride was a good deal younger than Luka, who in 1875 was about forty years of age. She may have been as young as twenty. But there would have been plenty of Batlhaping families only too keen to have their daughter, of any age, marry the son and heir of their *kgosi*. The bride's name was Masehoro, a Motlhaping of the Marumo branch.[15]

Revd William Ashton (LMS) and his wife in their front garden, probably in Barkly West.

14 *LMS*, Ashton, Kuruman, 26 November 1872.

15 P–L Breutz, *The Tribes of Kuruman and Postmasburg* (Pretoria 1963) p175

William Ashton performed the wedding ceremony at Dikgatlhong and has left us a record of the occasion. People came from all over the region. There had been heavy rains that year and the Harts River in April was in full flood, too full for wagons to cross. Nevertheless, people were determined to be there. Some swam the river; others waded with children on their shoulders and their best clothes on their heads. That was at the weekend. By Monday, however, the bride had still not arrived. She lived only a day's journey away, but her home lay across the Harts River. Ashton takes up the story:

Kgosi Khama's bride also wearing white at her wedding in 1896.

After a messenger had been sent, who turned back the next day without crossing the river, the bridegroom in-spanned his wagon, and set out on the Tuesday to go and look after the young lady, and returned on the Thursday morning, bringing her with her mother and a few friends. He had had great difficulty in crossing the river. The wagon was so deep in the water that the wedding party had got considerably wet; but, very prudently, they had left the toilet arrangements till they should arrive [at Dikgatlhong], and they managed to keep their wedding clothes out of the water. Those of the bride were handsome and expensive, including, what are now becoming common even among the Bechuanas, the wreath of flowers and veil. [16]

As we shall see later, Masehoro was a spirited young woman who bore him at least one son that we know of. She and her son stood by him to the end, through all the troubles to come.

The general note of optimism that Ashton had noted earlier among the Batlhaping commoners seemed for the moment to have been justified when Southey's land auction turned out to be a failure. Very few farms were sold and even fewer were paid for. Among the handful of exceptions were Francis Thompson, who bought two farms that he called Cornforth Hill, bordering the Harts below Boetsap, and George Paton who bought several farms just upstream from the old Helmore dam. Most potential colonial buyers, however, found that nearly all the best land between the Vaal and the Ghaap

---

[16] *LMS*, Ashton, Kuruman, 11 August 1875; *The Chronicle of the LMS*, March 1876, pp53–4.

Botlasitse of Phokwani and Waterboer of Griquatown attending a meeting with Southey at Barkly West in 1874 with land agents Arnot (right) and Wright (left); photograph by the Gray Brothers.

escarpment was already in full occupation by local African farmers; and they had no confidence that Southey's government had either the will or the ability to force the 'natives' from their land. Southey's failure to settle the land question and make land available for sale to white colonists was one of the underlying reasons why he was replaced as Lieutenant-Governor at the end of 1875.[17] But before he left the colony, he set up a Land Court that he hoped would finally sort out the conflicting claims to the land of Griqualand West.

In February 1876 the Land Court sat at Barkly West to hear evidence of the land claims for the Harts–Vaal territory. William Ashton, who was by then living in Barkly West, saw this as a final chance to get justice for the Batlhaping by having their claims properly heard in open court. Ashton arranged for both Jantjie and Botlasitse to attend the court, with himself acting as advocate, witness and interpreter.

The evidence that they and others presented to Judge Stockenstrom at Barkly West made it clear that if the Batlhaping had been properly heard five years earlier at Bloemhof, the land north of the Vaal could never have been awarded to Waterboer and thence to Britain. The claims of the land speculators were totally discredited. Indeed those of Theodore Doms were so exposed in open court that he left the territory for the Transvaal and was not seen again in Griqualand West. It was not Stockenstrom's role, however,

[17] Shillington *Colonisation*, pp70–74.

to undo what had already been done. While confirming Jantjie's right to the farm Dikgatlhong, he simply ruled that further provision would have to be made for those Batlhaping in occupation of so much of the territory between the Vaal and the Ghaap escarpment.

Stockenstrom's Judgement seemed to vindicate Ashton's faith in the ultimate integrity of British rule. Encouraged by Ashton, Jantjie dared to believe that natural justice would at last prevail and his people's claims to land within Griqualand West would now be honoured. Luka was not so easily convinced and his interpretation of colonial rule would ultimately prove more accurate.

Luka was not present at the Land Court hearing in Barkly West. He was away on a hunting trip somewhere in northern Botswana. He had been on a similar expedition in 1875. It is not known how successful that venture was, but the one he went on in the early months of 1876 was a serious financial failure. Expeditions such as this required quite a few companions, mounted on horseback, several wagons, at least two guns per person, preferably quality rifles, and many pounds of ammunition. Luka was set up with equipment, on credit, from a trader in Kuruman, on the assumption that he would be able to repay the debt on his return with an ample supply of ivory, ostrich feathers and furs. It is not known how far he travelled on this occasion, but numerous contemporary white hunters who wrote about their exploits in this period were going as far as the Okavango delta, the Chobe River, the Zambezi valley and the Ndebele kingdom, now under the rule of Lobengula. With the widespread use of guns since the 1850s, suitable game was becoming increasingly wary and scarce.

Whatever the details of his hunting trip, Luka returned in May 1876 seriously in debt to the trader in Kuruman and he spent the next few months travelling with several companions around the villages of the *morafe*, seeking financial help. In doing so he was, in his view, merely exercising his father's traditional authority, collecting tribute from the people. This was done on the principle that in return the Batlhaping *kgosi* would help and protect his subjects in their own time of need. The colonial authorities, however, chose to interpret Luka's action as illicit tax collection.

J G Donovan was the first to file a complaint. He had set up a trading store at Boetsap and he complained that Luka and about twenty mounted men had come to his store demanding brandy and threatening him and his employees. Donovan, who was already in dispute with Luka over his claim to Donderbosch, had been appointed field-cornet for the region and there was undoubtedly distrust between the two men. When they confronted each other in the formal atmosphere of a Land Commission ten years later, however, Donovan's story changed. Then there was no mention of threatening behaviour. He merely claimed that Luka had halted on a ridge above the store and that Donovan had ridden up to him. Luka, who had heard about the judgement of Stockenstrom's Land Court (March 1876), said that Donovan would have to vacate Boetsap as it was Batlhaping land. In his evidence to the Land Commission ten years later Luka, more or less confirmed this version of the incident, adding that the Batlhaping did not collect taxes, and the only dispute was with 'a man named Metzler', probably an employee of Donovan.[18]

Back in 1876, however, Donovan had exaggerated the encounter and built it up into a scare story as though Luka were threatening and terrorising the neighbourhood.[19] The new Administrator of Griqualand West, Major William Owen Lanyon,[20] responded to Donovan's complaint by writing to Jantjie at Dikgatlhong informing him that he had no right 'collecting taxes from persons within the Province [of Griqualand West].' Ashton translated the letter for Jantjie when the latter went to Kuruman in early July to pay Luka's trading debt.

Jantjie and Luka assumed that the 'persons' referred to in Lanyon's letter meant white men only and Luka wrote a reply in Setswana. The gist of Luka's letter, as they later told Ashton was: 'We have collected no taxes from white men. Are not the Bechuanas Jantjie's people? And we have yet to learn why our country has been taken from us by the English.' Ashton was uneasy with Luka's taking the initiative in communicating direct to government without seeking his prior advice. It was the beginning of the missionary's realisation that Luka would be guided by his own judgement rather than that of the LMS. Nevertheless, he appreciated the depth of feeling of Jantjie's people that were 'exceedingly sore and are quite unwilling to listen to any explanation of British Laws.'

> The Imperial Gov't has committed a gross injustice in including Jantjie's country in that taken over by them from Waterboer … and that injustice debars the Bechuanas from either respecting the Gov't or submitting to it, if they can possibly get beyond its reach.[21]

---

[18] *CA*, BBLC 9, *Land Commission*, Luka evidence.
[19] *Diamond News*, 5 August 1876.
[20] Lanyon succeeded Southey in January 1876. The post of Lt-Governor was downgraded to that of Administrator in anticipation of Griqualand West's absorption into the Cape Colony.
[21] *LMS*, Ashton, Kuruman, 13 July 1876; comment made before the August meeting at Dikgatlong.

On this occasion the Griqualand West Attorney-General, Sidney Shippard, whom Lanyon described as 'incorrigibly idle',[22] did not think Luka's letter worthy of a reply. And as to the question of the land belonging to Jantjie's people, Shippard commented:

> The idea of Jantjie's royal rights to minerals and precious [stones] is ludicrous in the extreme – and it is a little trying to have to waste ink on such a subject.[23]

The following month, August 1876, Jantjie summoned what turned out to be the last major meeting of the Batlhaping at Dikgatlhong. The purpose of the meeting was to discuss the land situation and what action they should take to protect their own interests. It was also perhaps to impress upon the government the strength of feeling amongst the people over the land issue. When Lanyon got wind of the meeting, he decided to put in an appearance. Lanyon was a military martinet who believed that 'firm handling' was the only thing that 'natives' understood. He saw this as an opportunity to curb Luka's assertion of independent authority within the colony. Arriving at Dikgatlhong accompanied by six armed police and Sidney Shippard, Lanyon took an authoritarian stance. Ignoring the land question which he must have known was uppermost in Batlhaping minds, he informed Jantjie that he no longer had any political authority in the colony. He then berated Luka for 'collecting taxes'.

One can see that tax collection was foremost in Lanyon's mind; in June he had announced that 'natives' within the colony would be charged a 'hut tax' in line with practice in the Cape Colony. Clearly he wanted to ensure that there would be just one tax-collecting authority and that would be the colonial state. In fact no hut tax was actually collected until 1879, by which time any Batlhaping political opposition had been thoroughly crushed.

Recalling the event ten years later, Luka protested:

> I am not aware that I ever collected money from any of the Bechuana people [in 1876] … It may have been grain, skins, or karosses. … It is only a law of the present day [1886] … that there is such a thing known as collecting taxes.

As far as his father was concerned, recalled Luka, it was from the time of that meeting with Lanyon that Jantjie Mothibi 'saw that he had been turned out of his [own] country.'[24]

---

[22] *TVL*, 596/12, Lanyon to his brother Charlie, 12 February 1877.
[23] GLW 92, No.2475, Minute of Attorney-General Shippard, September 1876.
[24] *Land Commission*, Luka evidence.

CHAPTER SIX

Tension and resistance in the colony
1876–1878

After Lanyon had departed from the meeting at Dikgatlhong in August 1876, Jantjie announced that he was moving to the Langeberg, that remote mountain range northwest of the colony near the borders of the southern Kalahari.

It was an indication of the depth of his despair at the humiliating way that he had been treated in front of his own people. To go to the Langeberg – the furthest western reaches of the old *morafe* – was symbolically as well as literally to get as far away as possible from British colonial control. But although the people were now more in tune with the despair of their leaders, they felt that this would be too drastic a move. They would prefer to go to the old traditional capital of Dithakong. All of this talk of a major move, however, was more an expression of frustration than a practical reality. In the event Jantjie went to join Luka and his other sons at Manyeding.

Now in his eightieth year, Jantjie hoped to live out his remaining years peacefully sewing karosses at Manyeding, under the protection of his son. He was, however, to be disappointed in this humble ambition.

Lanyon returned to Kimberley satisfied that his bodyguard of six police had suitably impressed Jantjie with his authority. In time-honoured colonial fashion, he reported to his superiors that the 'natives [were] peaceful':

> On the whole I think the interview was satisfactory, and I do not contemplate any further trouble from Jantze [*sic*], or indeed from any of the natives either within or without the Province.'[1]

Lanyon's administration decided that land should be designated for 'native locations' and Attorney-General Shippard was given the job of deciding which farms should be set aside for this. Shippard was guided by the principle that the minimum amount of land should be selected and it should

---

[1] *Great Britain Parliamentary Papers* (*GBPP*), C.1748, No.66, enclosures 1–4.

only include those farms that contained a large settled African population and arable land that was already under regular cultivation. Thus most of the extensive grazing land, so important to the Batlhaping rural economy, was to be excluded from the 'native allocation'.

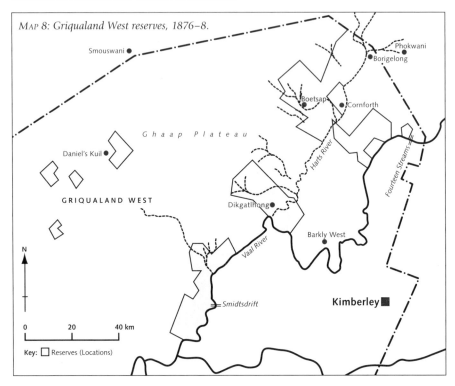

MAP 8: *Griqualand West reserves, 1876–8.*

Within these new confines it would not be many years before the land became overgrazed, rendering the rural 'reserves' little more than suburban 'locations'. Indeed the word 'location' was officially used to denote the land thus set aside. And along with the lost grazing land went most of the valuable timber resources of the district. George Paton, writing in January 1875 estimated that farms in the Barkly West district contained upwards of a thousand wagon-loads of timber each. Batlhaping access to this resource was now severely restricted.

Meanwhile Major Charles Warren of the Royal Engineers was appointed to go through the Land Court records, the Bloemhof Blue Book and anything else he considered relevant, to make a definitive decision on all the rival claims to land within Griqualand West and issue title deeds as he saw fit. It was a job he completed with the efficiency of an engineer during the course of 1877. William Ashton, writing a few years later was to aptly sum up the Batlhaping attitude to Warren's land settlement:

> Instead of allowing the decisions of the late Judge Stockenstrom to be confirmed, which refused to allow the claims of the Land Jobbers to Janjes [*sic*] country, Sir Bartle [Frere] sent Col. Warren with unlimited power to give the country to whom he liked, to pacify the Clamour of the Europeans.[2]

Luka and Jantjie were not the only Batlhaping leaders frustrated at the colonial seizure of their land. Botlasitse in particular was angry at the way his people were divided by the colonial boundary. He considered that his *morafe* stretched from the hills around Phokwani to the Harts and down the valley past Borigelong, now within Griqualand West, as far as Boetsap and Thompson's farm of Cornforth Hill. Botlasitse's people had been removing surveyors' marker flags and knocking down their stone beacons along the border region since the surveying work was first begun in 1873. After the failure of the Stockenstrom judgement to deliver them any justice, the Phokwani leaders decided to take the law into their own hands.[3]

News of the Bapedi defeat of the Boers[4] in August 1876 had filtered down to the region and probably provided some inspiration for more assertive action. In October 1876 Botlasitse's half-brother, Andries Mothibi, came to the old town of Borigelong, now a mere shadow of its former self, and began collecting tribute from the Batlhaping of the former *morafe*. At the same time he ordered all white colonists to get off Batlhaping land.

Lanyon too had heard of the Boer failure against the Bapedi. In a private letter to his father he observed:

> It is an anxious time for those who are in the advanced posts of civilization out here, for native troubles are springing up, which may at any time require prompt measures. With a small force to suppress anarchy, such matters must be dealt with at the outset, otherwise the flame of disaffection spreads and becomes unmanageable.

Despite Lanyon's belief in 'promptness and activity' as 'the only way to deal with native questions', it was not until November that the Barkly West magistrate Campbell set out with six police to arrest Andries Mothibi. He managed

---

[2] *LMS*, Ashton, Barkly West, 1 July 1880.
[3] Shillington *Colonisation*, pp74–75.
[4] The Bapedi–Boer war took place around Lydenburg, 600 kms away in the eastern Transvaal.

to effect an arrest, but he then found himself surrounded by an angry crowd of about two hundred men, many of them armed. They rescued Andries, and Campbell retreated hastily to Barkly West to report his failure. Lanyon was away in the Free State at the time, visiting President Brand in Bloemfontein. When he got back in mid-December he heard of the rescue of Andries Mothibi and, interpreting it as a riot, promptly set off with fifty police 'to arrest the beggars'. It was the sort of expedition that Lanyon relished, as he confided to his brother:

> I should not be surprised if they gave some trouble, and possibly may go on the shoot, if they do they will find they are not dealing with Boers.[5]

When he got to Borigelong, however, Lanyon found that Andries Mothibi had heard of his approach and had promptly moved across the border, which was only a few kilometres away. Nevertheless, Lanyon searched the town and discovered seventeen men whom he decided had been in the crowd that had rescued Mothibi. These were arrested, marched to Barkly West, and 'cast into prison'. As Lanyon informed his father:

> I went with fifty men, so the demonstration put a little proper fear into the native mind. ... I was struck with the enormous number of natives in that district; if they chose to combine they could be very troublesome. ... A vacillating policy or anything like a sign of fear would soon raise a storm which could not be readily allayed, and we should be having a repetition of the Transvaal trouble.[6]

Lanyon set up a police post on Thompson's farm and in February 1877 the constable there reported an increase in cattle stealing from both Batlhaping and white colonists along the border region. The cattle were being taken across the border to Phokwani and even as far as Taung. Lanyon decided that a punitive raid on Phokwani itself might be necessary and he sent the acting magistrate of Barkly West, G R K Bradshaw, on a secret mission to spy out the best route from Kimberley to Phokwani.

Bradshaw and the police constable from Cornforth Hill donned plain clothes and pretended they were on a hunting trip. On crossing the border, their disguise was easily seen through and they were arrested and taken before Botlasitse at Phokwani. Botlasitse had them escorted to the edge of town where they were told to leave Batlhaping country and not come back.

5 TVL, 596/11, Lanyon to his brother Charlie, 17/12/1876.
6 TVL, 596/11, Lanyon to his father, 25/12/1876.

The two spies, however, had already achieved their objective, and after visiting Mankurwane at Taung they returned to Griqualand West.

Bradshaw reported to Lanyon that the best route from Kimberley by which to make a swift attack on Phokwani was not to travel up the Harts valley past Borigelong, but rather to follow the Vaal as far as Fourteen Streams and cut across from there to Phokwani. Lanyon kept this in mind for future action that he felt sure would be needed before long.[7]

Luka, meanwhile, had been careful to keep well clear of the conflict between Botlasitse and the Griqualand West government. In the early months of 1877 he went on another long-distance hunting trip and this time it seems to have been reasonably profitable for there was no mention of debt.

Luka returned to Griqualand West in July to discover the people in a state of great agitation. The government had been conducting a census, not only of all people in the colony, but also all their livestock. The government claimed that the census was simply to build up a register of potential white voters for the Cape parliament in anticipation of the colony's impending annexation by the Cape. But the fact that they were also counting black people (who would not have the vote) as well as their livestock made it clear that the government did indeed have ulterior motives. The Batlhaping were quite right in their conviction that this was a preliminary both to defining the boundaries of the 'locations' and to setting up a tax register, and they were determined not to co-operate.

The census was conducted hurriedly in the Barkly West district over a three-week period.[8] It was carried out by local field-cornets, each accompanied by several armed police. On the approach of the census officials, most people fled from their homes, driving their animals before them. Along the north bank of the lower Vaal below Dikgatlhong, Field-Cornet Honey found the headman 'Chugo' 'insolent'. He refused to answer the official's questions saying he was answerable only to Jantjie, not the British government. Honey estimated Chugo's village as housing as many as five hundred people. About a hundred people lived under the western end of nearby Mosesberg with a further eighty living on the flat-topped mountain where Luka was born. All of the above, reported Honey, had plenty of ground under cultivation and 'immense droves of cattle and goats.' Elsewhere around Mosesberg he

---

[7] CA, GLW 101, No. 702, (Secret) Bradshaw to Lanyon, Cornforth Hill, 6 March 1877.
[8] CAD, GLW 104, No.1447: reports of census officials.

found several villages with an estimated combined population of up to four hundred, all of them uncooperative and 'answerable only to Jantjie'.

There seemed to be some coordination in this resistance, for the reaction of the Batlhaping was the same throughout the country. Jantjie had not been asked for his co-operation and was out of the country at Manyeding. Up the Harts valley his half-brother Matsemane confronted the officials on his behalf. He refused to give any information and said that he spoke for all the people from Fourteen Streams to Thompson's, to Dikgatlhong. Field-Cornet Corus issued Matsemane with a summons for refusing the census, to appear before the magistrate at Boetsap on 13 September.[9]

This was the atmosphere into which Luka returned in July 1877. He went down to Dikgatlhong only to discover that his old enemy, A W Greef, had taken over his house and put in one of his white employees, a German named Schmidt, to live there. Luka had an altercation with the man which culminated in him physically pushing Schmidt out of the house. Schmidt immediately reported the incident to the Barkly West magistrate who, without further enquiry, issued a warrant for Luka's arrest on a charge of assault. But before the warrant could be effected, Luka left the colony and returned to Manyeding.[10]

That September, anticipating that Matsemane would not answer his summons to appear at Boetsap before the end of the month, Acting Magistrate Bradshaw made a hurried attempt to arrest him. But Matsemane was fore-warned of his approach and managed to escape across the border. He made his way to Manyeding where he joined Luka and Jantjie. There were now two people at Manyeding with a colonial warrant hanging over their heads.[11]

Following the census troubles, the colonial government employed Sam Edwards as 'British Resident among the Batlhaping'. Edwards was the son of former LMS missionary, Roger Edwards, who had been an early colleague of David Livingstone among the more northerly Batswana in the 1840s. Edwards had been brought up a fluent Setswana-speaker and the government appears to have felt that he of all people should be able to persuade the Batlhaping to accept their movement into 'native locations'. Edwards, however, was no more successful than any other government official in this endeavour.

On the advice of William Ashton during 1877, the government reluctantly agreed to pay Jantjie a pension of £200 a year. Shippard intended this to be

---

[9] GLW 104, (1447) Report of Field-Cornet Corus, Spitzkop, 15 June 1876, and minutes.
[10] *UW*, Mackenzie Papers, A75/2, (draft) Mackenzie to Lanyon, 5 October 1877.
[11] GLW 104, (1447) G Bradshaw (Acting RM), Barkly, 23 October 1877.

a salary for Jantjie to act as government 'headman' at Dikgatlhong where he would help to persuade his people to submit to government wishes. Jantjie, and Ashton, saw the pension as poor compensation for loss of land and political authority. Shippard insisted that it would be paid only on condition that Jantjie lived permanently in Dikgatlhong. Jantjie agreed to accept the money, but he never accepted Shippard's conditions. Ashton regularly applied for the payments on Jantjie's behalf, in half-yearly instalments, and Jantjie came into Barkly West to collect it, but he no longer lived permanently in the colony and he never acted as 'headman' for the government.[12]

During the latter months of 1877 a small but steady stream of people began to leave the colony and head for the freedom of Batlhaping country north of the border. Some went to Taung, others to Manyeding or to the old Batlhaping capital of Dithakong and other villages towards Kuruman.

Tension within the colony mounted over the Christmas and New Year period. Within the Barkly West district white wood-riders[13] indiscriminately stole loads of firewood from designated 'native locations'. And Bradshaw reported in early January 1878 that Francis Thompson had 'something like a hundred loads [of firewood] on his farm [at Cornforth Hill], which to my own knowledge were cut at [Botlasitse's] Poquanee [sic].'[14] Botlasitse's people responded to these thefts of firewood by raiding for cattle across the border. Several white settlers near Fourteen Streams had their cattle taken, with Botlasitse claiming it was rent for their use of Batlhaping land.

Farms like Francis Thompson's, Cornforth Hill, often doubled as trading stores to the local people.

On 11 January 1878 Matsemane came down from Manyeding to assess the situation, but he was spotted by the constable at Cornforth Hill and arrested. Thompson swore out an affidavit asserting that this was the man who had resisted the census officials the previous year. Matsemane was marched off to Barkly gaol where he was imprisoned for two months.[15]

---

[12] *LMS*, Ashton, Barkly, 20 January 1877.
[13] People who transported wagonloads of timber for firewood to supply the mines.
[14] GLW 114, No.17, Minute of G Bradshaw, 17 January 1878.
[15] *UW*, A75/2, Ashton to Mackenzie, Barkly West, 23 February 1878.

Francis Thompson and his wife in 1850.

Following Matsemane's arrest, several of Botlasitse's brothers and sons came down to Cornforth Hill and threatened Thompson. Botlasitse's son and heir, Galeshewe, allegedly sat on the bar in the farm's store and demanded brandy. The gist of the message to Thompson was that the country belonged to the Batlhaping and they were going to clear the white people out of the country. Thompson reported the incident to the authorities in Kimberley, and Lanyon decided to act against Botlasitse.[16]

It was a time of rising tension throughout southern Africa. In the eastern Cape the colony was involved in its ninth and final war with the Xhosa. Initially the war had gone badly for the colonial forces and in the first week of January 1878 troops were rushed to the scene from all over British South Africa. Lanyon's contribution was to send Major Warren to the Eastern Cape in command of 110 troops of the Diamond Fields Horse, a volunteer regiment raised in Kimberley. This left Lanyon as the only professional military officer remaining in Griqualand West. But he relished the opportunity to star in his own little war:

> ... to be in a position of having to decide whether it is to be war or not, and war against overwhelming odds, where a reverse or an incautious act might prompt all the other niggars [*sic*] to join against us, is one which does not often fall to the lot of one placed as I am.[17]

He intended to exact a fine from Botlasitse, but, he confided to his father on the eve of his departure, it 'would be more pleasant' if the 'graceful savage' chose to put up a fight.

Lanyon departed from Kimberley on 21 January in charge of 150 white volunteers and about a hundred black troops recruited earlier in Kimberley. As they passed through Barkly West, Ashton tried to persuade Lanyon against the raid, predicting, accurately as it turned out, that it would bring down all sorts for trouble for the colony. Lanyon, however, pressed on regardless, picking

---

16   *GBPP*, Confidential Print (African 151), enclosure in No. 12, Lanyon to Barkly, 31 Jan. 1878.
17   TVL, 569/13, Lanyon to his father, Kimberley, 20 January 1878.

up fifty more white volunteers from Barkly West itself.[18]

Botlasitse was forewarned of their approach and vacated Phokwani, leaving behind women, children and old men who could not easily flee, and a large number of milch cows. Lanyon (*right*) restrained his troops from burning and raping, but he ordered that every house be broken into and searched. In this way he collected a large number of guns, most of them old flintlocks but a few of them good rifles. He then gathered up all the cattle, 445 in all, and took them as a 'fine' back to Kimberley where they were slaughtered and sold for meat.

Lanyon was delighted with himself. He wrote glowing reports of his 'victory' to his superiors and was rewarded with promotion to Lieutenant-Colonel. Ashton and the missionaries of Kuruman, however, condemned Lanyon's action as little more than a cattle raid that would cause great hardship for the people and provoke even more retaliation. Revd John Mackenzie, now the senior missionary at Kuruman, wrote a warning letter to Lanyon a week after the raid:

> I am told that Botlasitse … threatens that he will have English blood for his cattle: he will fall upon individuals or families and put them to death.[19]

Botlasitse had retreated to Modimong in the hills northeast of Taung and it was there that Luka went to visit him soon after Lanyon's raid.

Luka regarded Lanyon's raid as an unwarranted act of aggression and he promised Botlasitse his support in any future conflict with the colonial authorities. So far Luka himself had been careful to avoid open conflict with colonial authorities. Where there had been confrontation it had been with individual colonists such as Greef and Donovan whom he considered were acting unjustly. He knew, however, that there was an arrest warrant still outstanding against him. After the example of Lanyon's raid on Phokwani, Luka presumed that he would be next in Lanyon's sights, and he was determined that he would resist any commando that Lanyon might send against him. He began calling the Batlhaping to arms to defend themselves from an impending colonial raid. Among those summoned to Manyeding for potential military service were men whom the missionaries had been employing

[18] *LMS*, Ashton, Barkly, 8 February 1878.
[19] *UW*, A75/2, Mackenzie to Lanyon, 1 February 1878.

to finish building the new training seminary – the Moffat Institute – at Kuruman (*above*).

It was from this point that both Ashton and Mackenzie began to turn against Luka. They had never totally trusted him: Luka was clearly not as pliant as his father. From his base at Barkly West, Ashton wrote to Mackenzie at Kuruman in early February 1878:

> The Govt. will hold Janje [*sic*] responsible for what Luka has been doing in calling the natives to arms to help Botlasitse – or even for what they have done in arming & in turning out to resist the Commando. I think it is well for the people that Luka can no longer rule them within the Province; & those who are beyond it, who are still subject to his caprices, will in time find out that they are no better off than those who are British subjects... [20]

Despite Ashton's opinion, in the months that followed, an increasing number of Batlhaping from within the colony began to gather at Manyeding and looked to Luka as their leader. Matsemane, who was released from Barkly gaol on 12 March 1878, went straight to Manyeding and agreed to act as Luka's 'lieutenant'. Luka's father, Jantjie Mothibi, however, was still *kgosi* and as such was ultimately responsible for calling the people to arms. He came under considerable pressure from both Ashton and Mackenzie to put a stop to it. Jantjie was persuaded by the missionaries that some peaceful resolution was still possible and in April he ordered the troops at Manyeding to disperse.

Luka accepted his father's ruling; but by calling the men to arms he had made it clear to all, both within the colony and beyond, that any armed colonial incursion into independent Batlhaping territory would be met by armed resistance.

---

[20] *LMS*, Ashton, Barkly West, 8 February 1878.

CHAPTER SEVEN

Rebellion and the Battle of Kho

1878

Although Luka had accepted his father's ruling and had ordered his forces at Manyeding to disperse in March 1878, he probably believed that he would soon have to summon his men together again; it seemed unlikely, following Lanyon's attack on Phokwani in January, that Griqualand West's Administrator would leave arrest warrants against Luka and Matsemane outstanding without trying to enforce them. That probability was greatly increased with the outbreak of rebellion in Griqualand West in April 1878.

The catalyst that set off the Griqualand West rebellion was rooted in a small group of Xhosa who, originating from what was to become the eastern Cape Colony, had been settled at Prieska on the south bank of the lower Orange River for about two generations. This group had felt the pressure of the colonial land grab from the 1850s as the Cape Colony extended its northern boundary to the Orange River and they began to make use of the grazing land west of Griquatown, between Prieska and the southern Langeberg. This group also engaged in general acts of banditry. Having been squeezed out of their grazing lands south of the Orange, they were to lose out again in the 1870s when Warren's land settlement of Griqualand West refused to recognise any Xhosa land entitlement north of the Orange River.

Some early Xhosa successes in the ninth (and final) Cape-Xhosa War of 1877–78 appear to have inspired their distant cousins, the Xhosa of the Prieska region. By March 1878 there were rumours circulating in Griqualand West and beyond that the Prieska Xhosa were urging the Griqua and Batswana that now was the time to strike against their white oppressors. While the Batswana beyond the colony were hesitant about taking drastic action, many of the Griqua within the colony had few such qualms.

The Griqua under Nicolas Waterboer had trusted the assurances of their lawyer, David Arnot, that their entitlement to land would be best protected by British rule. They were soon disabused of this trust. Under Arnot's guidance much of the land of the supposedly 'Griqua territory' had been sold many times over before the British even annexed the country. And the Griqua found that many of the titles that they had supposed to be secure were challenged by rival claimants, many of them colonial speculators, in the Land Court of 1875–76. In Warren's land settlement of 1877, Griqua titles were often denied when they were challenged by plausible white claimants. And finally, those titles that were recognised were frequently mortgaged through debts to white-owned liquor stores. Even in Griquatown itself at least one Griqua liquor store owner of many years standing was denied a licence to operate, that same licence then being granted to a white claimant. The man's Griqua and Batlhaping employees were later to be found among the 'rebels'. As William Ashton remarked in June 1878: 'The Griqua have had much to complain of in the administration of what has passed for British Laws'; adding, 'but nothing to justify rebellion.' That final point was clearly a matter of perspective.[1]

In April 1878 a group of Prieska Xhosa joined with disaffected Griqua and dispossessed Khoesan hunters and herdsmen and launched their rebellion. They conducted a number of raids on colonial cattle farms and trading stores in the southwest of the colony. Some herdsmen and a few colonists were killed, and large herds of cattle and flocks of sheep and goats were driven off to the southern Langeberg.

Driving goats in the dry, dusty environment of the Langeberg today.

The Langeberg had already acquired a reputation among colonists as a haven for stolen livestock that would then be traded westwards to Namaqualand in southern Namibia. It is not clear whether these early 'rebels' regarded this as a conscious act of political rebellion against the colonial state or more simply as a defiant return to the freer days of pre-colonial banditry.

Lanyon, however, reacted with predictable enthusiasm, viewing it as

---

[1] *LMS*, Ashton, Barkly West, 13 June 1878.

another opportunity for a quick war against 'the natives'. He was not deterred by Warren's continued absence in the eastern Cape. Indeed he may have welcomed it as another chance to show what he could do on his own. Warren was expected back before the end of May, but Lanyon could not wait that long. He gathered a small force of enthusiastic white volunteers – all eager for some easy loot – and launched what he considered to be a lightning strike against the rebels in the Prieska region.

It was early in the dry season, after a year of severe drought, and Lanyon's force kicked up a conspicuous column of dust in the still cool air. Thus the whole of the southwest of the colony was forewarned of his attack and all that Lanyon's strike succeeded in doing was to drive the rebels into the Langeberg, beyond the colonial boundary. They were joined there by further disaffected Griqua who were certainly bent on rebellion.

Lanyon returned to Kimberley confident that he had scored another victory and awaited Warren's reinforcements. Warren, similarly promoted to Lieutenant-Colonel for military service against the Xhosa in the Eastern Cape, hurried north to rejoin Lanyon in Griqualand West. Immediately upon his return to Kimberley the colony's only two professional military officers gathered their volunteer forces and set off for the southern Langeberg, determined to clear this stronghold of all rebels, stock thieves and gunrunners. Establishing a base camp at Griquatown, they left the rest of the colony unprotected from any further rebellious action by its widely dissatisfied subject population.

So far, apart from a few isolated individuals, the Batlhaping as a whole had not taken any rebellious action within the colony. One reason for this was that most of those with a grievance against the government and the behaviour of its colonists had already left the colony, especially after Lanyon's cattle raid on Phokwani. They had gone to join Botlasitse at Modimong, north of Taung, or to join Luka at Manyeding. The majority of Batlhaping, however, remained within the colony and were busy using their wagons to carry firewood to the Kimberley market where firewood prices were approaching £20 per load. Ashton was kept busy issuing 'passes' to Batlhaping wood-riders that vouched for their good character and allowed them free access to the otherwise restricted urban centre of Kimberley.

On Saturday 25 May, Colonels Lanyon and Warren were approaching the southern Langeberg when a small rural trading store in the northern border region of Griqualand West came under attack. James Burness, his wife and brother lived at the store just north of Daniel's Kuil. Burness was a local field-cornet, responsible for pointing out the surveyor's beacons to the new owners of the land between Daniel's Kuil and the northern border. He was also master of the cattle pound in Daniel's Kuil. In both of these capacities he had come into conflict with local Griqua and Batlhaping. There were clearly local grievances against James Burness, perhaps not enough on its own to provoke an attack, but if there was to be a general uprising, then Burness was clearly an obvious easy target.

On the evening of Friday 24 May, from his house on the edge of the trading compound, Burness's African assistant saw some armed men circling the store. He slipped away unseen and hurried through the night to the house of a neighbouring colonist, John Chapman, to alert him about what he had seen. In the early hours of the following morning Chapman rode over to the Burness homestead. As he approached the place he dismounted and crept to within sight of the store where he witnessed the attack.

He estimated that there were twenty men surrounding the building when one of the Burness brothers came out onto the verandah to remonstrate with them. He was shot dead where he stood. His brother grabbed a shotgun, but he was shot in the doorway of the store. Mrs Burness was shot as she bent over the body of her dead husband. Chapman, quickly mounted his horse and made his escape. Some of the attackers pursued him briefly, but then gave up. After thoroughly looting the store the raiders made off northwards across the border to Koning. Here they settled down to enjoy some liquor and other spoils of war.

The exact identity of the Burness raiders is not known for sure, but judging from the second-hand reports from the missionaries of Kuruman, they appear to have been a mixed band of dissidents from both within the colony and beyond. There were some Griqua, a Morolong from Kimberley named Solomon, a few other assorted Africans from Kimberley, at least six Batlhaping, one of whom was said to be a Church member from Kuruman, and a number of Batlharo. The Batlharo were a branch of the Batswana, not directly related to the Batlhaping. They lived mostly in the drier regions to the north and west of Kuruman and in the Langeberg, the mountain range south-west of Kuruman that was reputed to be the ancestral home of the Batlhaping.

Koning, where the raiders now gathered and where *Kgosi* Mothibi had briefly established his town in the 1820s, was in the 1870s mostly a Batlharo settlement, coming under the authority of *Kgosi* Morwe, who lived down-stream from Kuruman at the town of Batlaros. The Burness raiders had the sympathy of Morwe, and the town of Batlaros had already become a safe haven for livestock stolen from the colony. Indeed, it was pursuit of stolen livestock that brought Luka to Kuruman at about the same time that the Burness murders were taking place.

In May, shortly before the Burness raid, John G Donovan had sent a message to *Kgosi* Jantjie at Manyeding complaining that some cattle and horses had been stolen from the colony and asking Jantjie to look out for them. Jantjie appeared to know about the matter already for he sent three men straight to a Batlharo village where they saw the stolen livestock. But the village headman, Mashow, refused to allow them to recover the animals. According to Luka's second-hand account Mashow said: 'I am Motlharo and am not going to acknowledge orders from the Batlhaping and allow them to go through my country as they like.'[2] In this he was, he said, acting under the orders of *Kgosi* Morwe. Furthermore, Mashow said, if the white men came to Jantjie asking where the cattle and horses were, he was to send them to Morwe.

When Jantjie's emissaries reported back to Manyeding, the aging *kgosi* made the three-hour horse-ride into Kuruman to consult with the missionaries. Mackenzie told Jantjie that he must assert his authority and arrest Mashow and his fellow stock thieves; but Jantjie pointed out that he had no power to arrest them as they were Batlharo, under Morwe and he, Jantjie, had no authority in that district.

Unlike his father, Luka by this time had no great faith in the missionaries, or their advice, but he was prepared to co-operate with the colonial authorities when he felt it was justified to do so. It happened that a week or so earlier Luka had arrested a Motlharo who was passing through Manyeding with a horse that Luka knew had been stolen from one of the Griqualand West surveyors. But a local Manyeding man helped the arrested horse thief to escape during the night and they both made off to Batlaros, taking the stolen horse with them. On Jantjie's return home from the missionaries at Kuruman, Luka sent his brother Olebile to Morwe at Batlaros to enquire about the stolen horse. According to Luka, Olebile failed to regain the horse, but he brought back a message from Morwe:

> You tell Jantjie Mothibi that he is to attack all the missionaries and shop-keepers in the country and kill the last one, so that there is not one left in the country. I will do the same here.[3]

---

2 CA GLW 130/6,7 Luka's account of the war of 1878, translated and transcribed in Kimberley gaol, 12 June 1879. 'Motlharo' is the singular form of Batlharo.
3 CA GLW 130/6,7 Luka's account, Kimberley gaol.

According to Mackenzie's contemporaneous account, as reported to him by Jantjie, Morwe had added that he expected Jantjie to kill the Kuruman white men first as he was the senior *kgosi*, and then he himself would feel free to kill the other white traders in Batlaros. This was Saturday 25 May, the day of the killing of the Burnesses. Considering the number of Batlharo involved, it is possible that Morwe had already heard of the attack. If so, then his message to Jantjie shows he considered the Burness raid as the signal for a general uprising, but he wanted to ensure that Jantjie and the Batlhaping were also involved and that they struck the first blow.

As Olebile arrived home from Batlaros, news of the Burness murders had not yet reached Manyeding. Nevertheless, as soon as he heard Morwe's message, Luka decided he must go immediately to Batlaros to forestall the killing of any white traders there. But he was suffering a severe fever at the time and was unable to mount his horse. His father persuaded him to rest until the morning when the two of them would go there in the wagon.

On reaching Kuruman next day, Sunday 26 May, Jantjie stopped off to report Morwe's words to Mackenzie while Luka went on to Batlaros to deliver a message from his father. The message was that Morwe must not do what he had threatened, but that if he intended to fight he must send the colonial government notice to that effect. Jantjie evidently wanted to ensure that any who attacked the white people should firstly openly declare war so that the wider population would not suffer the consequences. According to Luka, Morwe admitted that he had sent the previous message, but that he would now take Jantjie's advice and not fight. It seems that Morwe only wanted to join in if there was a general uprising, and he was not prepared to initiate anything on his own. Luka returned to Kuruman and delivered Morwe's message to Jantjie, whereupon father and son returned to Manyeding, having done what they could to calm the situation.

That night, however, Sunday 26 May, John Chapman rode into Kuruman with the news of the Burness shootings. He had spent much of the previous day and night hiding in the bush before making his way by a circuitous route to the supposed safety of Kuruman.

The missionaries and European traders of Kuruman were convinced that they would be the next target for attack. The mission had made itself vulnerable by attracting around it a number of major trading stores, and most of these dealt heavily in arms and ammunition. Chapman and the other traders at Kuruman had between them up to 1,800 pounds of gunpowder, a similar quantity of lead and at least 500 guns. This in itself was reason enough for

Part of the extensive Moffat Institute built in 1875–78 by the LMS, displacing local villagers.

potential 'rebels' to launch an attack on Kuruman.

Mackenzie (*right*) advised some of the more vulnerable members of the European community to move into the newly completed Moffat Institute, just across the river from the mission itself. As if to confirm Mackenzie's suspicions, Morwe rode up to Kuruman with a considerable body of men. They camped on the outskirts of the mission and rode through the settlement conspicuously armed with guns.

Quite apart from the attraction of the arms and ammunition, half of which was hastily buried while the rest was moved into the Moffat Institute, the building of the Institute itself had provoked considerable resentment among the local population. The building was designed as a seminary to train local Batswana missionaries, but when it was begun in 1875, Mackenzie had ordered the clearing of the village of Seoding across the river from the mission station. This was a very different attitude from that of Robert Moffat when he had negotiated permission from *Kgosi* Mothibi for the original mission site in the 1820s. With the building of the Moffat Institute, no prior permission was sought and no compensation was offered the displaced villagers, merely some labour to help them rebuild their houses further north.

The size of the building itself suggested to many that the missionaries were intent on building a permanent base of political power in the country – as an outpost perhaps of the colony of Griqualand West. Indeed, the events of 1878 that were then unfolding appeared to justify this suspicion. Despite the protests of the missionaries to the contrary, it was ironic that the first use to which the new building was put was as an armoury and barracks to protect the men of God from attack by their own congregation.

The presence of the Burness raiders at Koning and the restless activities of

Morwe's Batlharo around Kuruman spread unease and rumour throughout the territory north of the Griqualand border. At Bothithong, an LMS station not far from Dithakong, the resident missionary, Alfred J Wookey, received a warning from a neighbouring *kgosi* that he was in danger of attack. That was on Sunday 26 May. The following day Wookey's deacon rode in from his cattle-post to see if the Wookey family was still alive.

As yet Wookey had seen no reason to become alarmed. He had been in Griquatown in April and had seen the unrest among the Griqua there, but that was in colonial territory, quite different from independent Batlhaping country north of the border. Besides, he knew that he was respected in the region and was valued for his medical knowledge and expertise. But then on Wednesday 29 May he received an alarmist letter from Mackenzie telling him of the Burness murders and hinting that Kuruman itself was expecting imminent attack. Wookey advised his wife to prepare for evacuation while he rode into Kuruman to assess the situation for himself, leaving his wife and family under the protection of the local *kgosi*. At Kuruman the next morning, Wookey observed the state of high alert, and bowed to Mackenzie's advice to bring his family in to the relative safety of the Moffat Institute. Back in Bothithong by Thursday night, Wookey loaded up his wagon and departed with his family on the Friday evening, arriving in Kuruman twenty-four hours later.

When news of the Burness killings reached Manyeding, Jantjie sent a message to the raiders at Koning, advising them to stay where they were and to keep calm and peaceful. Although they followed Jantjie's advice for a couple of weeks, Morwe then countered this by pointing out that all Jantjie wanted was to hand them over to the *makgowa*, who were bound to come looking for them sooner or later. This was indeed almost certainly Jantjie's intention. Morwe, on the other hand, urged them to go to the safety of the northern Langeberg where they could seek the protection of the senior Batlharo *kgosi* Makgolokwe, who lived at Puduhush. Over the next couple of weeks the gang at Koning gradually dispersed. Some went to the Langeberg, some joined Morwe's camp around Kuruman, while a few, including the Morolong Solomon, joined Luka and Matsemane at Manyeding.

Within Manyeding, political opinion was sharply divided between the 'hawks' and the 'doves'. Jantjie was determined to avoid conflict with the *makgowa*, at almost any cost, but his over-dependence upon missionary advice was losing him authority over the younger members of the *morafe*. Luka appeared to take a more balanced approach. As ever, he respected his father's authority. Besides, he saw no point or justice in indiscriminately attacking *makgowa* traders and missionaries in independent Batlhaping country. They were after all living there under Batlhaping (or Batlharo) 'protection'. His attitude to the colonists of Griqualand West was that he would avoid initiating any conflict; but bearing in mind Lanyon's cattle raid on Phokwani, he was prepared to resist any unauthorised armed attempt to cross the border from the colony.

Luka's younger brothers, however, were clearly on the side of the 'hawks'. There was much antagonism towards Donovan, who was reliably reported to have shot dead a Motlhaping in the colony.[4] Olebile proposed raiding Donovan's place, slitting Donovan's throat and taking all his cattle. Luka intervened and managed to restrain his youngest brother. Solomon on the other hand, as a Morolong, saw himself as a free agent and he showed no such restraint. He led a raiding party to Klein Boetsap. Donovan and Hunter managed to flee the scene, leaving Solomon to loot some cattle and horses. Luka's younger brothers, meanwhile, having missed out on the Boetsap raid, led a looting party to Wookey's deserted mission station and a trading store at Bothithong, forty-five kilometres north of Manyeding. There was not much to take, but they returned with some looted cattle.

Jantjie, despairing of the behaviour of his younger sons, left Manyeding and went into the sanctuary of Kuruman. His arrival in Kuruman and his sons' raid on Bothithong was interpreted by Mackenzie as a sign that reliable 'native authority' within the territory had finally broken down and he assumed a state of siege. Under Mackenzie's direction, all the Europeans of Kuruman, missionaries and traders, moved into the Moffat Institute, which, with its iron roof, was believed to be safe from attack by gun or fire.

Mackenzie then sat down and between 1 and 10 June he composed a long letter to Colonel Lanyon, detailing recent events and what he believed to be their background.[5] He argued that Jantjie could no longer exercise authority, as evidenced by his inability to arrest the Burness murderers, and he urged the case for an extension of British protection over the region. This was something that the British government had indeed been considering ever since they had assumed authority over the bankrupt South African Republic (now known as the Transvaal Colony) in 1877.

---

4 *LMS*, Ashton, Barkly West, 23 July 1878.
5 A J Dachs, *Papers of John Mackenzie* (1975) pp108–112, quoting from Mackenzie Papers (UW).

The kind of protection that Mackenzie proposed was a far more tentative form of colonisation than had hitherto been British practice in South Africa. Mackenzie now spelt out in more detail the advice contained in his warning letter to Lanyon following the Phokwani raid. Mackenzie proposed the setting up of a network of British commissioners who would work alongside each of the main Batlhaping *dikgosi* who resided beyond the Griqualand border. These advance agents of British colonialism would advise the *dikgosi*, boost their authority, co-operate with general British policy and ensure that the Batswana generally did not come into conflict with any white person, either within the colony or beyond. In his February letter Mackenzie had contrasted this with Lanyon's policy of 'raid and fine':

> The one policy reminds one of the rude blow of a big, flat-headed hammer; the other is the quiet action of the thin end of a crow-bar. The one shatters everything to pieces; the other moves and changes without destroying.[6]

Mackenzie's letter was sent via Ashton in Barkly West for forwarding to Lanyon who was out of Kimberley at the time.[7] Judge J D Barry had been left in charge in Kimberley and he forwarded the letters to Lanyon, recommending the sending of a force to the relief of Kuruman as an 'absolute necessity'.[8] He had already ordered the surveyor John H Ford to assemble a force of fifty to one hundred mounted volunteers. Barry proposed that these should go to Kuruman first and then on to Koning to arrest the Burness murderers. They could then join Lanyon and Warren at Khosis to the west of Koning, but only 'if you approve'.

Lanyon received these letters in Griquatown on 16 June and he immediately responded by ordering that Ford's force should initially go only as far as Daniel's Kuil and Boetsap, well within the colonial boundary. Theirs was to be a 'demonstration' of force. This would give moral support to Mankurwane who appeared to be trying to bring Botlasitse's people under control by capturing some of the cattle that had been 'lifted' from the colony. It appears that Lanyon did not altogether trust Ford's military competence. In fact there was nobody left in Kimberley with any military experience, only 'gentlemen' dangerously eager for some 'sport'.[9] Those with any military experience were already in the field, with Lanyon and Warren in the Langeberg.

[6] Dachs, *Mackenzie* (1975), p105; from copy forwarded to LMS, 1 February 1878.
[7] Lanyon was based at Griquatown from where he and Warren were operating against the Griqua in the southern Langeberg.
[8] *Jagger Library*, J D Barry Private Letter Book.
[9] *LMS*, Ashton, 23 July 1878.

At the same time as attempting to restrict Ford's movements, however, Lanyon also gave Ford the discretion he had been hoping for. If 'something else' arose, Ford was permitted to cross the border, although only with prior clearance from Mankurwane, and he spelt out the 'something else':

> If the safety of the persons & property of British subjects at Kuruman itself are in jeopardy you are authorised to proceed thither for the purposes of protection.

His final instruction, however: 'You are to do nothing which may provoke hostilities.' was wasted on the eager amateurs of Ford's commando.

It took Ford ten days to gather and equip an initial force of seventy-five mounted Europeans, ten European infantry and twenty-five Mfengu and Zulu They left Kimberley with three wagons of supplies and passed through Barkly West on 21 June where they were joined by five more Europeans and seven more Africans. Ashton, who personally urged Ford to make haste to Kuruman, commented in a private letter to Mackenzie:

> I quite expect they will make a mess of it. ... Ford, the Commandant, has not had the least experience in this sort of work, and talks very big about what he will do. ... I hope he will not make matters worse, by bringing in, as prisoners, people whom he will find fleeing before him out of sheer fright, and thus leave behind him a greater hatred to the British Government than there is at present.[10]

But it was worse than Ashton feared; Ford was eager for a fight and was in no mood to take prisoners.

Meanwhile, on 21 June, the day that Ford left Barkly West, Lanyon's force at Campbell came under attack from the direction of Daniel's Kuil, well within the colony. Lanyon immediately wrote to Barry telling him to order Ford to proceed immediately to Daniel's Kuil, adding, 'I do not think it is advisable to go to Kuruman under present circumstances.' Barry, however, did not receive this instruction until late on Tuesday night, 2 July. Although he sent an urgent message to Boetsap within the hour, it was already too late to stop Ford.

As Ford had proceeded up the Harts to Boetsap, he had sent Sam Edwards ahead to Taung to get Mankurwane's permission to cross the border. By 30 June Edwards was back in Boetsap with permission granted and with a letter from Mackenzie warning the force to take care in coming up to Kuruman, for Luka intended to fight. This suited Ford who was, in his own words, 'burning for a fight'.[11] As he wrote to Barry on 30 June, 'If you wish to prevent me from fighting you must be sharp.' The following day Ford led his force across the border into independent Batlhaping territory.

With the missionaries and traders of Kuruman urging a colonial 'rescue' mission from Griqualand West, Luka and the Batlhaping at Manyeding prepared for the worst. They were well aware that a force was being assembled to come in pursuit of the Burness raiders. Luka assumed that the force would be led by Colonel Lanyon, the man who had conducted the raid on Phokwani six months previously. Luka himself expected to be a target for arrest, on the basis of the warrant for assault taken out against him by Donovan's employee the previous year. According to a trader who moved into Kuruman on 18 June, Luka had said that 'he does not wish to be taken.'[12]

On 24 June Luka's father came down to Manyeding from Kuruman and made one last attempt to prevent a war. According to Revd John Brown, who heard it from Jantjie himself later that night:

> The old man got up in a meeting when they were talking about sending out a Commando, and said that he hoped that if any of them went out on such an errand none of them would return from it. Leaving his curse thus hanging over them he left the meeting.[13]

Jantjie turned up at John Brown's house in Kuruman at seven o'clock that night asking for a room for himself and his belongings.

Jantjie's warning seems to have been heeded, for there were no rash 'commandos' sent out from Manyeding to anticipate trouble. Nevertheless, the following Monday, 1 July, news reached Manyeding that a large armed force had crossed the border the previous night and set up camp a few kilometres from the boundary line.

For the events that followed we have two sources of evidence: the report of Commandant Ford to Colonel Lanyon and, unusually, an account by his opponent, Luka Jantjie himself. It is one of those rare occasions when we have Luka's own version of events, albeit in English translation. His words were recorded while Luka was being held in Kimberley gaol the following year and so one might expect a certain degree of self-justification in his account. In

---

[11] UCT, *Jagger Library*, Barry Private Papers, Ford to Barry, 30 June 1878.
[12] Lanyon Private Papers, enclosures in Barry to Lanyon, 28 June 1878.
[13] LMS, Ashton, 23 July 1878, quoting a letter received from John Brown.

fact the two opposing accounts coincide remarkably well.

Luka takes up the story as news reached Manyeding of Ford's crossing of the border:

> Matsemane said to me that we had better go out and spy and see where the commando was going to. Eleven of us went out scouting on horseback [on the morning of Tuesday 2 July]. All of these men with the exception of myself were subsequently killed in the fight at Dithakong [on 24 July].
>
> We eleven went scouting and saw the commando at Kho. We were near some stone kraals when we saw *makgowa* coming. Matsemane wanted us to go into the stone kraals and fight the *makgowa* as they came up. We refused to do this. The *makgowa* came on towards us and called on us to stand or halt. But Matsemane would not let us halt, and then the *makgowa* fired on us. We returned the fire by firing five shots. No one was killed or wounded on either side by the firing.
>
> We retreated then, and met nineteen of our men on foot. At this time the *makgowa* who had fired on us were joined by the main body of *makgowa*. When we got on a little rise, the large number of our men ran away, as they saw the English commando. Eighteen of us remained. Then the *makgowa* fired on us a second time. This was about three o'clock in the afternoon and they continued firing at us until sunset.[14]

The implication of Luka's story is that he did not want to fight if he could avoid it. It should also be remembered that Luka was the only survivor of the battle at Kho who lived beyond the following three weeks. His was thus the only Batlhaping version of events. Nevertheless, bearing in mind his restraint hitherto in dealing with colonial officialdom, it is likely that he would not have authorised the first shot; but at the same time, he had called the men to arms to defend the remaining Batlhaping *morafe* and he was also intent on defending himself from colonial arrest.

According to Luka it was Matsemane who was most strongly bent on fighting the *magkowa*. From Ford's account we learn that it was Sam Edwards, who called on them to halt. This would have been delivered in Setswana, so they all understood what he said.[15] It sounds from Luka's story that he would have preferred to have heard what this advancing column wanted and what their intentions were. But Ford's men, like Matsemane, were so keyed up for a fight that it is highly likely that if Luka's men had indeed immediately halted,

---

[14] *CA* GLW 130/7 Luka's account, Kimberley gaol, 12 and 14 June 1879.
[15] BPP, C2220, pp25–6, Ford to Colonial Secretary, Mazeppafontein near Manyeering, 4 July 1878

they would probably have been fired upon in any case. As it was, once the firing had been started by the advancing column, Luka was just as ready as the rest to return fire and withdraw to a defendable position.

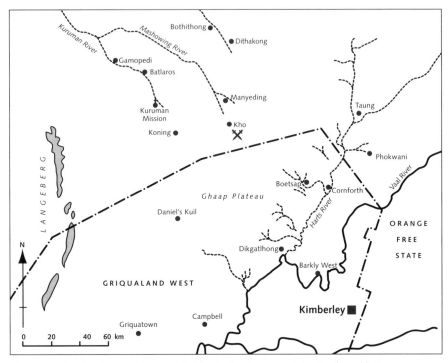

MAP 9: *The Battle of Kho, 2 July 1878: Luka's Batlhaping versus John Ford's Barkly Rangers.*

Ford's own report confirmed Luka's account that Ford's forward scouting party had started the shooting. A small group of five mounted men, including Sam Edwards, had gone ahead of the main body. When they saw Luka's scouting party, Edwards had called on them to halt, but almost immediately Captain D'Arcy of the Barkly Rangers ordered his men to fire. They did so enthusiastically and then pursued Luka's retreating troop, firing as they went, almost as if they were on a sporting hunt. Their sport was interrupted, however, when they were confronted by the main body of Luka's men who pinned them down under heavy fire. Edwards was sent back to urge the main force to move up quickly, and Ford brought up a further thirty men, leaving the rest to guard the camp.

Firing went on for several hours, throughout the rest of the afternoon. Although his force outnumbered the Batlhaping by nearly two to one, Ford's men came off the worse from the conflict. The Batlhaping were all experienced hunters, and according to a report in a Cape newspaper, they 'fought like mad and were splendid shots.'[16]

As the light faded, both sides withdrew. Ford had suffered five men killed and four seriously wounded, among them his own son, shot through the body. Many others had minor wounds. Stretchers were brought up and the able bodied carried the dead and wounded back to camp, leaving behind a number of guns and other equipment. Ford himself was shot in the lower leg and had to be carried back to camp.

Luka's men had suffered one killed and several wounded. Luka himself, like Ford, was shot through the left leg, below the knee. Unlike Ford, however, he managed to mount his horse and ride back to Manyeding. He arrived home late at night. By then he had lost a lot of blood and was too weak to ride any further. According to his own account, Luka told the women and children of his household to make their way to a place of safety, which they did that night.

> The next morning a wagon belonging to Mosete came and took me away and brought me to where the women were at a place called Ishlarapan.[17]

The 'Battle of Kho' was related by Luka's great-nephew in Manyeding a hundred years later as a great victory for the Batlhaping over the invading English.[18] In reality it was little more than a minor skirmish; but whatever its scale it was a clear victory for Luka and his men. The next day, one of the victors rode into Morwe's camp near Kuruman waving a pistol recovered from the scene. This prompted a number of Batlharo to hurry to Manyeding with three empty wagons that they hoped to fill with loot. Within the mission at Kuruman, however, there was some concern for the wounded, as Luka explained:

> At this time my father Jantjie Mothibi had gone to the missionaries at Kuruman. It was there that he heard I was wounded; the missionaries also heard so. A missionary named 'Waha' [Wookey] and Willie Chapman[19] came and dressed my wound at … Ishlarapan. The Bechuana washed off the dressing the white people had put on my leg, and put some medicine of their own on.
>
> After this the missionary said he wanted to go back to the white camp, but I would not let him go until I furnished him with a man named Mabate to escort

---

16 *Cape Argus Supplement*, 30 July 1878.
17 CA GLW 130/7 Luka's account, Kimberley gaol, 12 and 14 June 1879.
18 Author's interview with Molehabangwe Jantjie, grandson of Olebile Devolk Jantjie, Manyeding, March 1978.
19 Son of the trader John Chapman.

him to Kuruman as there were Bechuana camps between the place we were at and the white people's camp. We left [Ishlarapan] after the missionary had gone and went to a place called Mahlarene.

Alfred Wookey's (*left*) account of this meeting differs slightly from that of Luka and adds some interesting detail. According to the missionary, Olebile had come into Kuruman and requested that Wookey come and attend to his brother's wound. On arrival at Ishlarapan, however, Wookey found that he and Willie Chapman were not particularly welcome. Indeed, Luka's mother 'told us most insultingly to go back to where we had come from.'

Under the circumstances, the tense atmosphere that greeted the two British men was understandable: the Batlhaping had recently been attacked by a British force, apparently allied to the missionaries at Kuruman; a number of men had been shot and Luka had been badly wounded in his leg. Olebile, however, persuaded them to stay and they dismounted and went to see Luka.

We found him in the enclosure in front of a hut, and sat down and talked with him for some time. I asked him whether even now we could not open up some communication with the English, as they had not come to fight, and try to come to some amicable settlement with them; as he was only bringing certain ruin on his country by fighting. His answer was No, they meant to fight it out; and not even I would be allowed on any account to go past his people, as they would murder anyone who should attempt it. Neither would they allow us to touch his wound or give him medicine, as they said our intention was to poison him.[20]

According to Wookey, it was Olebile who saw to it that the two white men got back safely to Kuruman.

On Wookey's return to Kuruman, Jantjie decided that since his sons had fought a battle with an army of the British, he could no longer stay with the missionaries at Kuruman. His place was with his family where he would share whatever fate befell them.[21] So he joined Luka and his wife and other members of the family at Mahlarene and they all made their way to Dithakong. Luka's son Dikare, also known as Dokwe, would have been about

[20] *LMS*, Wookey, Kuruman, 27 August 1878
[21] *Cape Argus*, 8 August 1878, Revd John Brown to Editor, Kuruman, 16 July 1878.

sixteen years of age at the time. It is not known whether he accompanied his father and grandfather, but he probably did. Luka's brothers Kaelo and Olebile, however, remained at Manyeding where preparations were made to repel Ford's column that was now expected to advance from its camp near the border.

Ford's troops remained at their border camp for three days, burying their dead and tending to the wounded, with the assistance of one of the volunteers who was a surgeon. They moved on towards Kuruman on Friday 5 July, carrying their wounded in the wagons. They moved slowly, keeping a tight formation and forming a secure camp each evening. They passed Manyeding on Sunday 7 July where they came under steady fire, but they did not have the strength to launch the full revenge attack that Captain D'Arcy would have liked. Afterwards they boasted to the Cape newspapers that they 'scored' ten killed,[22] but this was sheer bravado, to cover for their humiliation at Kho. More reliable evidence claimed that only one of Luka's men was killed in the Manyeding skirmish.[23]

Ford's column finally rode into Kuruman on 9 July. His thoroughly chastened bunch of amateur volunteers were in no fit state for further military adventure under the current leadership and the most that they could do was to turn the Moffat Institute into a combination of hospital and military barracks. To his credit, Mackenzie refused to turn the Institute's Batswana students out of their dormitories and the white volunteers and Zulu auxiliaries alike had to sleep in wagons and tents.

During the following week, the Battle of Kho claimed its sixth white victim with the death from his wounds of John Ford's son. Willie Chapman rode to Koning with some fellow traders, imagining that they could retrieve some stolen cattle. Chapman was shot dead by a herdsman who was presumably protecting his animals from theft. Following this latest death, a vengeful troop of Barkly Rangers from Ford's column rode over to Koning and killed the first twenty Africans that they saw, driving the rest of the Koning population in the direction of the Langeberg.[24] With the arrival of Colonel Warren in Kuruman on 15 July, a little more discipline was imposed upon this dangerous band of armed colonists.

---

[22] *Cape Argus* Supplement, 30 July 1878.
[23] *Cape Times*, 8 August 1878, Letter from J Tom Brown, Kuruman, 16 July 1878.
[24] *Cape Argus*, 17 August 1878.

CHAPTER EIGHT

Dithakong and capture
1878–1879

Luka and his father would have arrived in Dithakong on about 8 or 9 July while his brothers, Olebile and Kaelo, arrived shortly afterwards, together with Matsemane and the defenders of Manyeding. They were greeted by Merwe,[1] the local *kgosi* of Dithakong who agreed that he and his people would stand by them in their common cause: the defence of the Batlhaping *morafe*. Soon after Luka's arrival at Dithakong, news would have reached the historic capital of the killings at Koning to avenge the death of Willie Chapman. It must have been clear to those gathering at Dithakong that a major battle with colonial forces was probably now unavoidable. And with news of the imminent arrival at Kuruman of reinforcements from Kimberley, that probability became a certainty.

The Administrator of Griqualand West, Colonel William O Lanyon, had returned to Kimberley on 4 July 1878 with a troop of volunteers who had seen service in the Langeberg. On learning of Ford's crossing of the border for the relief of Kuruman, Lanyon expressed no criticism until, three days later, he learned of the reverse at Kho. Then he loudly proclaimed that Ford had disobeyed orders; this was not strictly true, but it was probably an attempt on his part to distance himself from this perceived damage to British prestige.[2] Having sent off a letter to his father complaining how tiresome it all was, Lanyon re-gathered his volunteer force of 120 men and set off for Kuruman. Following the route taken by Ford, he found Boetsap sacked and looted and Manyeding deserted. Lanyon rode into Kuruman on Wednesday 17 July and immediately ordered a march on the Batlharo village of Gamopedi.

Ever since the arrival of Ford's battered column the Batlharo *Kgosi* Morwe had been professing his loyalty to the English. He claimed that the 'Basuto' responsible for the Burness murders had gone down the Kuruman valley to Gamopedi where they were living under the protection of *Kgosi* Ikaneng. It

---

[1] Not to be confused with Morwe, a Batlharo *kgosi* based at Batlaros during this period.
[2] TVL, 596/13, Lanyon to his father, Kimberley, 8 July 1878.

is possible that one or two Basotho from Kimberley had been among the Burness raiders, but this was probably an attempt by Morwe to save himself and his people from Lanyon's wrath by shifting the blame onto 'foreigners' from Kimberley rather than any Batlharo under his authority.[3] It did, however, place his fellow *kgosi*, Ikaneng, directly in the firing line.

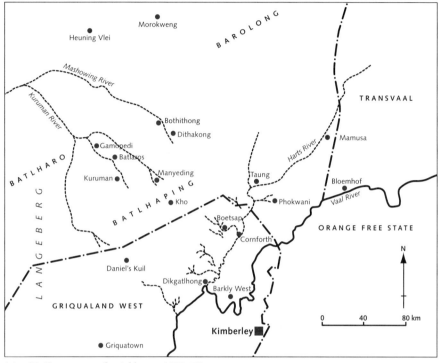

MAP 10: *Batswana and neighbours, 1878–79.*

Leaving Warren at Kuruman with half their combined forces, Lanyon left for Gamopedi that evening with the remainder of the troops and one of three field guns that they had brought from Kimberley. After a night march Lanyon's force reached Gamopedi at dawn whereupon, with no attempt at negotiation, he immediately ordered six artillery rounds to be fired into the village. Placing his Zulu auxiliaries in the front line, Lanyon then ordered an advance in skirmishing order.

The Gamopedi residents had never been on the receiving end of artillery before, and the large-scale killing and the obliteration of much of their village in a matter of minutes must have had a devastating effect. Nevertheless the survivors held their ground and initially kept the advancing men at bay,

[3] TVL, 596/10, Lanyon to Executive, Kuruman 20 July 1878.

killing two Zulu and seriously wounding a number of white men. With so many of the Gamopedi defenders killed in the initial artillery fire, however, the remainder were too few to hold off Lanyon's force for long. After an hour of hard fighting *Kgosi* Ikaneng ordered a retreat, leaving the village open for Lanyon's volunteers to joyfully loot. Amongst the rubble of the village Lanyon's men counted more than fifty Gamopedi men killed. Women and children are not mentioned in Lanyon's report; but as it was a surprise attack at dawn, it is likely that there were many women, children and elderly in the village, and a lot of these would have died or been wounded by the indiscriminate artillery fire.

Back in Kuruman two days later, Lanyon wrote a report to the Executive of Griqualand West in Kimberley. He asked Judge Barry to inquire from the Cape authorities whether, if he captured any 'murderers', they could be tried and executed in Kuruman, adding that 'the missionaries think the effect would be most wholesome amongst the natives.' In the same letter Lanyon boasted that at Gamopedi they had captured 600 cattle, 3000 sheep and 20 wagons. This was a gross exaggeration, presumably partly intended to boost Lanyon's personal prestige, after Ford's fiasco. But it was probably also to encourage more white men in Kimberley to volunteer for this kind of service, for unlike the Zulu recruited in Kimberley, white volunteers were not paid a wage for their service in the field. They were paid a share of the loot captured from the enemy: a popular motive for volunteering for 'action against natives' beyond the colonial border. When the Gamopedi loot finally came to auction in Kimberley on 1 August, the real amount consisted of 320 cattle, 1,500 sheep and goats, eight horses and two covered wagons.[4]

News of the slaughter at Gamopedi appears to have strengthened the resolve of those Batlhaping gathered at Dithakong to make a stand at the old historic capital, and further armed men came in from Bothithong, Batlaros and various villages across the region. A few more came in from Griqualand West where white volunteer forces had been ransacking villages in an over-eager hunt for 'rebels' (and loot).[5]

Jantjie Mothibi was the senior *kgosi* present at Dithakong, but he had by this time effectively abdicated authority to his eldest son. As the victor of Kho and the son of the leading *kgosi* present, Luka would in any case have

---

[4] TVL, 596/10, Lanyon to Executive, Kuruman, 20 July 1878; *Diamond Fields Advertiser*, 31 July 1878.
[5] *LMS*, Ashton, Barkly West, 4 August 1878.

The stone enclosures at Dithakong: (a) the steep slope at rear (b) well-suited to defence (c) the ridge.

assumed a leading role in the planning of the town's defences, even though he was still partially immobilised by his wounded leg. He and the other leading men present decided to make their stand on the ridge to the south of the town *(see map 11, overleaf)*. They realised that the town's houses themselves would never withstand artillery fire, and they concluded, rightly as it turned out, that if they took up a defensive position among the old stone enclosures on the ridge, the enemy would approach from across the northern plain. The back of the ridge was sufficiently protected by the steep slope down some fifty metres to the dry riverbed of the Mashowing.

The assembled people at Dithakong had nearly two weeks to prepare their defences. The rough stone circles that dominated the ridge had probably originally been built as animal enclosures, remnants of a settlement from an earlier century. Each enclosure measured about five metres across. They were formed from local granite blocks using a dry-stone walling technique so it was fairly straightforward to adapt them for military purposes. Luka and

Kgosi Merwe ordered the strengthening of the northern-facing outer walls at the base of the ridge while all along the crest the walls were reshaped to create a complex network of stone circles and well protected inter-connecting passages.

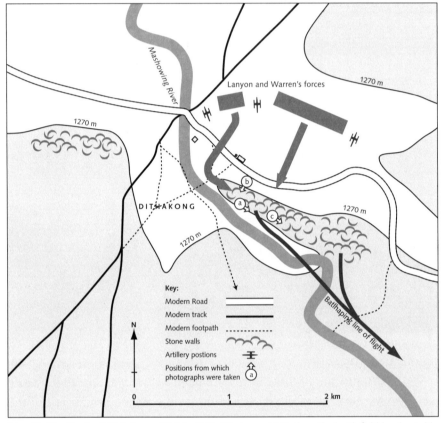

MAP 11: *The Battle of Dithakong, 24 July 1878 (photos on p109 show the battlefield landscape)/*

On Tuesday 23 July, Merwe received a message from Lanyon who had moved his force of about four hundred men up to Bothithong. The message demanded the immediate surrender of 'the Burness murderers'. The Batlhaping, however, were confident of the 'impregnability of their fortress,' and, with the victors of Kho among their ranks, they were buoyed up with the belief that they could cope with Lanyon's force as successfully as they had with Ford's. Thus Merwe sent a reply to the effect that 'what had been done had been done, and they would abide the consequences.'[6]

---

[6] Memo by Lanyon, Kuruman, 30 July 1878; Lanyon to Frere, Kimberley, 24 August 1878; in *British Parliamentary Papers* (GBPP), C.2220, pp120, 161–2.

Merwe ordered the immediate evacuation of the town of Dithakong and while the armed men of fighting age took up their positions behind the stone defences of the ridge, most of the civilians moved away to distant villages to await the outcome of the impending battle. Luka was still in no fit shape to fight, and so he too left Dithakong in a wagon with his father.

The defenders of Dithakong would have spent that night under a clear winter sky in their defensive positions on the ridge, no doubt huddled for warmth under their karosses on top of modern coats and trousers. It is not known how many defenders there were at Dithakong that night, but it is likely to have been at least five hundred. In the cold light of dawn on Wednesday 24 July they would have seen the rising column of dust in the northwest that indicated that Lanyon's force had left Bothithong. As anticipated, Lanyon drew up his men on the northern plain from where they had a clear view across gently rising ground to the well defended ridge.

Remaining just beyond the range of rifle fire, Lanyon readied the three field guns and began his artillery barrage at about ten o'clock. A steady fire of explosive shells onto the ridge was maintained for three hours. The defenders could not return fire as the enemy was out of range. All they could do was crouch down behind their stone defences and hope that enough of them would survive to engage the enemy when the advance finally came. It must have been an unnerving time for the defenders and most of their casualties were lost during this bombardment.

At one o'clock in the afternoon the artillery ceased firing and Lanyon moved one section of his force round to the western end of the ridge. As soon as that section began to move forward towards the ridge, Lanyon ordered a general advance along the nothern front. The only surviving eyewitness account of the action is that of Lanyon himself, and he reported that

> The enemy were well armed and had plenty of ammunition. Being hunters their fire was well directed, and had they been rashly attacked our loss might have been very heavy. ... It is certainly the most formidable place we have yet attacked as the whole place was a network of walls in every direction. ... [and] they fought to the last in a most desperate manner.[7]

The Batlhaping, however, were not fighting the rash amateurs of Ford's command and Lanyon and Warren's advance was steady, careful and relentless. The ridge was finally taken after an hour of what Lanyon described as 'the hottest fire we have yet experienced.' The network of some five hundred

---

[7] *GBPP*, C.2220, pp120, 161–2.

Colonel W O Lanyon and Colonel C Warren (seated 2nd and 3rd from left) with the kind of irregular troops who required 'rewarding' with loot after fighting for the colonial government.

stone enclosures was 'obstinately defended … Even after they were driven out of the place' reported Lanyon, 'they continued the fight and fired upon our men from every available spot.'

The bodies of thirty-nine defenders were found among the stone walls, including those of Matsemane and the other members of Luka's scouting party at Kho. At the time Lanyon claimed that Luka's brother Kaelo was among the dead, but he was later confirmed alive. An unspecified number of the surviving defenders were captured, but most seem to have made their escape down the steep slope at the rear of the ridge and out along the dry riverbed to the southeast. Lanyon had lost two white men and two Zulu killed and about a dozen wounded.

That evening Lanyon camped at Dithakong and as his men gathered up the loot of sixty-seven wagons and several thousand cattle, about two hundred women and children came into the camp now that the fight was over. As Lanyon had ordered the seizure of all the livestock and food in the town, these people were obviously now dependent upon him for their survival. Wanting to offload this responsibility, Lanyon sent them off walking the one hundred kilometres to Taung with a single wagon of provisions, a hundred milch goats and some slaughter sheep. He released two male prisoners to drive the wagon.

While the fighting had been going on at Dithakong, Luka and Jantjie had travelled east to Morakwane, in the hills to the north of Taung. They were joined there by their wives and other members of the family, including in due course, Kaelo and Olebile, who had been among those fighters to escape from Dithakong. A week later Mankurwane made a move against Botlasitse, to impress Lanyon of his loyalty to the British, and Luka's party decided it would be wise to move further away to the north. Aware that they were now fugitives from a colonial version of justice, they travelled northwest, through the Barolong town of Morokweng, before crossing the Molopo River and finding temporary sanctuary in the Bangwaketse country of what is now southern Botswana.

Lanyon and Warren, meanwhile, made no immediate attempt to capture the Jantjie family. Their more pressing concern was to scour the cattle-posts of Dithakong and Manyeding for loot with which to pay their volunteer troops. When the loot was finally gathered together and offered for auction in Kimberley there was so much of it that it took a week to sell. The auctioneer's advertisement (*opposite*) details all the property that was on sale. This huge auction gives some indication of the relative wealth accumulated by the Batlhaping over the previous decades. It was also clear that its seizure would seriously impoverish the survivors.

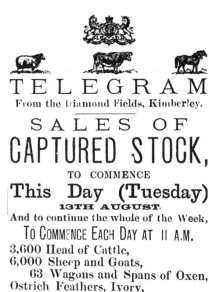

TELEGRAM

From the Diamond Fields, Kimberley.

SALES OF

CAPTURED STOCK,

TO COMMENCE

This Day (Tuesday)

13TH AUGUST.

And to continue the whole of the Week,

To Commence Each Day at 11 A.M.

3,600 Head of Cattle,
6,000 Sheep and Goats,
  63 Wagons and Spans of Oxen,
Ostrich Feathers, Ivory,
Karosses. Rifles.

Selling the looted Batlhaping property.

When Lanyon got back to Griqualand West, he learned that while he had been fighting in the north, certain members of Botlasitse's family had conducted a murderous raid into the colony. On 18 July, the day after Lanyon had attacked Gamopedi, a number of Botlasitse's brothers and sons led an attack on Thompson's farm at Cornforth Hill. According to Thompson's son, F R (later to be nicknamed 'Matabele') Thompson, (*right*) there were about two hundred raiders, thirty of them mounted. He claimed that he himself was shot and wounded by Galeshewe, Botlasitse's son and heir. He had managed to hide in a ditch and escape down the Harts valley to the safety of Spalding's store at Spitskop some twenty-five kilometres away. His father and cousin were not so fortunate. Francis Thompson senior was killed, according to his son, by a ramrod thrust down his throat. F R's cousin William, captured while trying to escape, was stripped and seriously assaulted. He never fully recovered from his injuries and died five years later.[8]

The raiding party, which included about twenty-five assorted disaffected Africans from Kimberley and the Cape Colony, made their way back past Taung to Modimong. This put Mankurwane in an awkward position, as he knew that he would be expected by the British to act against his cousins. He captured the man who was said to be the leader of the raid, Morebonoke, a brother of Botlasitse. He also took a wagon and a small amount of the looted cattle. Mankurwane then sent a message to Lanyon, 'the Governor of all the Regiments which are at Kuruman', stating that he had Botlasitse and the other raiders holed up in a cave at Modimong and he requested assistance in the form of two cannon. The letter was written in Setswana, and was translated in Kuruman by Mackenzie, for, as Mankurwane explained, he no longer trusted his 'secretary', the irrepressible A W Greef: 'I wrote letters by Greef; but I do not get any answer.'[9]

Mankurwane's efforts, however, were not enough for Lanyon. Fresh back in Kimberley with his loot from Dithakong, Lanyon marched on Taung in the first week of August. As Lanyon approached, Mankurwane (*left*) made a desperate demonstration of 'loyalty' to the British. In an attempt to forestall any military action by Lanyon, Mankurwane launched an attack on Modimong in which thirteen of the twenty-five colonial Africans were killed. Only two Batlhaping were killed, a brother of Botlasitse and a headman. No other Batlhaping was hurt and Botlasitse and all the rest of his family escaped.[10]

William Ashton believed, probably rightly, that Mankurwane's attack on Modimong was part of an elaborate 'made up plan', the aim of which was:

[8] N Rouillard (ed), *The Autobiography of Matabele Thompson* (1936), pp40–53.
[9] TVL, 596/7, Mankurwane to Lanyon, Taung, 1 August 1878, translated by J Mackenzie.
[10] TVL, 596/2, Agnor Dumas to Lanyon, Taung, 6 August 1878.

to get these men [the colonial Africans] separated from the Batlhaping in the fight in order to make them a sacrifice to satisfy the English and thus to cover Botlasitse's escape.[11]

Lanyon too was unimpressed. He imposed a fine on Mankurwane of 1,000 cattle. Mankurwane protested at the unfairness and arbitrary nature of the fine, imposed as it was upon such a loyal ally of the English. It remained unpaid and Botlasitse and his family remained at large.

By the end of August Warren had defeated the remaining Griqua rebels in the Langeberg. On Lanyon's instruction, he then spent the next three months on a military tour of the region between the Griqualand West border and the Molopo River (the southern boundary of modern Botswana), arresting any remaining 'Burness murderers' and others known to have offered resistance at Gamopedi or Dithakong. Under threat of military reprisals he got most of the *dikgosi* to submit and ask for 'British protection'.

Some of the *dikgosi* submitted willingly, such as *Kgosi* Montshiwa of the Tshidi branch of the Barolong who lived around the headwaters of the Molopo River. Montshiwa sought specific British protection from encroachment by the Boers of the Transvaal, who were, from 1877 to 1881, under British rule. *Kgosi* Morwe of Batlaros, by contrast, failed to impress Warren of his loyalty to the British so Warren deposed him, installing his brother Bareki in his place. *Kgosi* Merwe of Dithakong was held responsible for the looting of the trading store at Bothithong in June. He was fined 150 cattle and held prisoner until the fine was paid. This would have been a difficult task as most of the Dithakong cattle had been looted by Lanyon in July. It is not recorded how long Merwe was imprisoned.

Warren spent a fair amount of time at Kuruman where he enjoyed some hunting by day and spent long evenings with John Mackenzie discussing the future of 'Bechuanaland'.[12] Warren approved Mackenzie's proposals for a gradual process of colonisation. This would be underpinned by guaranteeing Batswana farmers secure title to their land. Gradual political change could then be brought about by the use of Mackenzie's metaphoric 'thin end of a crowbar', rather than the more typical South African 'rude blow of a big, flat-headed hammer', the approach favoured by Lanyon.[13] In line

---

[11] *LMS*, Ashton, 3 September 1878.

[12] The earliest Setswana orthography was devised by Robert Moffat in the 1820s. Based upon his understanding of the dialect of the Batlhaping, he spelt the general word for the Setswana-speaking people as the Bechuana, which in modern orthography is Batswana. I have used the modern orthography except when referring to Bechuanaland.

[13] Dachs, *Mackenzie*, p105.

Kgosi Montshiwa of the Barolong in Mafikeng; a striking photograph by Revd Willoughby in 1895.

with Mackenzie's reasoning, Warren appointed appropriate 'crowbars' in the region, British agents to act as chiefly advisers: Captain Stanley Lowe at Batlaros, Cecil Coyte-King at Phokwani, Agnor Daumas at Taung and, a relative of Warren's by marriage, Lieutenant Christopher Bethell with the Barolong *Kgosi* Montshiwa at Sehuba and later Mafikeng.

Part of Warren's military tour of the region took him to the Barolong town of Morokweng where he fined *Kgosi* Bonokwani 220 oxen for allowing Luka and his family to escape. Thereafter, as Warren's net tightened around southern Bechuanaland, the more northern Batswana *dikgosi* sought to distance themselves from their 'troublesome' southern neighbours, and Luka and his family found they were no longer welcome in Bangwaketse territory. In April 1879 *Kgosi* Gaseitsiwe of the Bangwaketse had them escorted south where they were handed over to Montshiwa.

The Barolong *kgosi* had them escorted south to be handed over to the British authorities. He was rewarded with £5 for his 'expenses'. The prisoners were brought south via Kuruman where Mackenzie wrote to Warren, by then Acting Administrator of Griqualand West,[14] requesting that old *Kgosi* Jantjie be granted a free pass to return to retirement in Manyeding. Warren acquiesced.

Not knowing whether they would ever see their aged father again, Luka, Olebile and Kaelo left their wives and children in the care of the venerable old man while they themselves were taken by cart to Kimberley where, on 29 May 1879, they were incarcerated in the town gaol. There they joined Botlasitse, Galeshewe and various others implicated in the Thompson raid. These men had been handed over to the Griqualand West authorities by Mankurwane in November 1878 following a military threat from Colonel Warren.

---

[14] Warren's acting appointment at the end of 1878 followed Lanyon's transfer to the Transvaal – which the British had annexed as a colony in April 1877.

CHAPTER NINE

Prison, release and
the new *morafe*
1879–1881

Colonel Warren's military tour of southern Bechuanaland in late 1878 had been intended as a preliminary to a formal British takeover of the region.[1] This was part of the British Conservative government's larger plan to amalgamate the whole of the British colonies, Boer republics and independent African states of South Africa into a single British colonial federation. The British annexation of the Transvaal in 1877 had been a first step in that direction. The British, however, found that there was widespread opposition to their plans. The Boers of the Transvaal resented the takeover; the Orange Free State refused to comply; and even the Cape Colony was reluctant to co-operate. The Natal Colony's co-operation was dependent upon the removal of the perceived threat from their powerful independent African neighbour, the Zulu kingdom. In the end it was the Zulu destruction of an invading British regiment at Isandlhwana in January 1879 that finally shelved British federation plans, at least for the time being.

The Zulu victory at Isandlhwana created widespread panic in colonial Natal. Further afield it provoked a general unease among colonial settlers about having armed Africans within their midst. In Griqualand West, Warren ordered a general disarmament of all 'natives' within the colony. This was on the cards anyway after the rebellion the previous year, but it was implemented now with unusual haste. In the first two weeks of February 1879, F R Thompson (son of the murdered Francis Thompson) and local landowner Henry Green, acting for the Government, disarmed the Africans of Barkly West District, the former Dikgatlhong *morafe*. Altogether the Batlhaping of the district were forced to surrender 407 muskets, mostly flintlock, some

---

[1] 'Southern Bechuanaland' here refers to the Batswana territory that lay north of Griqualand West and south of the Molopo River (the southern border of the modern republic of Botswana). In due course this territory became the colony of British Bechuanaland, 1885–95, thereafter joined to the Cape Colony and thus part of modern South Africa.

percussion, five double-barrelled shotguns and 197 rifles, a number of which were modern breech-loaders. They were promised the return of the weapons in due course, or monetary compensation. In the event, neither was ever forthcoming, a fact that provoked considerable resentment. But that was in the future.[2]

Three months later, at the time that Luka and his brothers were brought into Kimberley, the political future of independent Bechuanaland remained uncertain. While it was still presumed that Griqualand West would be joined to the Cape Colony (a move completed in October 1880), it was unclear whether the British still intended to take over southern Bechuanaland. The colonial authorities in Kimberley were similarly undecided about what to do with the 750 prisoners of war that they had collected from within and beyond the colony during the course of 1878. They so crowded out the prison and the surrounding yard, that the majority of them were released in the early months of 1879. Most were indentured as labourers to white farmers in Griqualand West, the Cape Colony or the Orange Free State. Of these indentured prisoners, 253 were women, eight of them Batlhaping, the rest mainly Griqua and Korana. When Luka and his brothers arrived in May 1879, there were only about forty prisoners left. Twenty-five of these were waiting to be charged over the Thompson raid.

Acting Administrator Warren and Attorney-General Lord were agreed that those responsible for the raid on Cornforth Hill that had resulted in Francis Thompson's death should be tried for murder. The youngest brother and two of the sons of Botlasitse had been identified by the survivors, William and F R Thompson, as leading figures in the attack. Botlasitse himself was among the prisoners in Kimberley gaol, but it was known that he had not been directly involved in the Thompson attack.

In June 1879, twenty-five men were taken before the High Court of Kimberley and charged on three counts relating to the Thompson attack: murder; 'public violence or riot and assault'; and theft. They all pleaded not guilty to these charges but were retained in prison pending trial. At the first sitting of the trial court on Monday 4 August it was realised that there was no direct evidence to prove exactly who had killed Thompson senior as the two younger Thompsons, the only prosecution witnesses, had fled the scene before the killing. All twenty-five defendants were thus declared not guilty of the most serious charge, that of murder. They were then held over until the trial on the second charge, that of 'public violence or riot and assault'.

---

[2] CA, NA 184, 'Arms received from natives', Barkly West District, 17 February 1879.

Meanwhile, Warren and his Attorney-General fell out over what to do with Luka and his associates who were clearly not involved in the Thompson attack. As the victor of Kho, Luka had earned a certain notoriety in colonial Kimberley, no doubt some people remembering his attempts to control the early prospectors on the river diggings. Following Luka's interview by the authorities on 12 and 14 June 1879,[3] it was realised that he could not be implicated in the Burness murders. Indeed it seems to have been decided that the Burness murderers had probably all or nearly all been killed in the actions at Gamopedi and Dithakong, and that it was not worth trying to prove anybody else's involvement in that particular attack.

Attorney-General Lord, however, appears to have wanted Luka charged with the deaths of those who had died at or after the battle of Kho, which had included, among others, the son of Commandant Ford. Lord had been involved, along with Judge Barry, in the decision to send John Ford in command of an inexperienced volunteer force across the border to the 'relief of Kuruman'. This was an action that both Lanyon and Warren had at the time considered to be foolhardy and uncalled for. Warren appears to have taken the view that no good would be served by trying to bring a case against Luka, who could reasonably claim that he was acting in self-defence against an unprovoked attack. The dispute between Warren and Lord became quite bitter and ended in the dismissal of the Attorney-General.[4]

With no decision to go to trial, Luka and his brothers remained in Kimberley gaol as political prisoners, along with Botlasitse, the Batlharo *Kgosi* Morwe and a number of other prominent men. As Warren's successor as Acting-Administrator, James Rose-Innes, explained the following year,

> ... these men are all men of influence among the Natives and ... were implicated in the recent disturbances in and around this Province. In the interest of peace, therefore, and in order that they should not be in a position to use their influence in a manner prejudicial to the public interest, it was deemed most essential that they should be detained in Kimberley and in consequence of there being no other place available they were detained in the precincts of the Gaol.[5]

Kimberley gaol, attached to the court house, was designed as a holding prison for people awaiting trial and for local criminals serving short-term sentences, mostly for crimes associated with drunkenness, violence or the

---

[3] CA, GLW 130/6,7, Luka's account of 1878 war, Kimberley gaol, 12 and 14 June 1879.
[4] *UKNA*, CO 107/8, Governor Frere, despatch No.45, 27 May 1880.
[5] CO107/8, No 45, enclosure, Rose-Innes to High Commissioner Frere, Kimberley, 13 May 1880.

theft of diamonds. Long-term prisoners were usually sent to Cape Town to serve out their sentences. Conditions were therefore very basic, with multiple-occupancy cells, no beds, no exercise facilities and slop buckets for ablution. The food was the standard 'ration' supplied to most of the labourers who worked the diamond mines. It consisted of stiff maize-meal porridge, cooked with salt and water. To this might be added a little 'stew', mostly little more than the water from boiled bones.

The only concessions allowed the prisoners-of-war was that they were kept separate from the common criminals, they were not subjected to hard labour and they were allowed some 'extra rations', in other words, there might have been a little meat on the boiled bones. To a man like Luka, used to a diet of soured milk or yoghurt, fresh or dried meat – mostly goat or wild game – and *mabele* (sorghum porridge) with beans, pumpkin or various wild foodstuffs, this was very poor fare. Indeed, he later referred to the diet of maize-meal as food fit for feeding to one's horse.[6]

Meanwhile, on 3 and 4 October 1879 the trial took place in Kimberley of those still charged with the Thompson attack. The five men identified by the younger Thompsons as leading the attack were each found guilty of 'riot and assault' and were held over for sentencing. The remaining twenty men were found not guilty and were immediately discharged. Satisfied with these convictions, the authorities decided to drop the charge of theft, difficult to prove in any case.

The guilty men were sentenced on 6 October. Galeshewe, eldest son and heir of Botlasitse, was sentenced to twelve years. His brother, Gasebaatje, got ten years, as did Morebonoke (also known as Andries Gasebonwe) who was the youngest brother of Botlasitse, and, being only in his early twenties, was ten years younger than his nephew Galeshewe. The other two convicted men were Gert Jagers and Andries Wagenpad who also got ten years each.[7] All five convicted men were despatched to Cape Town to serve out their sentences.

By the end of the year 1879 there was still no decision with regard to the continued imprisonment of Luka and his brothers. Warren had been taken ill, which may have delayed decision-making, and he then left Griqualand West to rejoin his regiment in England. A young, newly-qualified lawyer, James

---

[6] *CA*, BCC/82, Luka to High Commissioner, 23 September 1890, with a translation by Revd J Tom Brown of Kuruman. I am grateful to Nancy Jacobs for reminding me of this observation. See her *Environment, Power, and Justice. A South African History* (2003) p100.

[7] *CA*, Records of the Griqualand West High Court.

Rose-Innes, who was later to become a prominent Cape parliamentarian, was appointed Acting Administrator for 1880, to oversee the final merging of Griqualand West with the Cape Colony. One of his tasks was to resolve the problem of the eight remaining 'state prisoners' still held in Kimberley gaol. In May 1880, Rose-Innes wrote to High Commissioner Bartle Frere in Cape Town:

> As peace has been restored and the country and the Native tribes now settled down, the members of the Executive Council [of Griqualand West] are of opinion that the necessity for detaining these men no longer exists and that the time has now arrived where they might be allowed to return to their Locations [*sic*] where their presence will not exercise any disturbing influence upon the Natives living there.[8]

Bartle Frere (*right*) approved their release and on 31 May 1880, a year and two days from the date of their incarceration, Luka and his two brothers, Kaelo and Olebile, walked free. The remaining political prisoners released that day were Botlasitse (referred to simply by his father's name Gasibone [*sic*]), Morwe (the deposed *kgosi* of Batlaros), Seimpe (a Motlharo cousin of Morwe), Solomon (the Morolong from Kimberley who had thrown in his lot with Luka at Manyeding), and a man named David Lynx (probably Korana).

Luka, Olebile and Kaelo were expected to go back to Manyeding and they were provided with a wagon and provisions for the journey. After the three brothers had left Kimberley, the Acting Colonial Secretary wrote hurriedly to Sam Edwards, still the Inspector of Native Locations for the Barkly West district, urging him to persuade one of the Jantjie brothers to reside at Dikgatlhong, the 'farm' that was still registered in their father's name.[9] Edwards spoke to them as they passed through Barkly West and Kaelo agreed to take on the role of maintaining a family presence at the old home town of Dikgatlhong. His two brothers, Luka and Olebile, may have spent a day or

---

8 *UKNA*, CO 107/8, enclosed in despatch No 45, Rose-Innes to Frere, Kimberley, 13 May 1880.
9 CO 107/8, in despatch No 54, Acting Colonial Secretary, Kimberley, to S Edwards, 1 June 1880

Threshing sorghum in a Batswana village in the 1890s; photo by LMS missionary, Willoughby.

two there with him before making a slow progression up the Harts valley to Boetsap and across the border, past the site of their brief triumph at Kho and on to Manyeding which they reached on 12 June. One can only assume that they received a hero's welcome all the way.

That November, Revd John Mackenzie reported from Kuruman to Rose-Innes that Luka and his brothers were busy sowing sorghum at Manyeding. This was presumably as a relief from the diet in Kimberley gaol, but they were also growing maize, possibly to sell in Kimberley, or as animal feed. According to Mackenzie, Luka was planning a trip to the north 'to borrow cattle'.[10] On the surface it appeared that life was fairly settled at Manyeding, while old *Kgosi* Jantjie was living at Tlharing, thirty kilometres further east.

Of the other state prisoners released on 31 May 1880, it was not recorded what became of Solomon and David Lynx. Morwe was to join his brother Bareki at Batlaros, though not as *kgosi*, while Seimpe, who had previously been living with his cousin Morwe at Batlaros, now went to join his elder brother Toto[11] at Puduhush in the Langeberg.[12] Toto became Batlharo *kgosi* in the Langeberg following the death of his father, Makgolokwe, in 1879.

So far as Botlasitse was concerned, the intention was that he should be given a suitable residence in the district 'around Taungs [*sic*] under Mankoroane [*sic*], but not recognised as Chief by Government.' Once out of prison, however, Botlasitse insisted on returning to Phokwani. Not surprisingly, he refused to recognise Mankurwane as his paramount; and as for the British not recognising him as chief, Botlasitse refused to recognise the British government and he treated British agent Coyte-King with disdain. On both counts, of course, Botlasitse was absolutely right. Mankurwane's paramountcy was a purely British invention, quite illegitimate in Batlhaping tradition; and the British government had never formally proclaimed its authority north of the Griqualand West border.

[10] Mackenzie to Rose-Innes, Kuruman, 10 November 1880, in Dachs, *Mackenzie* (1975) p15.
[11] Sometimes spelt Totwe. P T Mgadla and S Volz (eds) *Words of Batswana* (2006).
[12] CO 107/8, enclosures in Nos 45, 54 & 62.

To Coyte-King's dismay, Botlasitse turned much more favourably towards a Scottish trader named Smith, who had set up a brandy store in Phokwani: Botlasitse became a good customer there. Coyte-King was also concerned that Botlasitse was getting rather too friendly with a Transvaal trader named James Blignaut, who had set up a trading store between Phokwani and the Vaal. Besides supplying Botlasitse with brandy, Blignaut also reputedly traded in arms and ammunition.[13]

This was a region that Transvaal Boers had been moving into over the previous few years, in an attempt to stake a claim to the whole region up to the Griqualand West border, particularly now that the British government appeared unwilling to take it over. As Revd W Henry R Bevan, Anglican missionary to Phokwani, reported in March 1880: 'The Boers go on continually encroaching more and more and driving the Natives from one fountain after another.'[14]

In December 1880, an event occurred that had an important impact upon the region. Taking advantage of Gladstone's new British Liberal government's lack of enthusiasm for imperialism, the Boers of the Transvaal rose in rebellion against British rule. Objecting in particular to British taxes, collected so assiduously by their Administrator, Sir Owen Lanyon,[15] they raised the flag of the 'South African Republic' and laid siege to the administrative capital, Pretoria. The British badly underestimated the military ability of these rural Boers and quickly suffered a series of defeats, culminating in the battle of Majuba Hill on 27 February 1881. In this brief battle, the British lost two hundred men either killed or seriously wounded. Among the dead was General Sir George Colley, the High Commissioner for South-East Africa.

A chastened British government agreed to negotiate its withdrawal from the Transvaal, and in accordance with the Pretoria Convention of August 1881, the British restored the Boers to full internal self-government. This was not full republican status, as the British still retained control over external affairs. But the most important thing so far as the Batlhaping were concerned was that the western boundary of the Transvaal was redrawn to extend well into Batlhaping and Barolong territory. The Keate Award boundary of 1871, set by the British, had never been enforced by them and for years the Boers

13 CO107/8, reports from Coyte-King enclosed in despatch No 62 of 19 July 1880.
14 *SPGA*, Annual Report 1880 A, Revd.W H R Bevan, St Michael's, Phokwani, 31 March 1880.
15 Former Administrator of Griqualand West; knighted upon his promotion to the Transvaal.

Kgosi Botlasitse of Phokwani in c.1874, with satin waistcoat and staff of office.

had been extending their settlements ever further west, persuading or forcing local African residents to accept their presence.

The new boundary now recognised by the British extended the Transvaal's territory down the Vaal River, past Bloemhof and Christiana to the Griqualand West border at Fourteen Streams. It then extended north, halfway to the Harts valley, before curving around Phokwani and Manthe to meet the Harts just to the east of the Korana town of Mamusa *(see map 13, p113)*. This, however, was not the limit of Transvaal territorial ambitions.

The British withdrew all official presence from southern Bechuanaland in April 1881.[16] With the British gone, the newly resurgent Boers of the Transvaal eyed the valuable Batlhaping and Barolong arable and grazing grounds around the Harts and Dry Harts valleys and the Molopo basin. And they soon saw their opportunity in the exploitation of local conflicts in the region.

In June 1881, Luka's father *Kgosi* Jantjie Mothibi died at Tlharing. He was in his mid-eighties and his death was not unexpected.

---

[16] Major Lowe, who had been stationed at Batlaros, went back to policing duties at Boetsap; Coyte-King moved to Taung in a private capacity; while Daumas and Bethell remained as private advisors to Mankurwane and Montshiwa respectively.

Jantjie Mothibi had done his best to follow the Christian way, advocated by the missionaries. In the end he learned to his cost the contradictions between the Christian ideal of peace at all costs in which he wished so much to believe and the harsh reality of colonialism. The missionaries urged him to trust in 'British justice', a justice in which they themselves naively placed total trust, and that justice betrayed him. It was a contradiction that the missionaries of Kuruman never satisfactorily resolved. Over many decades they had deliberately weakened the structures of the old pre-colonial *morafe* and then they blamed *Kgosi* Jantjie for being weak – too weak to rule his people in a way that suited the colonial ambitions of the intruding *makgowa*.

Nevertheless, so far as the majority of the Phuduhutŝwana branch of the Batlhaping was concerned, Jantjie was respected as the eldest son of *Kgosi* Mothibi, who was himself the undisputed heir of the great *Kgosi* Molehabangwe. In fact, for more than a decade Jantjie had been the only surviving son of Mothibi. This alone had given him additional authority in the counsels of the Batlhaping. And now his eldest son and undisputed heir, Łuka, was the recipient of that authority.

There is no record of any great *kgotla* meeting at which Luka was formally acknowledged as the new *kgosi* of the Jantjie line. There was probably no need. In most important affairs he had in effect been acting for his father for more than a decade. His leadership abilities had already been proved, both in his efforts to protect Batlhaping property rights in the early days of the colonial intrusion as well as in the more recent war of 1878. The question that remained was just how wide within Batlhaping society his leadership would be acknowledged.

Mothibi's official senior blood line, that had passed from Petlhu to Gasebonwe and thence to his son Botlasitse, was in disarray. Botlasitse had been weakened by the absence of his sons in long-term imprisonment in Cape Town. Although he had defiantly resettled at Phokwani, Botlasitse's close relationship with the brandy traders did not enhance his reputation. The extent of his support was revealed by the fact that he did not manage to attract more than fifteen hundred people around him at Phokwani.[17]

Mankurwane had a following of more than five thousand at Taung; but he had lost credibility among many Batlhaping by allying with the colonial British and accepting from them a 'paramountcy' to which he was not entitled. Nevertheless Mankurwane had inherited a core of reliable followers from his uncle Mahura who had acted as his regent. Mahura's sons Bogosin

---

17 *SPGA*, Annual Reports, Africa, from Revd W H R Bevan, 1879–83.

Kgosi Mankurwane's capital, Taung, with stonewalled cattle kraal in foreground; note the wagons parked (right) and horses (left); photo taken in 1889, but probably little changed since 1880.

and Maŝwe had established a number of outlying villages in the Dry Harts valley north of Taung and they guaranteed up to a further ten thousand adherents who acknowledged Mankurwane's claims to political authority.[18] West of the Ghaap escarpment, however, Mankurwane's writ did not run true and it was here that the heir of Jantjie Mothibi could expect to receive support.

With limitations on the acknowledged power of Botlasitse and Mankurwane, Luka was left as the most widely respected leader of the Batlhaping west of the Ghaap escarpment. He appears to have willingly accepted this position and stressed the strength of his lineage by formally signing himself 'Luka Yañki Mothibi Molehabañwe'.

Kgosi Luka, now at the height of his powers, was in his mid-forties at the time. It is clear from the actions he took in the years following the death of his father, that the new *kgosi* was determined not to sit back and wait for whatever the future might throw at his people. He would strengthen what remained of the *morafe* and do his best to ensure that it survived in the rapidly changing world ahead.

The people that Luka considered to be under his protection included all those who had acknowledged the authority of his father and who now lived due north of the Griqualand West boundary, encompassing an area to the west of that occupied by Mankurwane's and Botlasitse's people (*see map 12 overleaf*). Taking a line in the east from the northernmost tip of the colony's border, this extended northwest across the Ghaap plateau to a point south of Dithakong, then west to Kuruman and back south along the Kuruman Hills to the Griqualand West border. Thus, enclosed within Luka's perception of the *morafe* lay Tlharing, Manyeding, Koning, the border village of Smouswani, and all the settlements in between. Significantly, it also enclosed Kuruman,

18 Shillington, *Colonisation*, pp129–30, 133–4 and 173.

which his grandfather Mothibi had never awarded outright to the missionaries. The total number of Batlhaping who acknowledged Luka's authority within this territory probably numbered less than ten thousand, but he had hopes of acquiring more adherents from within Griqualand West.

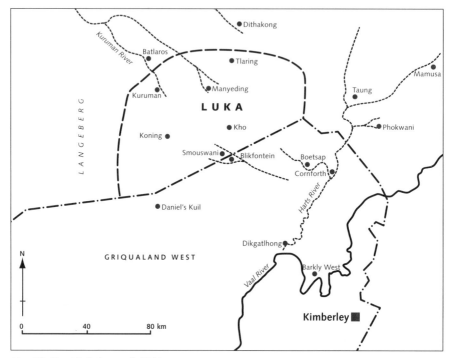

MAP 12: Kgosi Luka's morafe 1881.

The new *kgosi* appears to have given up on claiming any of the traditional territory that now lay within Griqualand West. He still considered, however, that the people within the colony, who had formerly acknowledged his father, still remained part of the *morafe*. And as the old *morafe* was now being re-established north of the border, he felt they should move north to join him. He also intended to claim by inheritance the 'farm' Dikgatlhong, which had been acknowledged by the colonial government as the private property of his father.

With these two aims in mind, *Kgosi* Luka travelled south to Barkly West in the first week of August 1881 to interview the resident magistrate.[19] It must have been a fairly tense meeting. Although Luka is believed to have spoken some Dutch/Afrikaans, he appears not to have spoken any English

[19] *CA*, NA 184, RM Barkly, 9 August 1881.

and always required an interpreter when conversing with British colonial officials. It is not clear who acted as interpreter on this occasion. It may have been Ashton or Sam Edwards, though by this stage the magistrate may well have employed his own local Setswana-speaking interpreter. Luka proposed to the magistrate that he be allowed to remove all the Batlhaping of Barkly West district from the colony to join him at his late father's town of Tlharing. The magistrate was horrified at the idea, presumably on two points: a mass migration would remove African labour from the colony, and it would strengthen a potentially hostile power just beyond the border. The magistrate vetoed the idea and informed Luka that he no longer had any authority in the district. This was probably pretty much as Luka had anticipated, but it was worth a try.

Luka then turned to the inheritance of his father's 'farm' of Dikgatlhong. Here he must have felt on firmer ground for it was registered as private property, something that the *makgowa* appeared to value more than human life! He was, however, quickly disillusioned. He was informed that although Dikgatlhong had been granted to his father as his personal property, that only applied to Jantjie in his own lifetime. Since he had now died, the property reverted to the state and it was being added to the general 'locations' that had been set aside for the local Batlhaping of Griqualand West.

Clearly, in what passed for British law in colonial South Africa, there were two different versions of private property: one for the *makgowa*, who possessed superior rights by virtue of their skin colour, and one for the indigenous Africans who had owned and worked the land for generations. The rights of the latter could be overruled at the whim of a colonial official.

Luka must have been furious. Nevertheless, he maintained the dignity appropriate to his new rank and he remained calm. There is no record of any outburst or threat and one can be sure that if there had been, it would have been reported. Thus Luka returned to the *morafe* north of the border with no new adherents at that time, although numerous individuals were to make the journey north in the years to come as they felt the increasingly harsh realities of Cape rule. What became of Kaelo, the younger brother left at Dikgatlhong the previous year, is not known, though it is thought that he may have died at Dikgatlhong in 1882.[20]

On his return to Tlharing and Manyeding after his unproductive visit to the colony, Luka made a point of strengthening his position north of the border by placing his loyal supporters at the various villages and cattle-posts of the

---

[20] Breutz, *The Tribes of the Districts of Kuruman and Postmasburg*, 1963, p175.

morafe. During the year that Luka had been in Kimberley gaol, Mankurwane had been encouraged by the British to assume authority over Jantjie's region and some of his placemen now found themselves expelled by Luka's men.[21]

Mankurwane was initially unwilling to push this issue into formal dispute, but from early 1882 his attitude changed as he found himself driven by the imperatives of war.

---

[21] BBLC 9, 10 & 12, for evidence of Luka, Mankurwane, Piet John and John G Donovan, April 1886.

CHAPTER TEN

War, land and the British
1882–1885

Kimberley market had opened up great opportunities for those who controlled the arable, grazing and forest lands of southern Bechuanaland. By 1881 the cattle owned by the wealthy men of Mankurwane's *morafe* numbered well in excess of fifty thousand. All the best arable lands of the upper Harts and Dry Harts valleys were fully utilised growing grain for Kimberley market. And those who had access to wagons used them for transporting firewood to feed the steam machinery of the diamond mines and the stoves and fireplaces of the town. All this put enormous pressure on the resources of the region, and the cattle-posts of Taung stretched far to the northeast up the west bank of the Harts.

The growing market in Kimberley stimulated agricultural production throughout the region.

Following the Pretoria Convention, Mankurwane deliberately extended his territory right up to the new Transvaal boundary. There Mankurwane's herdsmen clashed with the Korana of Mamusa. The latter had been forced by relentless Boer pressure from the east to bring their cattle across the

131

valley to the west bank of the Harts.[1] *(see Map 13 opposite)* In November 1881 Mankurwane ordered an all-out attack on Mamusa. This was partly an attempt to avenge the loss of some cattle and herdsmen in an earlier skirmish, but it was also an assertion of Mankurwane's authority in the region. Initially it had seemed an easy, disciplinary raid; but as Mankurwane's men rounded up the Korana cattle, they came under sustained fire from Boers stationed on the east bank. They were forced to retire to Taung in disarray, abandoning the captured cattle.

In launching his ill-advised attack on Mamusa, Mankurwane had provided the Transvaal Boers with the opportunity they sought to defy the strictures of the new Convention boundary.

Within weeks Mankurwane found himself under counter-attack in Taung. The Boers who had driven the Batlhaping back from Mamusa had quickly offered themselves as mercenaries in the service of the Korana chief, David Mosweu Taaibosch. By February 1882, several hundred Transvaal Boers were waging their own private war in search of loot in the land of the Batlhaping. In the opinion of Major Stanley Lowe, former agent at Batlaros and now of the Cape Mounted Police at Boetsap:

> The fighting [between the Batlhaping and the Korana] would soon finish, if left to themselves, and not urged on by a lot of unscrupulous white men, who have nothing to lose, and hope to get farms and loot at the cost of the Natives who may be beaten, if not from the victims also.[2]

Lowe's opinion of the mercenaries' intentions was confirmed the following month when they drew up an agreement to share out the land and loot of the Batlhaping. The agreement was drafted by the unscrupulous Theodore Doms, acting as the Korana chief's 'private secretary', and the Christiana storekeeper G J van Niekerk, who styled himself the 'Administrator of the territory of David Massouw [sic]'.[3] Each 'volunteer' would receive a minimum of one farm, to be cut out of Mankurwane's territory to the west of the Transvaal boundary. And any 'volunteer' who employed a substitute to fight for him, would receive an additional farm for each man employed.

Clearly Mankurwane stood to lose most of his *morafe* to white settlement, and he called in the Batlhaping of the Dry Harts valley to come to the defence of Taung.

---

[1] For discussion of the background to the Bechuanaland wars, see *Colonisation*, pp123–43.

[2] CA, NA 188, Lowe to Revd Bevan (at Phokwani), Boetsap, 13 February 1882, enclosed in CC Barkly West of 20 February 1882.

[3] TVL, S/29, *Krijgsraad Notulen*, May 1882.

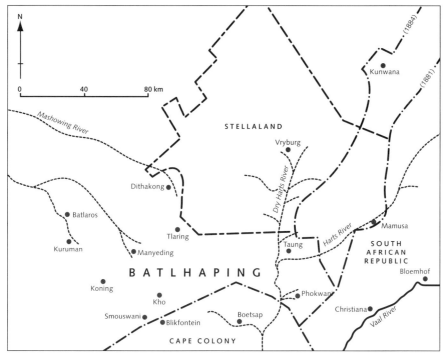

MAP 13: The Bechuanaland wars, 1882–84.

∼ ∼ ∼

Kgosi Luka Jantjie hoped to avoid involvement in a war that was nothing to do with him. Apart from his antipathy towards Mankurwane, he believed the war to be foolish and unnecessary. Why should Africans fight each other when it was well known that the real danger came from the white men?[4] Thus, when Mankurwane appealed to him for military support in the name of Batlhaping solidarity, Luka refused his appeal. He found, however, that it was impossible to remain aloof from the war for long.

The trouble started in the early weeks of 1882 when Mankurwane began recruiting his own white mercenaries from Kimberley, offering to pay them £4 or an ox a day, or a farm for three months service. Mankurwane had reasonably presumed upon the support of his ally and 'protector', the British government. The British, however, betrayed him. Anxious above all else to avoid any further open conflict with the Boers of the Transvaal, the new High Commissioner and Cape Governor, Sir Hercules Robinson, forbade any British citizen from engaging as a mercenary beyond the colonial border. Mankurwane, loyal ally of the British, was to be abandoned to his fate.

[4] BBLC 9, Evidence of Luka, April 1886.

So as not to upset the profits of the Cape merchants, however, no ban was put upon the supply of arms and ammunition to the war-torn region. And the gunrunners of Kimberley who supplied Mankurwane's forces tended to demand payment in the form of firewood licences. Firewood, in high demand by Kimberley's mining magnates, was the most profitable resource of the moment. The steam pumps and hoisting gear of the diamond mines were consuming five hundred wagonloads of firewood a week.[5] Most of the timber had already been stripped out of Griqualand West, and the wood-riding agents of the mining companies had their eyes on the woodlands of southern Bechuanaland. It was this which brought Luka's old adversary, John G Donovan, to Taung in mid-1882.

Donovan was a man who was always alert to a good speculation; but on this occasion, besides working for himself, he was also acting as firewood agent for his friend Cecil Rhodes, the Cape Member of Parliament for Barkly West district. As one of the most powerful mining magnates on the diamond fields, Rhodes had great need of a steady supply of fuel and the unscrupulous Donovan was happy to have a guaranteed market for the huge quantities of firewood that he expected to take from Mankurwane's country.

When Donovan arrived at Taung to offer his services as supplier of ammunition and general 'wood agent' for Mankurwane, the town was under siege by up to five hundred white mercenaries, mostly from the Transvaal. But it was not a tight siege. Donovan and any other white men who were acting as mercenaries or agents of Mankurwane, such as Coyte-King and G D Smith, had no difficulty passing through the cordon. The siege seemed to be aimed at looting the cattle of the Batlhaping and stealing the firewood of the region. The Korana chief David Mosweu had long since lost control of his mercenaries. As British agent Stanley Lowe remarked in August 1882:

> I cannot help believing there is a combination of a lot of white men to get
> possession of [Mankurwane's] country; not only those who are openly against
> him, but those who are supposed to be his friends. It is strange that in the
> fighting against the Boers, who are reputed such good shots, no white man on
> Mankoroane's [sic] side has been hit, and those of the Boers who have been hit
> have been shot by natives.[6]

Donovan supplied Mankurwane with an unspecified amount of ammunition and in return was made his chief wood agent, with authority to issue

---

[5] For the role of firewood in the conflict, Shillington, *Colonisation*, pp136–43.
[6] *GBPP*, C.3419, pp73–4, Lowe to CC Barkly West, 6 August 1882.

Mankurwane and his councillors posing assertively for this photograph by the Grays of Kimberley.

wood-riding licences in his name. And as Mankurwane's position grew more desperate, he promised farms as well as wood-cutting licences to anybody who would supply him with ammunition.

Through July the mercenaries tightened the noose around Taung and on 26 July 1882 they forced Mankurwane to sign a treaty of capitulation. According to the terms of the treaty, drawn up by Doms, the mercenaries were all to receive farms in Mankurwane's country. This applied even to Mankurwane's own agents and mercenaries, such as Coyte-King, G D Smith and J G Donovan. Before the treaty could be enforced, however, High Commissioner Robinson protested to the Transvaal government about this clear breach of the Pretoria Convention.

Believing that the British were finally coming to his aid, Mankurwane withdrew from discussions with his enemies and restarted the war. It was a forlorn hope. The British did nothing to help him, and Mankurwane, anxious that his people should disperse to their ploughing lands before the rainy season, signed a second treaty of submission on 29 September 1882.[7]

Peace, however, did not return to the region. Throughout the following year, as the mercenaries laid claim to a vast tract of territory to the north and northwest of Taung, the Batlhaping did their utmost to prevent them from taking possession of the land, and isolated acts of violence continued. In March 1883 the mercenaries proclaimed the region to be the 'independent republic of Stellaland'.

[7] Shillington, *Colonisation*, pp134–6.

135

They established a small township that they named Vryburg (Freetown) at the northern end of the Dry Harts valley to act as their centre of government. But Stellaland at this stage was only a republic on paper. Batlhaping resistance ensured that the mercenaries and land speculators who had bought many of the original land claims were unable to take possession of them. Thus, although the siege of Taung had been lifted, fighting continued across the region, with most of the mercenary attacks taking the form of cattle raids and the looting of firewood.

Further north, Montshiwa's Barolong found themselves in a similar predicament. Rival branches of the Barolong had rashly sought Boer help to secure the arable lands of the Molopo basin. As with the Batlhaping–Korana conflict, the Barolong became enmeshed with white mercenaries from the Transvaal. And those mercenaries were soon fighting their own war against Montshiwa, in an attempt to establish an independent 'republic' to the west of the Transvaal boundary. Montshiwa was forced to sign a treaty in October 1882. The mercenaries designated a large area south of the Molopo as the 'republic of Goshen'. But the Barolong succeeded in preventing the mercenaries from taking possession of their land, and fighting continued throughout 1883.

The western boundary claimed for Stellaland had stopped just short of Luka's country, but this did not free *Kgosi* Luka from the ambitions of Mankurwane's principal arms supplier, J G Donovan.

～ ～ ～

When Luka had first got out of gaol in 1880 and was passing through Barkly West on his way home to Manyeding, Donovan had accosted him and proposed that he become Luka's legal agent. Luka had brushed with Donovan before, and he refused him outright, pointing out that those who employed agents tended to lose their land.[8]

Then a few days before Luka's visit to Barkly West in August 1881, Donovan had been in the Barkly magistrate's office where he had managed to arrange to have the border farm Blikfontein registered in his name. Blikfontein was an old Batlhaping cattle-post to the north of Dikgatlhong. It fell just within Griqualand West, across the border from Smouswani. Between them, Blikfontein and Smouswani were reckoned to hold some of the best acacia woodland in the whole of the border region.

One of Luka's men, Mokoning, had been living at Blikfontein for some

[8] BBLC 9, evidence of Luka.

Wood-riders' wagons throng Kimberley with firewood to drive the water pumps vital to the mines.

years. He had been cutting wood from there and transporting it to Kimberley market. Now that Donovan had title to the farm, he issued Mokoning with an order to quit and move into one of the 'locations' of the Barkly West district. With Luka's approval, however, Mokoning moved across the border and settled at Smouswani where he continued riding firewood to Kimberley.[9] But Donovan's ambitions were not limited to Blikfontein. He had his eye on Smouswani itself and many other properties beyond the border and it was this that had brought him to Mankurwane in 1882.

Thus, when Donovan demanded payment from Mankurwane for ammunition and legal services, he insisted that he be paid in land and wood licences beyond the boundaries of the illusory 'republic of Stellaland'. He reminded Mankurwane that he was 'Paramount of the Batlhaping'. He should therefore ignore Luka, son of Jantjie, and grant Donovan farms and exclusive wood-cutting rights in the western region where Luka had re-established his *morafe*. Mankurwane complied and granted Donovan rights to a huge tract of land at Smouswani as well as the wood-cutting rights for Koning. He told him, however, that he would have to deal with Luka himself.[10]

The following month, October 1882, Luka crossed the colonial border to Blikfontein where he reported to Corporal Rawstone of the Cape Border Police. According to Rawstone, Luka had heard that Donovan intended sending men and wagons to Smouswani to cut firewood for the Kimberley market. If that should be the case, Luka warned 'it would be the cause of creating disturbances between the whites and his people.'[11]

The Griqualand authorities, however, declined to intervene and Mankurwane continued to give out farms and wood-cutting permits for land and forests in Luka Jantjie's territory.

Luka then took the extraordinarily bold step of recruiting a party of Boers

[9] BBLC 12, Evidence of Donovan.

[10] See BBLC 9, 10 & 12 for evidence of Luka, Mankurwane, A W Greef and Donovan.

[11] *CA*, NA 188, Enclosed in CC Barkly: Rawstone to Lowe, Blikfontein, 8 October 1882,.

from Griqualand West to help keep Donovan's men at bay. It was a clever move, but one fraught with danger. Luka was well aware that Mankurwane's white allies would have little compunction about shooting Luka's people if they tried to challenge them. On the other hand, Luka appears to have calculated, Mankurwane was much less likely to allow his British allies to shoot fellow white men – especially Boers, following the recent Anglo-Boer debacle in the Transvaal in 1881.[12] The danger for Luka in employing Boers, however, lay in the potential future problem of preventing them from staking a permanent claim to any land on which he allowed them to settle. Luka was thus careful not to promise them any land as Mankurwane had rashly done. All he did was allow them to settle at Smouswani and Koning on a temporary basis, to graze their cattle and cut a limited amount of firewood on the understanding that they would protect the region from Mankurwane's and Donovan's woodcutters.[13]

The ferry at Schmidtsdrift near Barkly West bringing livestock and wood across the Vaal river to feed the insatiable Kimberley market.

The move certainly strengthened Luka's position. In December 1882 his men seized some wagons brought into the country on wood permits from Mankurwane. Luka announced that he was holding the wagons until the wood was paid for. The following month some of Mankurwane's men were expelled from Koning by 'Luka's Boers', and by January 1883 there were up to a dozen Boers camped in tents at Smouswani on permission from *Kgosi* Luka.

---

[12] Despite the amicable peace agreement (Pretoria Convention), distrust and tension between Boer and Briton remained high through the early 1880s.

[13] *LMS*, Wookey, Kuruman, 12 January 1883; *GBPP*, C.3686, Enclosed in No.16, Rawstone to Lowe, Blikfontein, 13 January 1883.

Donovan was furious that he had been thwarted and he drafted a letter for Mankurwane to send to Governor Robinson in Cape Town. The letter complained that 'Luka's Boers' were squatting on 'Mankurwane's land' (Smouswani) and conveying wood to Kimberley that should have belonged to Donovan and to Mankurwane on a half-share basis.[14] Robinson at this stage did nothing about it; but it is probable that Donovan's motivation in prompting and drafting Mankurwane's letter was to stake a prior claim to this land in the event of a future British takeover of the region.

Luka, too, seems to have been looking to the future. In 1883 he sent his own men to plough land on his personal behalf at Smouswani, Koning, Klein Koning and numerous other arable sites around the region. In staking a personal claim to the ploughing lands of the *morafe*, Luka, like Donovan, may have had in mind the possibility of a future British takeover of the region. If that happened and judging by the experience of Griqualand West, a personal land claim would have a much better chance of being recognised by the British than any general claim based on communal Batlhaping occupation.

In understanding Luka's action here one should also bear in mind that in Setswana culture there was no clear distinction between the personal and the communal in the property of the *kgosi*. A wealthy *kgosi* attracted adherents to whom he could offer material security in the form of arable land and *mafisa* (loan) cattle. And a *kgosi*'s political authority and ability to protect his people was judged by his personal wealth and the size of his following. It appears that Luka was trying to marry the duties of a traditional *kgosi* with the 'modern' reality of capitalist private property.

The missionaries Wookey and Ashton interpreted Luka's action as an attempt to abuse his position and accumulate personal property at the expense of his people. The missionaries, however, had their own interests at stake. For some time there had been rumours in missionary circles that Luka was planning to use 'his Boers' to take over the arable land at Kuruman.[15] Hitherto the missionaries seem to have assumed that this was theirs to allocate to members of their congregation, much in the manner of a traditional Batlhaping *kgosi*. Their anxiety over Luka's intentions, therefore, probably stemmed from the fact that as the new senior *kgosi* in the western region, Luka was trying to reassert the level of chiefly control originally exercised by his grandfather, Mothibi, and which his father Jantjie had allowed to wane.

[14] A75/2, Mackenzie Papers, (Copy) Mankurwane to Robinson, 3 February 1883; BBLC 12, Evidence of Mankurwane, and BBLC 8, evidence of 'Massa' (Mašwe) Mahura.

[15] *LMS*, Wookey, Kuruman, 12 January 1883; A75/2, *Mackenzie Papers*, Ashton to Mackenzie, Barkly West, 7 June 1883.

~ ~ ~

If Luka really was anticipating a colonial annexation during 1883, his fears were well founded. Although Mankurwane's appeal for British help or protection from marauding Boers had been turned down in 1882, two influential men were working hard during the course of 1883 to persuade the British government to change its policy. They were the Kimberley mining magnate, Cecil Rhodes, and the Kuruman missionary, John Mackenzie. Both men urged their cases from very different viewpoints.[16]

Rhodes' main concern was the uninterrupted supply of cheap African labour for the diamond mines. Many of these workers came from Mozambique and the eastern Transvaal and the Transvaal Boers had a reputation for waylaying Kimberley-bound workers and forcing them into unpaid farm work. So the Mozambican workers travelled west across the northern Transvaal, avoiding the main areas of Boer settlement. They then went south through Bechuanaland, skirting the Transvaal's western boundary. Fighting in Bechuanaland had already interrupted Rhodes' flow of labour, and now van Niekerk proposed levying a tax on all labourers passing through 'Stellaland'.

From June 1883 Rhodes persistently urged Governor Robinson to annex Bechuanaland to the Cape Colony, having already persuaded van Niekerk to agree to this in principle, provided all Stellaland land claims were recognised. By the end of 1883 Robinson was urging just such a policy on the British government in London.

Mackenzie approached the issue from a very different perspective. Mackenzie believed in the inevitable spread of European settlement into southern Bechuanaland; but what he had learned from the rebellion and war of 1878 was that the Africans of Bechuanaland must be guaranteed title to their land – for a minimum of at least ten years. Loss of land in his view created rebellious subjects. European settlement must therefore be restricted and carefully controlled. The kind of speculative land grab that had created Stellaland was anathema to Mackenzie. He favoured a British imperial 'protectorate' rather than annexation by the Cape. He had no interest in Rhodes' labour problems.

Mackenzie was on leave in England during 1883, and he used his time there to campaign on behalf of the Batlhaping and Barolong who were suffering the uncontrolled ravages of Boer mercenaries and white land speculators. He campaigned in the press and used the influential network

[16] For Rhodes and the annexation of Bechuanaland, Shillington, *Colonisation*, pp149–61.

of missionary supporters to whip up criticism of the British government's inaction.[17]

It happened that the Transvaal leaders, Paul Kruger (*right*) and Piet Joubert were also in London in late 1883 to seek greater independence through a revision of the Pretoria Convention of 1881. Pressed by Governor Hercules Robinson for the Cape Colony, Mackenzie for the Barolong and Batlhaping, and Kruger and Joubert for the Transvaal, the British government decided on a compromise that they hoped would satisfy all three interests. They agreed to revise the Pretoria Convention of 1881 and grant Kruger and Joubert most of what they wanted.

Thus the London Convention of January 1884 allowed the Transvaal Boers renewed republican status and an extension of their western boundary as far as, but not including, the territory of Mankurwane and Montshiwa. To the west of this new line, the Batlhaping and Barolong lands, including the illusory 'republics' of Stellaland and Goshen, were to come under some form of British protection. Mackenzie's proposed minimal 'territorial govern-ment' seemed appropriate and so Mackenzie himself was appointed Resident Commissioner for this new 'protectorate' of Bechuanaland. And to appease Cape interests, the British intended this as a temporary arrangement before annexing Bechuanaland south of the Molopo to the Cape as soon as possible.

Rhodes, however, was horrified at Mackenzie's appointment. The former missionary's pro-African stance was unlikely to appease the Stellalanders and was thus unlikely to ensure the territory's smooth assimilation into the Cape Colony. Hercules Robinson, 'a man of weak will-power',[18] had come under the influence of Rhodes, and by the time of Mackenzie's arrival in Cape Town in March 1884, Rhodes had managed to get Mackenzie's position changed to that of 'Deputy Commissioner'. This reduced Mackenzie's independence to determine policy and made him directly answerable to Robinson.

Mackenzie reached Taung in April 1884, and to Mankurwane's evident relief he proclaimed this region of southern Bechuanaland to be a British 'protectorate'.[19]

[17] *The Times* 28 November 1883, 15 January 1884.

[18] According to S M Molema, *Montshiwa, Barolong Chief and Patriot* (1966), p142.

[19] Mackenzie's protectorate of southern Bechuanaland was never officially confirmed by the

Luka arrived at Taung to find out what this new protectorate entailed. He was accompanied by a considerable party of councillors and elders. Mackenzie had distrusted Luka in the past as someone who was too inde-pendent-minded, unlike his more pliant father. But Mackenzie now took Luka's high-profile presence as a symbol of a widespread acceptance of the new protectorate: 'His presence showed confidence in the Protectorate – that under it justice would be done to all.' Revd A J Wookey (also LMS) wrote in April 1884 to Mackenzie that 'Luka would make a capital kind of chief... It would give him something to do and keep him out of mischief.'[20]

It is unlikely from his previous experience that Luka had that much trust in British precepts of justice, but he must have felt that he and his people had a better chance with a Setswana-speaking former missionary at the helm. Mackenzie promised that land claims would be looked into and the Batlhaping would have all the land that was rightly theirs restored to them.

Luka's reaction to this promise was not recorded, but he must have been heartened by Mackenzie's basic standpoint. Mankurwane was on less sure ground. He had been issuing title to western Batlhaping land that clearly was not his to give away. His agent Donovan was particularly concerned as he stood to lose most of his claims that fell within Luka's territory. Donovan kept Rhodes in Cape Town well informed of Mackenzie's proposals.

As Mackenzie proceeded up the Dry Harts valley, he saw with his own eyes the full extent of arable land that Mankurwane's Batlhaping stood to lose if the Stellalanders were guaranteed their land claims. His urgent telegram on this to Robinson directly contradicted Rhodes' bland assur-ances that Stellaland claims were all in vacant unused land. In Vryburg the Stellalanders received Mackenzie's proclamation of the British protectorate in stony silence. And as soon as he had moved on towards Mafikeng, the cattle rustling and wood stealing resumed.

In Mafikeng the British protectorate was welcomed by Montshiwa, but the Goshenite mercenaries showed their contempt for Mackenzie's authority by conducting a cattle raid from their base across the nearby Transvaal border, even while the Deputy Commissioner was still in Mafikeng. Mackenzie lacked the power or resources to recruit more than a handful of police, and with no force to back him up, his protectorate lacked all effective authority in the region.

British government and is not to be confused with the Bechuanaland Protectorate (north of the Molopo River, the future Botswana), declared in September 1885 at the same time that Mackenzie's southern 'protectorate' became the Crown Colony of British Bechuanaland.
[20] J Mackenzie, *Austral Africa*, Vol I, p270; Wookey 25 April 1884, Dachs *Mackenzie* p180.

Rhodes (left) in Bechuanaland; standing from left, Sir F Carrington, Rev J Mackenzie, General Sir Charles Warren; centre (hat in hand), Sir Gordon Sprigg, Cape Premier on four occasions.

Mackenzie's form of African-friendly 'territorial government' depended crucially upon the co-operation of the Batswana *dikgosi*. At this critical moment, therefore, when peace had not yet been firmly established in the eastern region, the Deputy Commissioner set off on a circuitous route through southern Bechuanaland, getting the specific agreement of the principal *dikgosi* to the establishment of the British protectorate. He visited Kuruman and Manyeding. Luka is not specifically mentioned in Mackenzie's correspondence on this visit, but one can assume what his attitude would have been. If he was to be forced to surrender complete political independence, then Mackenzie's proposals for security of land tenure would be an acceptable way forward.

Mackenzie did not get as far as the Langeberg, but even so his journey through the central part of southern Bechuanaland meant that he was out of touch with events in the eastern region for more than a month. This turned out to be a grave tactical error. In his absence, fighting in the eastern zone resumed with renewed fervour, as the Stellalanders sought to establish a firm presence before Mackenzie's return. As a result, by the time Mackenzie returned to Taung at the end of June, his protectorate was in disarray. His announcement that he was setting up an immediate enquiry into all land claims in the region effectively sealed his fate as Deputy Commissioner, and with it any chance of a fair distribution of land within the territory.

With van Niekerk and Donovan keeping Rhodes in telegraphic touch with what was going on, Rhodes was able to convince Governor Robinson that Mackenzie's presence and policies were the cause of the continued fighting. Mackenzie was thus recalled to Cape Town where, in early August, he was obliged to resign his commission. He was replaced by Cecil Rhodes.

Rhodes hurried north to Vryburg where he guaranteed all Stellaland claims without further investigation, and peace was restored. His attempt to do the same with the Goshenites, however, failed, mainly because of the effectiveness of Barolong resistance, which had kept the mercenaries pinned back along the Transvaal border. With the newly independent South African Republic (Transvaal) threatening to annex the whole of the Barolong lands of Goshen, Rhodes informed Robinson that a full military presence was the only way to enforce British authority west of the republican border.

Having refused to allow Mackenzie to raise an adequate police force, the British government now agreed to Rhodes' request for a large-scale military expedition. The British change of heart, however, had nothing to do with white seizure of African land in Bechuanaland. They had been forced into this decision by wider international strategic concerns. In one of the early acts of the notorious European scramble for Africa, Germany had declared a protectorate over South West Africa (Namibia) in August 1884. The prospect of a hostile German–Transvaal alliance across the 'road to the north' through Bechuanaland was too much for the British. And having decided on a full British military expedition to Bechuanaland, the obvious man to lead it was newly-promoted General Sir Charles Warren.

≈ ≈ ≈

Warren arrived in Cape Town in January 1885. Determined above all else to avoid open conflict with the Boers of the South African Republic, he led his large and well equipped military expedition on a slow advance northwards through eastern Bechuanaland. It took him two months to get from Fourteen Streams on the Griqualand border through Taung and Vryburg to Mafikeng, which he reached on 11 March 1885. In the process he met the Boer President Paul Kruger of the South African Republic and secured his acknowledgement of British authority to the west of the London Convention boundary. Having lost Kruger's support, the Goshenites melted away into the Transvaal.

Sir Charles Warren, bemedalled.

With the British government now deciding to extend their protectorate northwards to forestall further German expansion, Warren was ordered north to seek the formal approval of the northern Batswana *dikgosi*. Impressed by the welcome that he received, and encouraged by Mackenzie, who accompanied

KING MANKORANNE RIDES DOWN WITH HIS ESCORT TO VIEW THE CAMP AT TAUNGS

a confab

One of Mankoranne's Escort

a courtier

*Drawings of the Warren expedition to Bechuanaland (from top)
Mankurwane and sketches of his people; raising the Imperial
flag in Vryburg; Warren flying the flag from a military balloon;
the perils of colonising Africa for the British soldier.*

145

him as special advisor, Warren devised an ambitious scheme for a vast imperial 'crown colony' that would combine the whole of Bechuanaland both
north and south of the Molopo River. Run along Mackenzian lines, it would
be quite separate from the Cape Colony and only parts of it would be available for limited white, specifically British, settlement.

Warren's proposals, however, were distinctly anti-Boer, a position totally
unacceptable to the important bloc of Afrikaners in the Cape parliament. To
compound the problem Warren and Mackenzie, back at Taung in July 1885,
announced the setting up of a formal enquiry into land claims, including
those in the region of Stellaland. This was to be a revival of the enquiry
that Mackenzie had started the previous August and which had precipitated
his recall to Cape Town. Once again, an enquiry into land titles, especially
one of which Mackenzie was part, was the last thing that the British wanted
at this moment. British High Commissioner and Cape Governor Hercules
Robinson, realising that he could not persuade the Cape parliament to agree
to the annexation of any part of Bechuanaland under these conditions,
proposed the division of Bechuanaland along the line of the Molopo River.
The area to the north of the Molopo would become a protectorate, with
minimal British commitment to its development, while the area south of the
river would become a separate imperial colony. Then in due course, once a
'satisfactory' land settlement had been established in the south, it could be
transferred to the Cape Colony.

Thus, on 30 September 1885 Bechuanaland north of the Molopo became
the Bechuanaland Protectorate,[21] while that to the south of the river became
the Crown Colony of British Bechuanaland. Just how 'satisfactory' the subsequent land settlement in the latter would be for Luka and his Batlhaping, will
be seen in the following chapter.

---

[21] This enabled the region to become, 81 years later, the independent Republic of Botswana.

Maps of southern Africa in 1880 (1 above) and 1885 (2 below) showing the evolving colonial frontier.

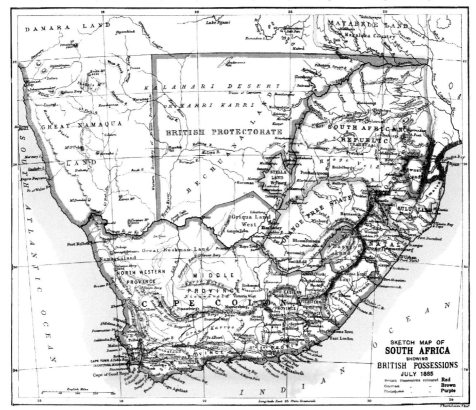

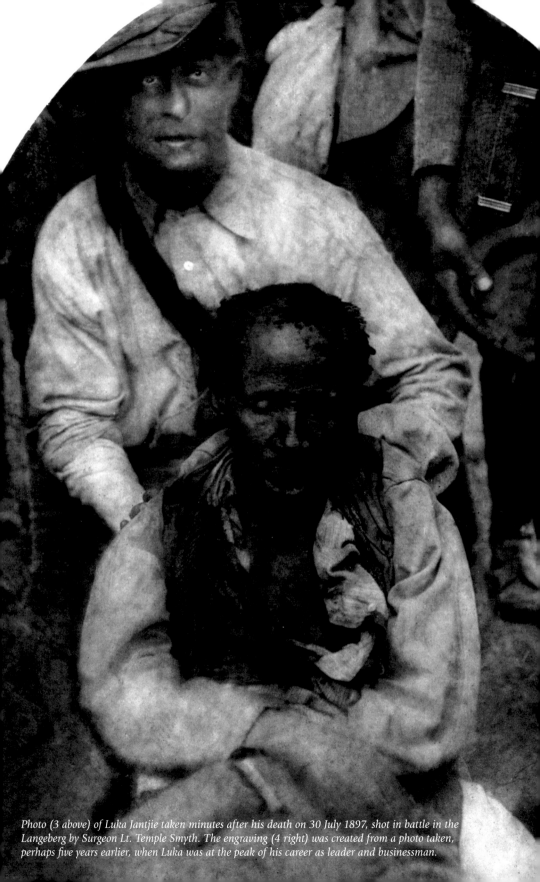

Photo (3 above) of Luka Jantjie taken minutes after his death on 30 July 1897, shot in battle in the Langeberg by Surgeon Lt. Temple Smyth. The engraving (4 right) was created from a photo taken, perhaps five years earlier, when Luka was at the peak of his career as leader and businessman.

5 Commemorative portrait of Luka Jantjie drawn by Judy Seidman, Johannesburg, 2010.

Robert Moffat's church (6 above) at Kuruman, largely unchanged since it was built around the time of Luka's birth. Inside the simple church (7 below) today which Luka will have visited on several occasions.

The school house at Kuruman mission (8 below) with desks outside. It was in a similar building at the LMS mission in Dikgatlhong that Luka was taught by Anne Helmore to read and write in the 1840s.

Griquatown today (9 above), not much bigger now than it was under the Griqua leaders in the mid-nineteenth century. A prospectors bag and tools, and the tin box where Alfred Beit kept his diamonds (10 right). 11 below is a Cape cart similar to one that Luka would have used and the kind of tin shack used by early diamond buyers in the Kimberley area.

Diggings at Kimberley in the early 1870s (12 above). By 1890s this became the 'Big Hole'. Now abandoned (13 below).

THE BATTLEFIELD TODAY

14 Photo taken from the colonial forward base camp at Gamasep Kopje in 1995.

Graves of
colonial troops

Mount Toto
1836m high

Luka's battle position
on Fighting Kopje

Twaai Kloof
behind the ridge

15 Luka's view from Fighting Kopje

Mt Toto

Fighting Kopje

The view (16 below) from Gamasep Kopje looking south across the battlefield to Fighting Kopje and Twaai Kloof.

The entrance (17 above) from the road to the modern farm in the Langeberg called Luca, and (18 below) a photo taken from within the farm looking westwards and showing the hills surrounding Twaai and Gamasep Kloof.

Twaai Kloof

19 Battlefield sketch of the 2nd colonial assault in April 1897. (1) Where Johnson began his climb (behind this hill is Toto's Puduhusch). (2) Peak of Mt Toto, which a few of Johnson's troops reached. (3) Artillery at entrance to Twaai Kloof. (4) Woon's troops hiding in a donga. (5) Pearce's store, where Lt Harris was killed. (6) Gamasep Kopje, where this sketch was made, and site of camp for colonial troops. (7) Schanze-lined hill which Woon failed to capture. (8) Fighting Kopje, where Luka led Batlhaping defence. (9) Water carts for thirsty colonial troops. 20 below, photo taken from Fighting Kopje, where Luka was killed, showing a defensive schanze in the foreground and looking up Twaai Kloof towards his village at the far end of the valley (the last dark green area).

One of several streams (21 above) in Twaai Kloof where Luka's people established their village in the Langeberg in the 1890s. It was these streams which filled with the stinking corpses of cows killed by rinderpest after its devastating arrival in April 1897. The remaining foundations of Pearce's store (22 below left) today, and (23 below right) a stone enclosure, originally a house, in Luka's village at the head of Twaai Kloof.

24 *The stone barrier (front) at the entrance to Luka's village in the Langeberg showing Fighting Kopje (centre) and Gamasep Kopje (right). It was along this path that Luka probably walked – early on the morning of 30 July 1897.*

Gamasep Kopje (25 above) where colonial forces established their forward camp, their artillery positions, and later their field hospital. Cattle (26 below) in the 1970s feed around one of the water sources in Twaai Kloof.

27 In the past Luka's people met under this tree in his village in Twaai Kloof; today, researchers check the site endeavouring to learn more about the history of what happened here over one hundred years ago.

Author, Kevin Shillington (28 above), studies Lt. Harris' grave at Gamasep in 1978. Archaeologist, David Morris (29 above right), records the gps position of Fighting Kopje in 2009. Artefacts (30 below) found on the Langeberg battlefield: (from left) parts of cannon barrel, cooking pot, tin, button, pottery and bullet.

Luka's Descendants

31 Tumo Dikare Jantjie
(Luka's great great great grandson)

32 Kgosienewang II Jantjie
(Luka's great great grandson)

33 Pitso Jantjie *(Luka's great grandson)*

34 Kgosienewang Jantjie *(Luka's grandson)*

35 This contemporary map of the South African War 1899–1902 also shows where the conflict between the Batlhaping and colonialists took place. Note that only two years after the campaign ended in 1897 many of the ancestral place names in the Langeberg have been obliterated. A large red crossed swords symbol shows where the 1897 siege was.

CHAPTER ELEVEN

The Land Commission
1885–1886

Before the recall of his Bechuanaland expedition in August 1885, General Warren had managed to set up his committee of enquiry into the Stellaland claims to the lands of the Batlhaping. Mackenzie had chaired the committee and it had heard evidence at Taung in the first two weeks of August.

The principal aim of the committee was to look into those claims that bordered the Dry Harts valley, the region that Mackenzie had the previous year described as 'the granary of Mankurwane's country'.[1] As a result of his enquiries Mackenzie drew up a report which showed that, if any justice were to be served, a large part of the Stellaland claims that Rhodes had so readily accepted the previous year would have to be rejected. Knowing the Cape government's opposition to this position, Warren telegraphed Mackenzie's findings direct to the British government in London on 22 August.[2] But it was already too late. He and Mackenzie had been forestalled by High Commissioner Hercules Robinson in Cape Town.

The previous day Robinson had telegraphed Lord Stanley, Secretary of State for the Colonies, with alternative proposals that were to become official British policy.[3] Warren and Mackenzie were to be withdrawn, and their land proposals overruled. Southern Bechuanaland was to become a crown colony, pending annexation to the Cape. And a Land Commission was to be set up under the presidency of Sir Sidney Shippard, former Attorney-General of Griqualand West and currently judge of the supreme court in the Cape and Hercules Robinson's legal adviser during the Warren expedition.

Kgosi Luka Jantjie had been among those who had gone to Taung in early August 1885 to give evidence to Mackenzie's land enquiry. He must have

---

[1] Shillington, *Colonisation*, pp171–3.

[2] GBPP, C. 4643, pp 16–17, *Further Correspondence re. the Affairs of the Transvaal & Adjacent Territories*, Warren to Secretary of State Stanley, Banksdrift, 22 August 1885.

[3] C. 4643, p 4, Robinson to Stanley, 21 August 1885.

been very frustrated to hear that Warren and Mackenzie were being withdrawn before the land question had been settled. If he was not already a cynic about British justice and colonial power, then this turn of events was enough to make him one. The arbitrary nature of the Crown Colony's proclamation on 30 September 1885 must have been reminiscent of Griqualand West's proclamation in 1871. Luka knew only too well the contempt shown towards African land rights in that Crown Colony and he was determined to uphold his own and his people's rights to justice.

Luka's concept of justice inasmuch as it affected his people in 1885, was primarily to do with their rights to land and their equal treatment within the new state. For generations the Batlhaping had lived a sparse existence in tune with their environment, dependent largely upon cattle and hunting for their subsistence. And cattle-raising in this harsh environment required relatively free access to a wide range of grazing land. Luka and his father had made few demands upon their subjects, allowing them a wide leeway to satisfy their own families' needs. Now, over the years as the cash economy increasingly intruded, the Batlhaping were making ever greater demands upon the environment as, with wider opportunities, their own material needs increased. Access to land was becoming more competitive, even within the Batlhaping *morafe*. Luka recognised this and respected the concept of private property in land, which in his view could co-exist in concert with communal grazing rights and a general principle that all families should have access to enough land to satisfy their basic needs.

Beyond access to land, however, respect was the vital component that underpinned Luka's concept of justice. Human respect was that shown to the individual and to figures of authority, regardless of origin or race.

It appears to have been these principles that guided Luka's actions in the months that followed the proclamation of the Crown Colony in September 1885. He knew he must take the initiative, be proactive in defence of his people's land and be well-prepared for any land investigation when it came. Thus during the month of October, *Kgosi* Luka drew up a list of 'places occupied by my people', and wrote it up into a formal submission that he intended to present to the government.[4] His list of villages, arable land and other settlements covered a wide range of territory to the east and southeast of Kuruman. The places named extended south from Tlharing, near the modern crossroads of Lykso on the Kuruman–Vryburg road. Most were clustered around Manyeding, but they also extended as far as the Griqualand

[4] BBLC 31, General Register No.74.

border to take in Koning, Klein Koning, Kho and Smouswani (*see map 13, p133*):

> [All of these] places in which I and my people are now living,' emphasised Luka 'were ploughing places of my people even when we lived at Dikgatlhong. We ploughed them before the war [of 1858] in which Gasebonwe was killed.

He went on to explain:

> I do not claim any distinct boundary lines. The Batlhaping have no boundaries. My country has been as far as my people extended.

He expanded on the 'no boundary' concept by pointing out that not everybody on this land owed full allegiance to him. At times some owed allegiance to different *dikgosi*, but that did not invalidate his claim that all of these places were the legitimate lands of Luka Jantjie's people. In other words, there was a level of fluidity within the Batlhaping concept of land usage, ownership and political authority. A man named Petrus, for instance, worked some of the land at Klein Koning. He had fought with Luka in 1878, but he had fought for Mankurwane in 1882. As Luka casually explained, 'Sometimes he is for me, sometimes for Mankurwane.' Similarly, he described shifts in population:

> At Bothethelesa there used to be only my people, but now there are also some of Bogosin's. At Matchutsening there are some of Bogosin's people as well as mine.[5]

In the past this fluidity had extended also to certain white people who wished to reside within the Batlhaping *morafe*. For instance, Luka had recently given permission to a man named Devenish 'to plough some of my land at Gakatsan, and years ago my father gave Agenbag permission to plough, and he has recently done so at Kaw.' But Luka was adamant on this key point:

> They were to live amongst us as we live. I have never given away any farms.

This was in sharp contrast to Mankurwane, who had indeed been giving away farms. Partly as a result of Mankurwane's machinations, a white man named Botha was, according to Luka, '[giving] trouble' at Mahukobong, while another named Armunsen had taken over the land of one of Luka's men at Kho.

The trouble stemmed, as Luka saw it, from the fictional British concept of Mankurwane's 'paramountcy':

---

[5] Luka refers here to Bogosiñ, eldest son of Mahura and first cousin to Mankurwane, also half-cousin to Luka's father, Jantjie Mothibi.

> I am a *kgosi* quite independent of Mankurwane. He has no right to give away my country.

Luka went on to explain the hierarchy of the descendants of Molehabangwe:

> Mothibi was the eldest son of Molehabangwe. The eldest son of Mothibi was Gasebonwe and Jantjie came next. Molale, father of Mankurwane, was Mothibi's younger brother, by a second wife of Molehabangwe.

In Setswana culture, the word 'eldest' as used by Luka here denotes seniority rather than a specific number of years. In fact, as reference to the family tree (*see p16*) shows, Jantjie was Mothibi's first-born son, by a few years, but Gasebonwe was born of the senior wife and so, after the early death of Petlhu, he became the 'eldest' son of Mothibi. Likewise, Mankurwane's father, Molale, was not only a younger brother of Mothibi in number of years, he was also born of a junior wife of Molehabangwe, and so was doubly 'younger' in Setswana terms. Thus, although Mankurwane was now ruling as an independent *kgosi* at Taung, in terms of Batlhaping hierarchy, far from being 'paramount', he was in fact junior to both the Gasebonwe and the Jantjie lines, that is, junior to both Botlasitse and Luka. Paramountcy – the right of one *kgosi* to speak for and above all other *dikgosi* – was not a concept that was practised by the Batlhaping. Even in the days of Molehabangwe's confederation of the late eighteenth century, it had been a voluntary union within the single *morafe* – a union that easily split apart in the years that followed. Thus Luka was claiming no paramountcy over Mankurwane, merely independence from him.

Early in November 1885 *Kgosi* Luka Jantjie went to Taung to present the land claims of his people. It was here at Taung that the administrator of the new Crown Colony, Sir Sidney Shippard, had set up his headquarters during the first few weeks of the new colonial regime, until the administration's buildings were ready for him to move to Vryburg. At this early stage in his administration Shippard was not prepared to grant the Motlhaping *kgosi* an interview, for this might have implied some special recognition of his status. Instead Luka's 'petition' was received by senior officers of the Bechuanaland Border Police (BBP).

The BBP had been set up by Warren in 1885 to ensure that Transvaal Boers made no further cross-border incursions into Bechuanaland. With the establishment of the Crown Colony, this militarised police force assumed a wider role, initially performing the main administrative functions of the new regime.

The original document of Luka's land claims, possibly written in his own hand, has not survived, but an English translation is preserved in the Cape Archives.[6] The translation appears to be in the handwriting of Captain J J Leverson, a former member of Warren's expeditionary force and a senior member of the new administration at the time. The translation was provided by J P McCarthy, an Irish colonist and one-time trader who was sufficiently fluent in Setswana to act as government interpreter. Luka's signature on the English translation, dated 11 November, was witnessed by Leverson and Lieutenant St Quintin of the BBP.[7] In formally signing himself 'Luka Yañki Mothibi Molehabañue', Luka clearly indicated his ancestry and position in the *dikgosi* hierarchy of the Phuduhutŝwana branch of the Batlhaping.

Luka was probably at this stage informed that his statement would be presented to a Land Commission that would start hearing evidence in the New Year.

≈   ≈   ≈

Sidney Shippard, Commission President

The Land Commission, under the presidency of Administrator Shippard, was established early in 1886 and began hearing evidence at Taung in the second week of March. As a starting point and in accordance with the Rhodes Agreement (of 1884), the Commission accepted all Stellaland land claims as a given. There was not much that either Mankurwane or the Mahura family could do about it. Their evidence of long-term occupation of the Dry Harts valley springs was recorded, but not acted upon. That left the land to the west of Stellaland, mainly Luka's country, as the only Batlhaping territory seriously open to dispute.

Kgosi Luka Jantjie travelled down to Taung in early March to defend his case for the lands of his people. He was not on good terms with Mankurwane, so it is unlikely that the Taung *kgosi* would have offered him a house to stay in. Luka had probably travelled from Manyeding on horseback, but he would

---

[6] BBLC 31.

[7] McCarthy was later to become Assistant Inspector of Native Reserves in the new colony, and St.Quintin was soon to become Inspector of Native Reserves.

have been accompanied by numerous councillors, retainers and servants. He would have taken at least one, if not several, covered ox-wagons in which to sleep for there would have been no indication how long the business of the Commission was likely to last.

Luka would have been pleased to note that the newly appointed resident magistrate for Taung was John Smith Moffat, son of Kuruman missionary Robert Moffat who had died in retirement in England a few years previously. Here at least was a colonial official who had grown up amongst the Batswana, was Setswana-speaking and knew something of their history and way of life.

Moffat took no official part in the proceedings of the Land Commission which were held in the office and court of the resident magistrate. This was a building of corrugated iron on a wooden frame that had been constructed at Taung the previous year. Most sittings were chaired by Sidney Shippard, assisted by Captain Leverson. They would have sat at a raised table at the head of the room with tables to the sides for official recorders and interpreters. There would have been further seating in the body of the court for claimants, witnesses and legal representatives. The whole business was conducted in a formal, courtroom manner. Those wishing to present claims made their submissions to the Commission; they were then open to cross-examination by any interested party who had reason to challenge their claims.

There is a portrait of Luka Jantjie, published as an engraving (*see 4 in plate section*), but clearly based upon a contemporary photograph, probably taken a few years after these events.[8] In it he is wearing a smart three-piece check suit, with buttoned waistcoat and watch chain, stiff collar and dark tie, held in place by what looks like a diamond pin. He wears a diamond ring upon the middle finger of his right hand. This is probably very much how Luka looked at he presented himself at the court of the Land Commission in Taung on the morning of 18 March 1886. A lot of people were depending upon him, and he would have dressed in a formality fit for the occasion. He was not presenting himself as a humble supplicant; here was the rightful ruler and representative of his people. As such he was at least the equal of any other man present, except perhaps recognising the higher authority of Shippard, the representative of the British government that was now in ultimate control of Bechuanaland.

---

8 For technical reasons the direct printing of photographs in newspapers was not of an acceptable quality until the late 1890s. The preferred method of printing was to make a copper-plate engraving, traced directly from the photograph. This then produced a very clear print of almost photographic accuracy. The technique was widely used in books, magazines and newspapers from the 1860s right through into the early decades of the twentieth century.

Luka Jantjie was to spend an estimated ten hours, spread over three days, giving evidence to the Commission. Although it was recorded in English as a contemporaneous translation from the original Setswana, the transcript of his evidence is the closest we can get to the actual words of Luka Jantjie, spoken spontaneously, in confrontation with his old adversary J G Donovan. On the first morning of the proceedings Luka responded to his questioners cautiously, mostly with minimal answers. But once the confrontation with Donovan began in earnest, the Batlhaping *kgosi* warmed to the task and gave as good as he got.

Captain Leverson opened the proceedings and, with J P McCarthy interpreting, invited the *kgosi* to make any statement that he liked. Luka considered that he had already made his statement, as submitted in writing to Leverson the previous November, so he responded:

> Have I to make many statements? I would rather that questions were asked me.
> *Leverson*: I supposed that you came in from Manyeding to make some statement.
> *Luka*: I would rather you asked me any question you like.
> *Leverson*: What are the names of the places you claim in the country north of Griqualand West?

Luka did not immediately reply to this question. Presumably he felt that he had already provided the information in his November statement. Leverson, however, appeared to want the names recorded here in the open court, so he read out each one of the places mentioned in Luka's earlier statement, asking after each name whether this was one of his. To each one Luka simply responded 'Yes.' And when asked why he claimed one of the places as his, he replied:

> It belongs to me on account of it being the country of my father Mothibi. The land belonged to Jantjie Mothibi.

Leverson then went on to question him about Bothethelesa, where a son of Bogosin Mahura lived alongside some of Luka's people. Luka explained that his father's people had come there first, after the war with the Transvaal Republic in 1858.

> *Leverson*: Did your father acknowledge that he was living in the country of Mahura?
> *Luka*: No, he was living in his own country – the country of Mothibi.
> *Leverson*: And did Mahura interfere with your father at all?

Luka: No.

Leverson: Is Mankurwane your head chief?

Luka: No, he is not my head chief; he is the son of my grandfather's younger brother.

Leverson: Was Jantjie Mothibi a higher chief than Mankurwane?

Luka: Yes.

Leverson: Who do you consider the head chief of all the Batlhaping?

Luka: The chief of the Batlhaping was Gasebonwe.

Leverson: And who is the head chief today?

Luka: At the present day the head chief is [Botlasitse] the eldest son of old Gasebonwe.

In raising the status of Mankurwane and Mahura and the issue of seniority within the *morafe*, Leverson was leading up to the case that was going to be argued by J G Donovan, for Donovan based his claims upon Mankurwane's right to give away land in Luka's country. Leverson finally got to the nub of the issue when he asked Luka whether he had ever had any transactions with Donovan. Luka replied:

No, not that I know of.

Leverson: Did Mr Donovan ever offer to be your agent?

Luka: Yes.

Leverson: When was that?

Luka: The first offer he made was when I was released from gaol.

Leverson: And what did he offer?

Luka: He asked me if I would accept him as my agent. I asked him what work he wanted to do for me, and he [Donovan] then referred to the [land] and said that as the chief Mankurwane was fighting at the war that afterwards he [Mankurwane] would take all the country.

At this point Donovan, who was in the court, shouted:

Deliberate lies!

Shippard: Do not interrupt, please.

Leverson continued:

What did Mr Donovan offer to do for you?

Luka: He also offered to sell the wood.

Leverson: What did you say to Mr Donovan?

Luka: I refused. I said 'No, I don't know what use an agent is. Your father had begun as an agent at a place called Kaklere, at Bethulie [in the former Basotho lands of the Orange Free State], and what has [Basotho *kgosi*] Lapoi got for that? Is he still alive, for that? Is Lapoi today still on his own ground? Has [Griqua chief] Adam Kok had an agent? And is Adam Kok today in his own country? Has the Chief Waterboer had an agent by the name of Mr Arnot; and is he still in his own country?' That was my answer to Mr Donovan.

Luka, clearly riled by Donovan's interruption, displayed an impressive knowledge of Donovan's personal history, to say nothing of wider southern African affairs. In his attempt to become Luka's agent, however, the notorious land speculator had not been put off by one rebuff and he had apparently approached Luka again after the war in 1884.

Leverson: And what did you say then?

Luka: 'You want me to take you as an agent, but a chief cannot take an agent until he has consulted his own people first. When a man wants to get an agent to act for him he first consults his own people, and should his people agree, he then considers what price the agent should ask, and what amount of money he would require.'

Leverson: Did you consult your people, and agree to accept Mr Donovan?

Luka: I consulted my people, but they would not agree to it, and nothing more came of it.

Leverson: Did anyone try to induce you to take Mr Donovan as an agent?

Luka: Mr Greef spoke to me with regard to Mr Donovan.

Leverson: Did Mr Donovan's brother ever speak to you about it?

Luka: Yes.

Leverson: Which brother?

Luka: Fergus.

Leverson: And what did he ask you to do?

Luka: He asked me if I had not come to the conclusion to accept his brother as agent.

Leverson: And when did this happen, and where?

Luka: It was at the time that this line was made that Mr Fergus spoke to me – where he was living at Blikfontein; the new – the Griqualand West line.

Leverson: How many years ago is that?

Luka: I can't remember.

Leverson: Was this before the war [of 1878], or afterwards, that Mr Donovan's brother spoke to you?

Luka: It was before the war.

At this point Leverson considered that he had finished his questioning. He had prepared the ground for Donovan. It was approaching midday and Leverson asked Luka whether there was any further statement that he wished to make as this time, to which Luka replied with a simple 'No.' The Commission President, Sidney Shippard, adjourned the court for the rest of that day.

The following morning *Kgosi* Luka Jantjie attended the court again. He knew that Donovan – the man who had called him a liar in court the previous day – intended to cross-examine him, and he came well prepared. It is possible that he had in the meantime spoken with Moffat, but he appears to have been informed primarily by his own understanding of justice and formal procedure, as practised in the Batswana *kgotla*. There is no evidence that he received any formal legal advice either before or during the Commission hearings. And the stand that he was about to take in court that day showed that he had no need of it.

Looking into a modern kgotla surrounded by the traditional wood palisade in Serowe, Botswana.

After some other witnesses had given their evidence, Luka Jantjie was called again. Donovan came forward and asked in a demanding tone:

You are the son of Jantjie Mothibi?

Luka ignored his challenger and instead addressed himself directly to the President of the court:

I wish to ask if I cannot ask a question before Mr Donovan cross-questions me.
Shippard: Yes, you can ask what you wish to know.
Luka: I wish to speak a few words.
Shippard: Yes, you can speak.
Luka: I should like to know whether it is a custom, or law, in any court that a man has a right to call another man a liar in court. I always thought that in a court men had a right to dispute with one another, but I was not aware that a man had a right to say to a man openly in court that he was a liar.

Shippard: Do you ask it as a question?

Luka: Yes, it is a question.

Shippard: He has not a right to do so. No man has a right to call another man a liar, and I also checked Mr Donovan when he said so.

This of course was not strictly true. He had not 'checked' Donovan for calling Luka a liar. He had merely told him not to interrupt proceedings. There is a tradition in Setswana history that Shippard acquired the name *Morena Maaka* ('Lord Lies'), through his dealings with the northern Batswana *dikgosi* in the 1890s.[9] It is tempting to suggest that the first germ of the idea for the nickname might be found here, in the Land Commission of 1886. Certainly it must have been clear to Luka that the court leaned in favour of Donovan.

With no further word of censure against him, Donovan recommenced his cross-examination:

Donovan: You are the son of Jantjie Mothibi?

Luka: Yes.

Donovan: Residing at the present time at Manyeding?

Luka: Yes.

Donovan: Where were you born?

Luka: I was born at Mosesberg.

Donovan: Where did you grow up?

Luka: I grew up … at Dikgatlhong.

Donovan: Where did your father come from?

Luka: I heard that my father came from Kuruman.

Donovan: With Mothibi?

Luka: Yes.

Donovan: Did they flee away from Kuruman?

Luka: He left Kuruman after the war which they had with the [Korana] chief Orta, and went down on account of starvation towards the Vaal River.

Donovan persisted in this line of questioning in an attempt to establish that Mothibi had abandoned the whole of the country west of the Ghaap escarpment, which the new colonial regime defined as 'Kuruman District'. If that were the case, argued Donovan, then his descendants had no right to claim it now. Luka, however, continued to deny that they had ever 'abandoned' the country. They had simply 'moved away' on a temporary basis, in the time-honoured manner of Batlhaping environmental management.

[9] Neil Parsons, *A New History of Southern Africa*, p182.

Donovan then quoted from a letter written by old Robert Moffat in 1871 that asserted that Mothibi had, in the missionary's view, 'fled' from Kuruman. Luka was evidently reluctant to challenge the opinion of so respected a figure as the late Revd Moffat, especially as his son, the magistrate, was probably present in the court. So he fended off the question by asking:

> Are those old things which occurred in those days to be brought up today?
> *Donovan*: Yes, because there are disputes about the Batlhaping country today.

In that case, thought Luka, he too could play at that game and he turned the tables on his questioner by posing his own set of questions:

> *Luka*: If that is the case, to whom did Amataku [Campbell] belong?
> *Donovan*: To the Chief Waterboer – (*addressing the court*) – he knows that perfectly well, and the English Government received it from Waterboer.
> *Luka*: It is generally known that the Griquas came from the Kaap [the Cape Colony]. And who were the owners before the Griquas? It was the country of the Batlhaping.
> *Donovan*: And the Batlhaping left it.
> *Luka*: Where did the Batlhaping go to?
> *Donovan*: They left it, and we found the Chief Waterboer in possession; and so it is with the Batlhaping country – certain chiefs left, and certain chiefs remained in the country and we found them.
> *Luka*: It cannot be proved that the Batlhaping ever left the country. How could they have left the country when Waterboer was reigning at Griquatown – when Mothibi and Mahura were [still] here [in Batlhaping country]?

Thwarted on that line of questioning, Donovan brought up the issue of A W Greef's old claim to Dikgatlhong in 1861. Donovan pointed out that Jantjie had submitted that case to Waterboer for settlement. Did that not show that Jantjie was a sub-chief to Waterboer? But on that occasion Waterboer had acknowledged that the Griqua had no right to sell Batlhaping land which had never been purchased by the Griqua in the first place. So Luka was easily able to brush aside Donovan's claim that the Greef case proved prior Griqua ownership of Dikgatlhong. And when Donovan tried to press the case that Jantjie had been a sub-chief of Waterboer, Luka dismissed the idea out of hand. None of the Batlhaping had ever paid taxes to the Griqua and none of them had ever recognised Griqua authority over them.

But the two adversaries were arguing different cases. While Luka was talking about people, his opponent was referring to land. Donovan was trying to turn what had been personal authority over one's own people into territorial authority – the authority of a nation state. Thus, when Donovan asked if Mothibi had got permission from the Griqua when they moved down from Kuruman, Luka replied:

> Why should he get permission from the Griquas when the country he occupied was Batlhaping country? … What questions are these? I have already told you that the Griquas were from the Kaap, and got permission to live in that country from the Chief Molehabangwe.
>
> *Donovan*: Were the Griqua ruling the country – were they in power at that time?
>
> *Luka*: Yes, but they were a different tribe. The Griqua only exercised rule over Griqua.

Then in an attempt to dismiss this line of questioning, Luka added:

> The time that the *Kgosi* Mothibi came into the country was before I was born. You yourself were not born then.

Donovan failed to shift Luka's stance on Batlhaping independence from the Griqua, so he shifted his cross-examination to the period of the early diamond discoveries. Donovan tried to argue that Theodore Doms, acting for Luka's father, had offered the whole of the country to the British government. Luka, however, denied that it was ever anything to do with the actual ownership of land:

> At that time, on account of the discovery of diamonds the diggers asked permission to be allowed to dig for diamonds in that country. … They did not ask for the ground; they wanted the right to dig for diamonds.

Furthermore, Luka vehemently denied that either he or his father had ever authorised Doms to sell land on their behalf.

Donovan then went through the events of the 1870s, including Luka's disputes with him over Donderbosch and Boetsap, his censure by the colonial authorities over the 'collection of taxes', and the time that Lanyon had come down to Dikgatlhong to tell Jantjie Mothibi that he no longer had any authority in the Barkly district. It was a fruitless line of questioning so far as Donovan's claims to land north of Griqualand were concerned; but it seems to have been an attempt to undermine the historic authority of Jantjie and thus his son and successor. Luka, however, was not intimidated. He stood his ground and answered most questions in the negative: 'No', 'I have forgotten' or on one occasion, 'I don't remember, but you can continue to speak.'

Donovan's cross-examination of Luka Jantjie that day, with its simultaneous translation of every exchange, must have lasted several hours and Shippard appears to have grown bored. When Donovan asked permission to quote from yet another document from the 1870s, he commented:

I suppose it is relevant.

Donovan: Yes. I will ask your Honour if the Commission will acknowledge the fact that Jantjie had no right to the Kuruman District.

Shippard: We really do not like to admit any facts, or anything whatever.

With that the President of the Commission announced an adjournment for lunch and the weekend, commenting that as he would be spending time the following week with his surveyor-general, Mr Duncan, hearings would reconvene on Monday morning under the chairmanship of Captain Leverson.

In the light of the subsequent report of the Commission it is clear from Shippard's remarks about not wishing to admit any 'facts' at the Commission's hearings, that the principal decisions about the division of the land had already been taken. Luka, Donovan and others were being allowed their days in court for the sake of appearances. Nobody would be able to claim they did not have a fair hearing, and Shippard's report would not be questioned like that of Judge Stockenstrom on Griqualand West. In the meantime, as the court continued to take evidence never intended for publication, Shippard consulted with his surveyor-general and between them the real decisions were made.

While Shippard and his surveyor-general discussed how best to allocate the land of the Crown Colony, the contest between Luka and Donovan entered its third day on the morning of Monday 22 March.

Donovan returned to his documents, this time quoting extensive passages from the Bloemhof Blue Book, which recorded the evidence of Jantjie Mothibi at the Bloemhof Arbitration of 1871. In his evidence on that occasion Jantjie had referred to the Batlhaping inheriting their land from the ancient *Kgosi* Tau, after whom Taung was named. 'Tau,' Jantjie was reported as saying, 'was the great chief of the Batlhaping, and the eldest of them all. He was a Barolong.' Clearly having no idea who Tau was, Donovan pounced on the reference to the Barolong, whom he knew now lived well to the north of the land that he was trying to claim:

Then according to Jantjie's word ... Tau was Jantjie's great chief [and] you have to look for ground from the Barolong, is that so?

With great patience, Luka attempted to explain what Jantjie was referring to:

> The country of the Batlhaping and Barolong is one, they formerly lived all
> together. Jantjie, in mentioning Tau, only mentioned the descendants of Tau.

But Donovan would not let the idea go and he persisted:

> Then you must look for your ground from the Barolong?

Luka's exasperation began to show:

> You cannot ask me that question because all that has taken place now had taken
> place then. We never had such a dispute until the white people came.

Abandoning this line of attack, Donovan pointed out that at the Bloemhof
arbitration, Jantjie Mothibi had only laid claim to land in the Barkly West
district. Therefore, implied Donovan, he made no claim to the land of the
Kuruman district – the land that Luka was now trying to defend. Luka's
response reveals both his exasperation and a yearning for a more certain
time, an idealistic past that possibly never was:

> Jantjie did not confine himself only to the district of Barkly, he mentioned the
> whole of the Batlhaping Territory … These disputes now only arise from the
> white people; the country belongs to the Batlhaping tribe in general, and before
> the white people came, they never knew what it was to have a dispute between
> sections of the tribes, the country belonged to one head, and that was the *Kgosi*
> Molehabangwe.

So Donovan tried a different approach. He got Luka to admit that Mahura
had, at times, gone to Kuruman and had exercised some form of power there.
Donovan must have thought he had won the contest. If Mahura had exercised power in the Kuruman district, then he must have been a superior chief
to Jantjie, and thus, by inheritance, Mankurwane rather than Luka must be
the ultimate chief of the Kuruman district. Donovan, however, was miscon-
struing the Batlhaping concept of power. In the days of Molehabangwe
among the Batlhaping power had been centralised and personified by the
kgosi himself. Under his successor, Mothibi, power became decentralised, but
there was still only one *morafe*. There were simply several *dikgosi* who exercised power within that single *morafe*.

As Luka explained to the court:

> The *Kgosi*, Mahura, never exercised supreme control over the country, but

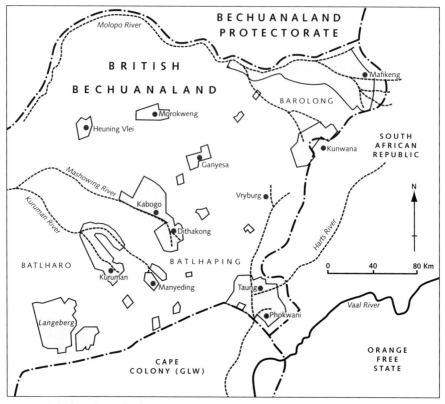

MAP 14: *British Bechuanaland reserves, 1886.*

whatever he did was for his elder brother Mothibi. ... When the *Kgosi* Mahura went to Kuruman, he exercised rule there, so did the *Kgosi* Jantjie, whenever he went to Kuruman, and also the *Kgosi* Gasebonwe when he went there, because the country belonged to them in general.

Donovan was still determined to establish that Mahura had some sort of power over the other *dikgosi*. He kept asking about meetings that Mahura may have called and whether or not the other *dikgosi* had been summoned to attend them. Luka, however, would not be drawn:

> *Donovan*: How many times did Gasebonwe visit Kuruman after 1828?
> *Luka*: I have already told you, I cannot answer such questions; anything referring to myself I can answer you.
> *Donovan*: Well, did he go there more than three times?
> *Luka*: I have already told you, you can ask someone who was there. I refuse to answer because I don't know.

Finally Donovan returned to the 1870s, but his line of questioning had clearly lost direction. By the end of the morning on that third day, Donovan had failed in his objective, which was to prove to the court that Mankurwane rather than Luka exercised ultimate power in the Kuruman district. Over three days of hard cross-examination, Luka Jantjie had patiently held his own in this battle of wits between the two protagonists.

Luka had indeed won a victory of sorts, for although in the final judgement of the Commission Shippard paid scant respect to traditional Batlhaping land rights and awarded Luka's people a very restricted amount of land, Donovan was not awarded a single farm in the territory claimed by *Kgosi* Luka Jantjie.

CHAPTER TWELVE

From 'murmuring' to boycott, British Bechuanaland

1886–1895

In September 1886 Luka Jantjie learned the final decision of the Land Commission.[1] From his point of view as *kgosi* of the western Batlhaping it was a devastating report.

The pre-colonial state or *'morafe'* that Luka had done so much to safeguard over the previous five years no longer existed. His people were allocated barely ten percent of the land between the Ghaap escarpment and the Kuruman hills. Most of the places that Luka had claimed in his November submission had been recognised, but not much more than the villages and the surrounding arable land was granted. Thus Smouswani, Koning, Grootfontein and Tlharing were all allocated to Luka's people, but they were each restricted to little more than twenty square kilometres. The large number of sites that Luka had claimed in the Manyeding and Bothethelesa region ensured a slightly larger allocation here; but like the others, it was still woefully inadequate for the Batlhaping's extensive cattle-grazing practices. The Batlhaping had been used to regularly moving their cattle across the poor grazing *veld* of the Ghaap plateau. This option was now denied them. They were restricted to communal 'reserves' and the land in between was declared 'vacant crown land', available for sale to white colonists.

Apart from the restricted nature of the land allocation, the thing that particularly riled Luka and other leading Batlhaping was the communal nature of the reserves. This supposedly followed 'African tradition'. In fact for several decades Luka and many of the other men of the wider ruling family of the Batlhaping had been treating their outstations as a combination of both their personal property and the places where they exercised traditional authority with all its reciprocal obligations. They used the wealth

---

[1] GBPP, C.4889, *Report of the Commission appointed to Determine Land Claims and to Effect a Land Settlement in British Bechuanaland.*

obtained from cattle-keeping, hunting, wood-riding and general trading to accumulate personal wealth, but also as a means of safeguarding the livelihood of their people. They saw no sharp divide between traditional wealth and power relations and the individual wealth of the capitalist system. They had therefore expected to be granted individual title to the 'farms' that they claimed as their own. The fact that they shared the usage of these farms with their people through traditional power relations should have been no bar to the granting of individual title. But Luka and his peers formed a new class of modern African that the government was determined not to recognise, and the Land Commission refused to recognise any African claim to individual title. White colonists, on the other hand, merely had to prove a few years of occupation to be granted individual title. Thus Armunsen got title to a 3,000 hectare farm at Kho, based upon the fact that Luka's father had given him permission to plough there on the understanding that he would live among the Batlhaping like one of them. But now the Batlhaping who also ploughed at Kho got nothing.

Considering the anger that Luka must have felt at the injustice and discriminatory decisions of the Land Commission, his letter of complaint to Shippard was remarkably restrained:

> I am Luka Yanki.
>
> I let the Chief [Shippard] know of my murmuring with regard to the country, because now there are no black men who have obtained farms, only white men. Now I say Chief, where can we go because all the country is a Location? And again, Chief, I wonder to see the Magistrate [Moffat] place the man Treboen as chief of Bothethelesa, he not being a chief, in spite of my notice and that of the council of the Batlhaping.
>
> This is my complaint.
>
> Greetings to Chief Shippard.[2]

Shippard's response was patronising in the extreme and merely added insult to injury. He claimed the reason he had not given individual land titles to any Africans was so that they would not fall into the temptation of selling their titles to white men who offered them money. The real motive, of course, was to make the maximum amount of land available for sale to white colonists; to nip the new class of modern African in the bud by destroying any chance

---

[2] CA, BCC 93, Translation of Luka to Shippard, 11 September 1886, Enclosed in 165G of 18 November 1886. Luka still spelt his Jantjie surname 'Yanki' in the phonetic manner taught him by the English missionary Anne Helmore.

of genuine African economic autonomy; and to ensure that Africans would not be able to live an independent existence within the reserves. Although he did not say as much to Luka, Shippard's intentions were clear: Africans in the new Crown Colony were to be a permanent working class, whose labour would be available to satisfy the needs of white colonists. Furthermore, Shippard pointed out to Luka, Treboen was the son of a headman appointed by Mankurwane, so Luka should have no objection. This last remark was in direct defiance of Luka's extensive evidence against Mankurwane's supposed seniority.

There was worse to come. In 1886 and 1887 Shippard issued two 'hut tax' proclamations. The tax was in effect a racially-based poll tax charged at the rate of ten shillings a year on every adult African man in the colony. An additional ten shillings was charged against each additional wife. In the absence of a census of the African population, colonial officials estimated the amount of tax due by counting the number of African houses in a village, and assumed one adult man per house. They referred derogatively to the traditional African circular house as a 'hut' – hence the term 'hut tax'. The second proclamation specifically ordered that the tax be paid in cash – a deliberate attempt to break African economic self-sufficiency and drive more people into the colonial wage economy.[3] White colonists, on the other hand, were charged no direct tax. They were subject only to the indirect taxes and duties charged on imported consumer goods. The fact that Africans also had to pay these indirect taxes was conveniently ignored. Africans, according to Shippard, were paying for 'the blessings of British rule'.[4]

In Luka's region the rate of tax collection was particularly low. Police sent to collect tax in 1887 found the Manyeding reserve populated almost entirely by women, children and old men. It was supposed that most men were away working in Kimberley. But Luka's people did not have a reputation for wage labour and they may well have simply been evading the tax collectors.

The colonial authorities hoped that the diversion of taxation from chiefs to government would undermine and fatally erode the political authority of the chiefs. In fact the reverse held true: the system served to highlight the chiefs as the champions of justice for the Batlhaping and the opponents of colonial government. And the more the Batlhaping felt the oppression and injustices of the colonial system, the more they looked to their traditional

[3] Proclamations 15 (BB) 1886 and 30 (BB) 1887, Shillington, *Colonisation*, pp204–7. There were twenty shillings to the pound (£).
[4] *GBPP*, C.7944, p5, Shippard, Annual Report, 20 September 1895.

dikgosi for leadership. Thus, when J S Moffat returned to the magistracy at Taung in 1895, he found that the 'tribal system' was still strong and remained, as he saw it, 'a bar to all progress.'[5] It was no coincidence that when rebellion finally came in 1896 and 1897, it was conducted under the leadership of the traditional *dikgosi*.

It is clear from his subsequent actions that Luka Jantjie remained determined to defend his own and his people's economic and political autonomy, within the limits of the new regime. Thus, as far as he was able, he would maintain the Batlhaping's basic cattle-raising culture; he would not be pressured into the indignity of colonial wage labour; and above all, he personally would not accept being treated as a second-class citizen in his own country.

It was Luka Jantjie's adherence to these three principles that shaped the way he coped with colonialism in the years ahead. And when resistance finally turned to open warfare, it was assumed by colonist and colonised alike that Luka Jantjie, albeit unwillingly, would be at the head of it.

≈ ≈ ≈

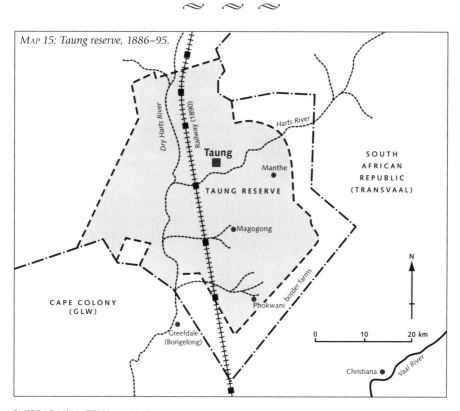

MAP 15: *Taung reserve, 1886–95.*

Dry Harts River

Railway (1890)

Harts River

Taung

Manthe

SOUTH
AFRICAN
REPUBLIC
(TRANSVAAL)

TAUNG RESERVE

●Magogong

N

CAPE COLONY
(GLW)

border farms

Phokwani

0   10   20 km

Greefdale
(Borigelong)

Christiana ●

Vaal River

5 *CPP*, G5–'96, BBNA, pp51–2.

167

To the east of *Kgosi* Luka's collection of reserves on the Ghaap plateau lay the 'Taung reserve', a single block of land in the southeast corner of British Bechuanaland (*see map 15*). Besides *Kgosi* Mankurwane's capital town of Taung itself on the north bank of the Harts, south of the Harts the reserve included the Bamaidi Batlhaping town of Manthe as well as *Kgosi* Botlasitse's town of Phokwani. All of this was separated from the Transvaal and Griqualand West by a string of border farms intended for sale to white colonists.

The Taung reserve contained a reasonable range of grazing and arable land and a number of useful streams, besides part of the Harts and Dry Harts rivers. The actual town of Taung housed about five thousand people and the northern half of the reserve would have been ample for the arable and grazing needs of this size of population. But the bulk of Mankurwane's (*left*) people had lived at the fertile and well-watered outstations that bordered the upper reaches of the Dry Harts valley. From these they were now expelled by the granting of the Stellaland farms to a few hundred white colonists. This meant that a further ten thousand people were now crowded into the Taung reserve. The result was immediate overcrowding in the northern half of the reserve.

Further south, around Phokwani, with Botlasitse's people numbering only a few thousand, overcrowding was not so apparent. The main hardship here lay in the lack of access to the Harts and Vaal rivers. Free access to the Harts was interrupted by white-owned border farms, while the Vaal was cut off by both border farms and the extension of the Transvaal as far as the Griqualand boundary.

In the early years of the Crown Colony the cattle owners of Phokwani lost a lot of livestock to cattle impounders who based themselves in the border farms. In the west, the owner of the border farm Hartigan, Harvey Smith, earned a comfortable living from impounding Phokwani cattle, and the herdsmen were obliged to accompany their cattle to the Harts River in armed groups. The only action that the colonial authorities took was to establish a police post at Schaapfontein, just to the north of Phokwani village.[6] It was not until 1891 that Harvey Smith's activities were curbed somewhat when he applied for a licence to open a store in Phokwani. On magistrate Stanley Lowe's recommendation, the licence was issued on condition that Smith allow Phokwani cattle free access across his farm to the Harts. Smith transferred his trading licence to Arthur Blum, who set up a store and began trading in Phokwani in 1891.[7]

Between 1885 and 1887 Luka Jantjie visited Taung several times, mostly to see colonial government officials about land issues. It is more than likely that on occasion he also paid a courtesy visit to Phokwani, to pay his respects to Botlasitse Gasebonwe, the senior *kgosi* of the Phuduhutŝwana branch of the Batlhaping.

Botlasitse was in need of Luka's support, for he lacked that of his older sons Galeshewe and Gasebaatje and his youngest brother Morebonoke (Andries Gasebonwe), all three of whom were still serving long-term sentences in Cape Town's convict prison. Botlasitse had become a frail old man, though he was only in his early sixties, just a decade older than his much fitter cousin, Luka. A photograph taken of him ten years previously (*see p125*) shows him to be very stout. Since then his overall health may have been affected by his fondness for Cape brandy. According to the Taung missionary, John Brown, Botlasitse had nearly died of its ill-effects on several occasions, and in 1883 he had suffered a 'paralytic stroke'. He had now given up the brandy; but he was sorely feeling the absence of his sons for so many years.[8]

In the early months of 1885, soon after the arrival of Warren's expeditionary force, the resident Anglican missionary at Phokwani, Revd W Henry R Bevan of Bloemfontein Mission, had written a petition in Botlasitse's name to the Cape Governor requesting the release of the *kgosi*'s sons. That petition had been supported by General Warren and John Mackenzie who thought the men should be released just as soon as the country was 'restored to tranquillity'. In December that year, three months after the establishment of the Crown Colony, Bevan wrote again for Botlasitse, this time to administrator

---

[6] CA, BCC 45 (265B), Moffat, RM Taung, 27 December 1886.
[7] Shillington, *Colonisation*, p216.
[8] *LMS*, John Brown, Taung, 2 December 1885.

Shippard, requesting his support for the release of the *kgosi's* sons:

> I think, Sir, that that time [of 'tranquillity'] has come now; for the whole country is happily settled under the Government of Her Gracious Majesty.[9]

However, neither Shippard nor Governor Robinson were very sympathetic and it was not until October 1887 that Galeshewe was finally reunited with his ailing father, having served eight years of a twelve-year sentence. Galeshewe (*below*) assumed control of the Phokwani polity and Botlasitse lived on in retirement until his death in March 1890.

≈ ≈ ≈

In the early months of 1888 Luka Jantjie visited Galeshewe in Phokwani to discuss the unsatisfactory nature of the land settlement and to try and develop a joint policy to alleviate their problems. There is no evidence that Luka and Galeshewe were ever particular friends. There was a certain distance between them. The Jantjie family may well have been wary of the Gasebonwes, ever since the troubles of 1858. Nevertheless, they were united in their opposition to Mankurwane's overbearing nature and his assumption that he was senior *kgosi* of the Phuduhutŝwana Batlhaping. Some sort of agreement to co-operate seems to have been reached between Luka and Galeshewe, but no specific policy was decided at this stage.

Meanwhile, tension was building in the Taung reserve as drought persisted through 1886 and '87 and grain harvests were almost non-existent. At the same time, the effects of overcrowding were becoming apparent. Mankurwane complained early in 1887 that shortage of grazing land had led to the loss of 800 cattle; but Shippard gave him no sympathy. He refused to countenance any extension of the reserve into the border farms, insisting that 'increased industry and thrift [was] all that he and his people need[ed] to ensure great prosperity.' And if that failed, asserted the callous administrator, there was

---

[9] *Botswana National Archives (BNA)*, HC 177/12, Letter written by Revd Bevan for Botlasitse, Phokoane [*sic*], 10 December 1885, in J S Moffat to Administrator, Taung, 19 December 1885.

African miners in 1870s with symbols of wealth, which (inset) F R Thompson's new labour system gradually took away in the 1890s.

always work on the Kimberley mines.[10] Some took up this option: at least they were paid in Kimberley, which was often not the case if they worked for local white farmers. On the other hand, those Phokwani people who were pushed into wage labour preferred working on white-owned farms in the Orange Free State. They avoided the Kimberley mines, which had recently introduced a closed-compound system for their African contract labourers, a system devised by their old opponent, F R Thompson:

> My plan was that the natives should be locked within the enclosure for three months, and have access to the mine only through a covered way.[11]

As a Phokwani resident explained to the magistrate Stanley Lowe:

> They would sooner go to prison than into a compound, where they are beaten, knocked about, and worse treated by the white overseers than they are in prison.[12]

And a number of the people in Phokwani had had several years' personal experience of prison life in Kimberley and the Cape Colony.

With the return of good rainfall in the 1887–88 season, every possible

10 Shillington, *Colonisation*, p208.
11 Rouillard, *Matabele Thompson*, p83
12 *CBPP*, C.5897, p47, Annual Report, RM Taung, 9 October 1889.

piece of land was brought into cultivation. But there were clashes over ploughing rights as the Dry Harts incomers ploughed what had hitherto been Taung grazing land. Mankurwane tried to assert his authority over the reserve by reviving initiation ceremonies, much to the consternation of Revd John Brown.[13] Initiation led to the creation of new *morafe*-wide age-grades or regiments (*mephato*) under the leadership of one of the sons of the *kgosi* and thus with loyalty to him and his dynasty. The LMS missionary was thus right to judge that the re-emergence of these 'heathen practices' was politically motivated and a potential threat to government authority. And Shippard's persistent refusal to address the land issue placed the blame for the mounting economic crisis firmly upon the colonial government.

There was a bumper harvest in May 1888; but that did not resolve the issue. Because there was such a huge surplus of grain that year, those with maize and millet to sell found that the rates they were offered by the local colonial traders fell far below the price that they had had to pay to the same traders to buy back their grain in the lean time of 1887. The following season (1888–89) drought returned and Revd John Brown compared the atmosphere in 1889 to that which had existed in 1878, following Lanyon's raid on Phokwani.[14]

It was into this atmosphere of tension and distrust that Luka Jantjie rode in June 1889 to take up residence at Magogong in the Taung reserve.

After the failed harvest of 1889 and the continued suffering of his cattle on the poor grazing of the Manyeding reserve, Luka decided it was time to seek better grazing land elsewhere. Leaving his brother Olebile in charge at Manyeding, he went down into Griqualand West to see if the Cape authorities would allow him to reclaim his father's old farm of Dikgatlhong, where his brother Kaelo appears to have died in 1882. This was denied him by the Inspector of Native Locations, William Hall, who was concerned at the very thought of having such a non-submissive *kgosi* in his domain.[15]

Considering Luka's experience of the colonial authorities there in the 1870s, it may seem surprising that he should even contemplate moving back to Dikgatlhong. Perhaps he only hoped to use it for grazing cattle and had no intention of personally living under the Cape regime. On the other hand, anticipating that he would be refused, he may have simply applied for the

[13] *LMS*, John Brown, Taung, 9 October 1889.
[14] *LMS*, John Brown, Taung, 9 October 1889.
[15] *CA*, Blue Book of Native Affairs (BBNA), G4–'90, Hall, Barkly West, 2 January 1890.

return of Dikgatlhong on a matter of principle, knowing that it was his by any normal rights of justice.

Luka had probably already decided that he would move to the Taung reserve, something that he would have negotiated with Galeshewe the previous year. While in Griqualand West he visited Boetsap and the Harts valley and found fifty families from the Mammutla and Shaleng locations who were prepared to go with him and settle in British Bechuanaland. Major Stanley Lowe, former head of the Bechuanaland Border Police, had some sympathy with the Batlhaping. He had taken over from Moffat as resident magistrate at Taung in 1887 and he agreed to Luka's settling in the Taung reserve.

Luka established a settlement of several hundred people by a spring at Magogong, south of Taung, midway between there and Phokwani. His arrival caused consternation among local white colonists. The missionary John Brown, in particular, was uneasy about having such a strong and inde-pendent-minded *kgosi* within the reserve.[16] The people he brought with him merely added to these concerns.

Most of those who followed Luka to Magogong had fought with him in 1878, including the (Morolong) Solomon who had been suspected of involve-ment in the Burness murders at Daniel's Kuil. A number of these people had been radicalised by their recent experiences under Cape rule in Griqualand West and they came to Magogong in defiant mood. As John Brown reported in October 1889, just a few months after their arrival in the reserve:

> Last week one of Luka's people was in Taung and was very impudent to one of the storekeepers – telling him that his chief would soon show the English to whom the country belonged.[17]

Whatever the expectations of some of his followers, however, Luka himself had no intention of stirring up trouble with the colonial authorities. He hoped, as he had always done, to peaceably coexist with colonialism, but at the same time to maintain as much of his political and economic autonomy as was possible within the new regime. Above all, he would *not* be treated as a second-class citizen, and it was perhaps this latter attitude which his more enthusiastic supporters interpreted as anti-colonial hostility.

The Magogong region offered far better grazing than Manyeding. Much of

---

[16] The LMS missionary John Brown is not to be confused with his colleague John Tom Brown who was based at Kuruman. The latter is referred to here as J T Brown or J Tom Brown.

[17] *LMS*, John Brown, Taung, 9 October 1889.

the soil on the Ghaap plateau was low in phosphate and close grazing of the coarse grass that grew there left cattle vulnerable to diseases such as bovine botulism. Luka would not have known about the chemical composition of the Ghaap soil, but he knew good grazing land when he saw it and that on some coarse grazing land the cattle were more prone to disease. Magogong offered quality grazing and access to the Harts only ten kilometres away. There was also sufficient arable land nearby for the settlement's immediate needs. This favourable situation, however, was not to last for long.

Train at Warrenton, 1895: the arrival of the railway in the 1890s brought change in many ways.

In March 1890, a mere nine months after Luka's arrival at Magogong, the government appropriated a 600 hectare strip of reserve land for the construction of a railway north from Griqualand West to Mafikeng and beyond. Cutting through the centre of the Taung reserve, west of Magogong, the rail strip included what Stanley Lowe described as some of the best arable land in the district. Crops were destroyed for which scant compensation was offered, and there was no compensation at all for the loss of land. For Luka's people it was a disaster. It deprived their cattle of direct and safe access to the Harts River. And worse was to come. With the rail link reaching Taung in August 1890, scores of white 'sportsmen' made day trips from Kimberley to slaughter what was left of the small wild game of the district.[18]

In spite of this, the settlement at Magogong continued to grow as people increasingly looked to Luka Jantjie for leadership and protection. Luka was making regular trips to Griqualand West to look after the interests of his people there. The Griqualand locations were suffering terribly from overgrazing. In spite of this, William Hall and F R Thompson of Cornforth Hill were intent on confiscating some of the location land and 'concentrating the natives' into a smaller number of locations. Under these circumstances it is not surprising that many were prepared to move to British Bechuanaland where they hoped to live under a slightly less oppressive regime. Hall dismissed them as 'disinterested natives', but he observed too that Luka Jantjie was 'evidently collecting his old following.'[19] Within two years of Luka's arrival

---

[18] Shillington, *Colonisation*, p219.
[19] Shillington, *Colonisation*, pp108–9.

Bangwato women housebuilding in the 1890s; Luka's people built similar thatched houses.

at Magogong more than a hundred houses had been built there, in the traditional style.

The migration of more of Luka's people to Magogong coincided with a general revival of initiation ceremonies at Taung. The missionary, John Brown observed early in 1891 that the ceremonies were on a much larger scale than before, with both young men and young women involved. The revival was led by Mankurwane's brother and sons, including professed Christians, at least one of whom had been to the Moffat Institute at Kuruman. Revd Brown was frustrated by the lack of concern shown by the colonial authorities:

> As a political movement it is anything but hopeful for the peace of the country. Its manifest design is to foster the power of the chief; and it is astonishing to me that the government cannot see what will be the inevitable result of this strengthening of the chief's power.[20]

According to John Brown, a number of Luka's people from Dikgatlhong in Griqualand West as well as from the Kuruman district were involved in the Taung ceremonies of 1891, including numerous married Christians.

Luka had never been initiated, and so was not in a position to conduct initiation ceremonies himself, even if he had wanted to. In any case, he probably did not feel the need to boost his political support; and he certainly would not have boosted Mankurwane's prestige by paying any attention to the ceremonies being conducted at Taung. However, so far as Phokwani was concerned, initiation ceremonies had never been abandoned. Botlasitse had never paid too much attention to missionary criticism and during his lifetime he had regularly conducted rainmaking, initiation and age-regiment formation ceremonies.[21] Galeshewe merely carried on the tradition.

[20] *LMS*, John Brown, Taung, 24 March 1891.
[21] *LMS*, John Brown, Taung, 4 December 1885.

Although the three *dikgosi* – Galeshewe, Luka and Mankurwane – did not always see eye to eye on matters of internal politics and relations with the colonial powers, they were united in their dealings with colonial traders.

Kimberley shops prospering in the 1890s and supplying mass-produced goods to the Batswana.

The penetration of industrial consumer goods into the rural areas had been greatly boosted by the development of the diamond fields. In the Taung reserve of the late 1880s most metal tools and utensils were imported rather than manufactured in the traditional fashion. Iron cooking pots – made in the British industrial cities of Birmingham or Glasgow – were rapidly replacing home-made clay pots in all but the poorest households. And the wearing of some degree of cloth clothing had become almost universal by the mid-1880s, although fur karosses were still widely used during winter months and at formal meetings in the *kgotla*.

Itinerant traders and resident storekeepers, therefore, provided an important service in the rural areas where they were also the sole source of consumer credit. But they tended to manipulate their monopoly position to their own advantage. They encouraged indebtedness by offering consumer goods on credit through the year, mortgaged against the potential harvest of individual farmers. And by insisting on barter rather than cash, the real price of goods and the true rate of profit were concealed from the African consumer.

This relationship between Batlhaping and trader stretched back to the 1860s when small-scale farmers in the Harts valley began selling surplus grain to itinerant traders such as John O'Reilly. Since the early 1870s the Batlhaping had been growing and selling grain on a regular basis for the Kimberley market, and, in the absence of large grazing lands and good

176

Molala, who succeeded Mankurwane as kgosi in Taung, with his wife and granddaughter in 1896.

hunting opportunities, growing grain for market had by the 1890s become the only way for many Batlhaping to avoid succumbing to the demands of full-time wage labour. But indebtedness to traders was in danger of destroying this last vestige of economic independence.

In the early 1890s Luka, Galeshewe and Mankurwane co-ordinated their efforts to break the traders' hold on African indebtedness. The new railway regularly brought Kimberley newspapers to the reserve so they were fully aware of the market prices for grain in the diamond city. During the winter of 1892 – after a good rainy season and heavy grain harvest – the three *dikgosi* ordered farmers in the reserve to demand payment in cash for their maize, millet and sorghum. The traders held out for some weeks until they realised that some of the reserve's African farmers were sending their grain by rail direct to Kimberley. So they raised their rates closer to the Kimberley level and agreed to pay in cash. As a result the farmers were able to pay off their debts and still have some cash left over. The traders' stranglehold upon the rural economy had been broken, at least in the Taung reserve. In what was one of South Africa's earliest examples of boycott as a weapon of peaceful resistance, the Batlhaping action in the Taung reserve in 1892 was a salutary lesson of the effectiveness of co-ordinated resistance to rural oppression.[22]

Unfortunately it was the only example of such well co-ordinated action. In November 1892 Mankurwane died, in his early seventies. He was succeeded by his son, Molala (*above*), who seemed a little unsure about his position with regard to his older cousins, Luka and Galeshewe. Although Mankurwane had been happy to accept the British promotion of his paramountcy, Molala did not seem prepared to push any claim over Luka, the eldest surviving grandson of Mothibi, or over Galeshewe, technically of the senior line.

---

[22] Shillington, *Colonisation*, pp221–2. The term 'boycott' was coined in Ireland during Irish resistance to British land policies in County Mayo in the west of Ireland in 1879–81. Captain Charles Boycott was the land agent for an absentee English landlord. His tenants refused to harvest his crops at reduced wages and Boycott was obliged to import outside labour and troops to protect them, all at a cost that far exceeded the value of the harvest.

Following the death of Mankurwane, Luka's status within the reserve would have risen, and as events unfolded, it appears that people looked increasingly to him for leadership in any confrontation with colonial authority.

Growing maize in the 1890s.

Ever since the seizure of the rail strip in 1890, Luka had been pressing the government for more land, to provide greater freedom for his people and safe grazing pasture for his cattle. Shippard, however, had always taken the view that the Batlhaping had no need for more land. If they couldn't earn a proper living from the land they had, then they could go out and work for wages in the colonial economy. Those who failed to do so were clearly lazy. But following the success of the Batlhaping's cash-for-grain policy against the traders, Shippard woke up to the fact that perhaps the Batlhaping were not just lazy after all. He was impressed by the fact that during the 1891–92 season they had grown double the amount of grain per hectare in the Taung reserve than all the white farmers of the Vryburg district. At last he seemed prepared to listen to Luka's request for more land, and he finally agreed to a meeting with the *kgosi* in Taung.

The meeting took place in Taung on 24 May 1893. It was attended by all three Phuduhutŝwana *dikgosi*, Luka, Galeshewe and Molala, as well as Kgantlapane of the Bamaidi Batlhaping. All complained of lack of grazing space in the reserve, but judging from the minutes of the meeting, Luka appears to have been the dominant participant.[23]

Luka had clearly given up on any revision of the land settlement. He announced that he intended to purchase land because that was the only way to get enough. Before Mankurwane's death the previous November he had tried to persuade the Taung *kgosi* to come in with him in buying some of the border farms around the reserve, most of which still remained unsold. But Mankurwane had been hesitant. At present, Luka explained to Shippard, there was simply not enough room at Magogong. His cattle had to cross the rail to get water from the Harts River and they often got killed on the line.

---

[23] BCC 114, Enclosed in 155G of 7 June 1893.

Ideally, Luka said, he would have liked to go back to Manyeding, but there they would have 'no place to send their cattle to.' So he had concluded that the best solution would be to go to the Langeberg mountain range or to its northern neighbour, the Korannaberg. He reckoned he would need the equivalent of two standard farms, about 6,000 hectares, and he was prepared to pay for it. When asked by Shippard if he would give up Manyeding in exchange, Luka said no, at least, not until he had seen the alternate land.

Luka explained that Galeshewe had agreed to join him in this land purchase scheme. Either they would buy the border farms by the railway or they would both go to the Langeberg. When asked again how much land he needed, Luka replied cryptically, 'as much land as would prevent our being crowded.' Shippard indicated that the only way they would get more land would be by exchange or purchase. He appears to have seen no reason why Africans should not be allowed to buy private land in the colony.

Despite Luka's reference to a joint venture, Galeshewe did not go in with him in buying land in the Langeberg. The Phokwani *kgosi* would have preferred to buy Hartigan, the valuable farm that bordered the Harts River, but Harvey Smith refused to sell. So shortly after the meeting with Shippard, Galeshewe bought two farms on the Transvaal border. And over the next couple of years Molala bought six further farms that bordered the Transvaal in the northern half of the reserve (*see map 15*). Although all these farms were private acquisitions, the *dikgosi* made them available to the general population of their *merafe*. This was in line with traditional practice by which the *kgosi* provided for his people. So far as the colonial government was concerned, these farms were not the private property of Galeshewe or Molala; they were simply part of the Taung reserve. They were thus subject to potential forfeit in the case of rebellion: an important point in the case of Galeshewe and Phokwani, as we shall see later.

Luka Jantjie, however, had set his heart on the Korannaberg where the grazing was sweet and he would be far from colonial interference. Shippard had indicated that he would need to check what land was available.

Sometime after the Taung meeting, Luka went to Kuruman to discuss land purchase with the resident magistrate, Scholtz, who was responsible for the whole of the Langeberg and Korannaberg region. It appeared that the only suitable privately-owned land lay within a huge tract to the northwest of Kuruman that had been set aside for the Bechuanaland Railway Company, a subsidiary of Cecil Rhodes' business empire. This was in part payment for the building of the railway line from Griqualand West to Mafikeng.

Within this area, Luka identified at least one farm that he wanted, east of the Korannaberg. It bordered the Gamogara, a seasonal river that flowed north from the Langeberg to the lower Kuruman. Scholtz explained that he would need to negotiate the purchase with the railway company. On this understanding Luka paid the magistrate £115 that he had collected from his people.[24] He then made his way back for a final season at Magogong.

The rains fell early that year and the reserve was extensively cultivated. When it came to the time to reap their bumper harvest the following May 1894, however, the farmers of the Taung reserve found that the traders had dropped their prices to half what they had been the previous year when there had been shortages.

Luka took immediate action. He initiated another boycott, the tactic that had been so successful two years previously. To the consternation of traders and colonial officials, Luka Jantjie ordered his people to refuse to sell their grain to traders at anything less than two shillings a bucket, the price that had been offered the previous year.[25] Luka's example was followed by Molala in Taung and Galeshewe in Phokwani. Molala sent word to Dithakong to tell the people there to follow suit. And emissaries went as far as the Langeberg to urge the Batlharo *Kgosi* Toto to do likewise. The rural traders who were the subject of the boycott were worried by these urgent messages being sent across the country. They feared they were attempts to 'incite the people to war'. And isolated rural police officers anticipated trouble.[26]

Back in the Taung reserve the boycott was not universally supported and Molala's resolve soon wavered. Luka, however, stood firm as he and Galeshewe enforced a complete boycott of Rickman's store in Magogong and Blum's store in Phokwani.

Some of Galeshewe's people tried to evade the ban, and Galeshewe fined one man an ox for allowing his daughter to sell some grain to Blum. Other Phokwani residents sneaked their wagons across the Griqualand border to 'Greefdale', the former site of Borigelong (now owned by A W Greef), where

24 BCC 72, Inspector of Native Reserves, St Quentin, 15 February 1895. For price comparison: a new wagon and span of eight seasoned oxen would have cost £110–150, and a rifle between £5 and £10, while the few senior chiefs who were on the government payroll – Mankurwane, Montshiwa and Toto – received £200 a year. Luka was not one of these.

25 There were twenty shillings to the pound (£) and a bucket contained four gallons or half a bushel, the standard measure of grain at that time.

26 *BNA*, HC 113/4, Scholtz (RM), Kuruman, 29 May 1894; *CAD*, NA 222, Police report, 21 July 1894, Civil Commissioner, Barkly West, 24 July; William Hall (INL), Barkly West, 4 Aug 1894.

A Batswana family and outspanned wagon; note the factory-produced 3-legged iron cooking pot.

they were able to sell their grain and buy brandy. In July, Galeshewe summoned his regiments to a grand hunt – a *letsholo* – such as his great-grandfather Mothibi would have done earlier in the century. But there was hardly any wild game left in the region, and it is likely that the *letsholo* was an attempt by Galeshewe to establish greater unity of purpose within Phokwani. Whatever Galeshewe's motivation, the gathering panicked the nearby Transvaal Boers who feared that rebellion was imminent. They hastily formed defensive laagers around their farms, which further added to the tension.[27]

In Magogong, Luka's people seemed more united behind the boycott. At the end of July they confiscated a whole ox-wagon full of grain, oxen and wagon included, that had been sent by the Bamaidi *Kgosi* Kgantlapane from Manthe for sale at Rickman's store.[28]

The price of two shillings a bucket that Luka and Galeshewe were holding out for was the equivalent of four shillings a bushel, the standard eight-gallon measure for grain. With very little grain available, because of the boycott, the price offered by storekeepers crept up to just over three shillings a bushel. It is not clear how long the boycott lasted, but when it finally broke later in the year, the market was so flooded with grain that the price fell by almost half.[29]

By that time, however, Luka was preparing for his departure to the Langeberg for what was to turn out to be the final chapter of his life.

---

[27] *UKNA*, CO 417/125, Report from Sgt. Taylor (BBP), 6 August 1894, enclosed in 'Confidential' of 29 August 1894; and *CAD*, NA 222, enclosures in CC Barkly, 24 July 1894.
[28] CO 417/125, Sgt. Taylor, Vryburg, 6 August 1894, in 'Confidential' of 29 August 1894.
[29] Shillington, *Colonisation*, p223, and p243, fn.39.

CHAPTER THIRTEEN

The Langeberg, rinderpest and rebellion
1895–1896

Although Luka's destination, the northern Langeberg, was the ancestral home of the Phuduhutŝwana Batlhaping, in recent decades its main occupants had been the Batlharo. The Batlharo claimed Bahurutshe ancestry in contrast to the Batlhaping's Barolong origins; but in broad terms the distinction was not that important. Batlhaping and Batlharo had been united as one in the days of Molehabangwe. And although that great confederation had subsequently disintegrated, Batlhaping and Batlharo treated each other like distant cousins – related, but following different *dikgosi*.

Land and cattle typical of the Langeberg, even today; dry and sandy, with wide open spaces.

The physical environment of the Langeberg was very different from that which Luka had been used to at Magogong. The latter possessed fertile soil and, in most years, high enough rainfall for extensive cultivation. The main problem for Luka had been lack of room for extensive cattle grazing. The Langeberg, by contrast, offered virtually opposite conditions. The soil was too sandy and average rainfall too slight for regular cultivation; but there were still wide open spaces for grazing large herds of cattle, provided that the cattle were managed carefully. The grass was of high quality, although sparse and prone to suffer quickly from over-grazing. Thus, successful cattle-raising in the Langeberg depended upon access to a wide range of cattle-posts and water that could be managed in rotation. There were plentiful springs in the *kloofs* (ravines) and foothills of the mountain range and those around the northwestern side made that area a particularly valuable grazing zone.

By the time of Luka's departure for the Langeberg, however, the free access to extensive grazing that he anticipated was already being restricted. In spite of this, a major attraction of the Langeberg must have been its remoteness from colonial centres of power. Earlier in the nineteenth century the mountain range had had a reputation as the home of raiding bandits, some of whom had troubled the Batlhaping at Dithakong and Kuruman, but by the late nineteenth century these bandits had been dispersed.

From his base at Puduhush in the northern Langeberg, *Kgosi* Makgolokwe had managed to keep his Batlharo from involvement in the Griqua rebellion that had raged through the southern Langeberg in 1878. A couple of years previously, Administrator Lanyon had offered Makgolokwe a present of a saddle and a bridle in exchange for the Batlharo *kgosi*'s surrender of some alleged Griqualand West stock thieves. As Makgolokwe's son Toto explained to Lanyon's envoy at the time, it was clear to the Batlharo that the British government wanted to treat them like Waterboer, that is, 'worm itself into their confidence and then deprive them of their country.'[1] Toto succeeded to the leadership of the Langeberg Batlharo on the death of his father in 1879 and he maintained this generally defiant and independent attitude right through the Crown Colony era. The colonial authorities of the 1880s and early '90s considered the Langeberg 'the most lawless part of the territory',[2] but from the Batswana perspective, it was far from lawless; it was merely remote from exploitative colonial law. And it was this, combined with Toto's defiant attitude that would have attracted a man like Luka Jantjie.

The Langeberg reserve, officially designated in 1886, was one of the largest blocks of reserve land in the colony. It enclosed the whole of the northern Langeberg: fifty kilometres north to south and stretching east of the mountain range by forty kilometres to the Gamogara River. The borders of the reserve, however, were not surveyed for several years and so for a while the Batlharo suffered little colonial interference. They were free to hunt and graze their cattle across the vast expanse of the northern Langeberg and Korannaberg and the lower Kuruman valley as far as the modern borders of southwest Botswana and Namibia.

[1] *CA*, GLW 97, Report of Sgt Heugh, December 1876.
[2] *UKNA*, CO 417/16, (No 366) Shippard, Vryburg, 23 September 1887.

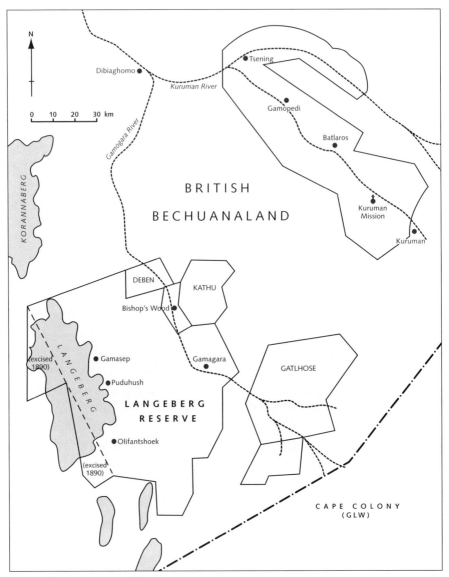

Map 16: The Langeberg, 1895.

When the surveyors did start work, in 1890, Toto's people tore down their stone beacons in the Korannaberg. Shippard himself had to come to Kuruman to meet Toto and explain to the Batlharo *kgosi* that the government was 'anxious to reserve to the Batlharo all land that they require and have been in the habit of using.'[3] Shippard, as usual, was not telling the

[3] CO 417/46 (No.710), Report of Surveyors, 21 June 1890; minutes of meeting between Shippard and Toto, 26 August 1890.

whole truth. Apart from denying the Batlharo access to the Korannaberg, he intended to exclude from the reserve the western foothills of the Langeberg itself. This land was blessed with many small springs and formed some of the best cattle-posts and arable ground in the reserve. Admitting that the Batlharo may lose a small, unspecified, part of their land, Shippard promised Toto an annual pension of £200 in compensation. This was enough to quieten the Batlharo for the time being, and the surveyors got back to work.

Lines were drawn on maps in 1891, but it was still a few years before it became clear to Toto (*above*) that the whole of the western edge of the Langeberg had been beaconed off for sale to white settlers. In late 1894, before any of this land had been sold, white colonists moved in and started evicting the Batlharo and others who were living there. Some of the evicted people were herdsmen from Toto's village of Puduhush on the eastern side of the mountain range; but many were recent immigrants from eastern Bechuanaland and from Griqualand West who had taken up residence at the springs along the western Langeberg. Whole villages, in all more than 150 houses, were destroyed, and 82 families were forced from their homes.[4]

The driving of ever more people into the confines of the reserve, however large, put severe pressure on the delicate ecosystem of the Langeberg. Not only was potential arable land very limited, but the reserve was becoming overstocked with cattle. As a result the grassland was in danger of being reduced to a barren wasteland once the Batlharo and Batlhaping herdsmen were denied the freedom to range widely in search of seasonal grazing.

The Batlharo, like the Batlhaping, were accomplished horsemen and as the evicted people and their livestock crowded into the reserve, Toto rode the 80 kilometres into Kuruman with a small body of armed men. The journey would have taken them most of a day. On arrival, Toto lodged a strong complaint with the magistrate about the illegal evictions. It was a time of rising tension in the colony. Rumour of impending rebellion was

4 *CA*, SGBB 30, Report of L Lanham, 3 December 1894.

Two photos of the Langeberg taken from Gamasep over 100 years apart: (a) shows massive denuding from over-grazing in 1897; (b) by 2009 the vegetation is green and vigorous.

widespread and it was known that Luka Jantjie was planning on moving to the Langeberg. Shippard decided he had better act swiftly and within weeks a special commission was set up to look into the Batlharo grievances.

As Toto explained to the three-man commission in January 1895, 'the water is too scarce in my location and there are too many people.'[5] But the commission did little to ease the tension in the Langeberg. They told the former residents of the western region that they could tend their crops for that season, but after harvest time in May they must leave. By then the government had started evicting residents from the Korannaberg and driving them too into the Langeberg reserve.

It was shortly after this that Toto heard of the impending annexation of British Bechuanaland by the Cape Colony.

The intensity of colonial ambitions that were pressing in on the southern Batswana in the 1890s needs to be seen in the context of Europe's 'scramble for Africa'. And in this respect it is useful to observe the options and strategy adopted by the northern Batswana (of present-day Botswana) in their attempts to combat colonial oppression.

In 1889 the British government had granted Cecil Rhodes' British South

[5] SGBB 79, Langeberg Reserve Commission, evidence of Toto, 16 January 1895.

Africa (BSA) Company a royal charter authorising it to colonise the territory of modern Zimbabwe: something that they carried out, by force, between 1890 and 1893. Critically for the northern Batswana, a clause in the BSA charter promised that the Bechuanaland Protectorate, that is, the territory north of British Bechuanaland, would in due course be transferred to the Company's rule.

By early 1895 the white settlers of the BSA Company considered they were in full control of the territory that they called 'Rhodesia', and Rhodes applied for the transfer to take place. The Batswana, led by Khama, of the Protectorate protested vigorously. When they had submitted to General Warren in 1885, they agreed to become a protectorate of the British queen. They understood this to mean protection from German (from Namibia) or Boer (from the Transvaal) colonisation, with minimal British interference in their internal affairs. So far, British administration and land seizures in the Protectorate had been minimal and the northern Batswana *dikgosi* were keen that it should remain so. They had never consented to being put at the mercy of a private company. They had seen the land and cattle confiscations and the brutality of Company rule in neighbouring Rhodesia and they wanted none of it. At the same time they were kept informed of events in the Crown Colony of British Bechuanaland and were aware of its impending transfer to the Cape Colony.

The three northern Batswana dikgosi, Bathoen, Khama and Sebele visit Shippard (seated on verandah) before heading to Cape Town to protest against the Protectorate's transfer to Rhodes' BSA Company. Standing, in white suit, Kwenaetsile, Bathoen's brother.

187

When their appeals to the British authorities in Cape Town were brushed aside, the three principal northern Batswana *dikgosi* – Khama of the Bangwato, Bathoen of the Bangwaketse and Sebele of the Bakwena – sailed to England to present their petition direct to the British government.[6] At first the Secretary of State for the Colonies, Joseph Chamberlain, refused to meet with them, so the *dikgosi* took their appeal direct to the British people. Aided by the missionary Revd Willoughby and a wide network of LMS sympathisers, the *dikgosi* toured the country making public speeches that revealed the true nature of BSA Company rule in Rhodesia. Their strategy whipped up such a public clamour that Chamberlain relented and came to terms with the *dikgosi*. In exchange for some concessions, which included colonial taxation, the transfer to the BSA Company was indefinitely postponed in November 1895. The Protectorate remained under British overrule, which allowed the *dikgosi* a certain level of internal freedom to run their own affairs and the country as a whole to become the independent Republic of Botswana seventy-one years later.

While the southern Batswana were well aware of these events, no such strategy was available to their *dikgosi* in their attempts to thwart the ambitions of Cecil Rhodes (*left*), Prime Minister of the Cape government since 1890. British Bechuanaland was a colony not a protectorate, and the distinction was important. A protectorate, at least theoretically, recognised certain rights of the indigenous population whom the colonising power was there to 'protect'. In a crown colony, on the other hand, the colonising power owned all the land and could deal with it, and its people, as it saw fit.

On 30 May 1895 Sir Hercules Robinson returned to South Africa as British High Commissioner and Governor of the Cape.[7] With his close political ally Cecil Rhodes now Prime Minister of the Cape, Robinson agreed the time was right to complete their plan of 1885 and transfer British Bechuanaland to the Cape Colony.[8] Montshiwa of the Barolong and Molala had got wind of this even before the arrival of Robinson, and in early May they petitioned

---

[6] Neil Parsons, *King Khama, Emperor Joe and the Great White Queen* (1998).

[7] Hercules Robinson had held the same dual position in 1881–89.

[8] For background and detail on the annexation, Shillington, *Colonisation*, pp183–6.

the British government against Cape annexation. They were particularly concerned about land security. Their fears of Cape rule were fed by the nearby example of Griqualand West where eviction from locations had reached a new intensity in April 1895.[9]

Luka Jantjie's signature does not appear on Molala's petition of 14 May, suggesting that he may already have moved away from the Taung reserve by then. He clearly had other things – his move to the Langeberg – on his mind and perhaps he recognised the futility of expecting fair consideration from the British government.

Luka Jantjie arrived in the Langeberg in August 1895. There is no direct evidence of exactly when he left Magogong for the 300 kilometre trek west-wards, but it would appear to have been several months earlier, probably in May or June.

At least one advance party from Magogong had arrived in the western region during 1894. In December a government land surveyor reported seeing about a hundred of Luka's people settled in a village on crown land in the lower Kuruman valley. They were some way downstream from the Lower Kuruman reserve at a place called Dibiaghomo. When questioned by Surveyor Theal, they said they were waiting for their *kgosi*, Luka Jantjie, whom they believed had bought two farms in the Korannaberg together with Galeshewe. In fact, no such transaction had at that stage formally taken place and Theal was concerned, not only about this illegal squatting, but also about the potential arrival of Luka Jantjie:

> I submit that this is a matter for enquiry as Lucas Jantjie's character is an unenvi-
> able one, and his presence in the Korannaberg will not improve the value of it,
> or the surrounding ground.[10]

Although a large number of people beyond Magogong looked to *Kgosi* Luka for protection and leadership, they did not all accompany him when he departed for the Langeberg in 1895. It is estimated that only two to three hundred people actually travelled with him at the time. This was about half the immediate settlement at Magogong.

The decision whether or not to follow their *kgosi* was left up to individuals

---

[9] For these Griqualand evictions: Shillington, 'Irrigation, Agriculture and the State…', in Beinart et al, *Plough to the Ground* (1986) pp321–25.

[10] CA, BCC 116 (8G), Report of Government Surveyor W M Theal, 20 December 1894.

and their motives would have been complex. Moving so far was a huge commitment. For Luka himself, besides seeking greater freedom from colonial interference, a large part of his decision to move was probably based upon the fact that he owned a considerable number of cattle. Additional healthy grazing land was always what he claimed he was looking for. Those who remained probably owned a lot less cattle individually than their *kgosi*. And now with his departure they would have slightly more room, for crops as well as for grazing.

Although Luka did not bring many people directly from Magogong to the Langeberg, a large number of people had been gathering there over the previous few years: from elsewhere in the Taung reserve, from Manyeding and from the locations of Griqualand West. Luka had made his final visit to Griqualand West in October 1894 and he would have told his people there about his intention to move to the relative freedom of the Langeberg.[11] The number of his direct adherents that eventually settled in the Langeberg by 1895–96 was in excess of a thousand.

Luka and his followers made their way slowly westwards during the months of June and July 1895. It was a major undertaking. They would have taken all their possessions with them, loaded high on numerous ox-wagons. Mounted on horseback and driving their cattle before them, they would have been lucky to have made as much as ten kilometres a day. Allowing for days of rest, and depending upon the route they chose, it probably took them three weeks to reach Manyeding, a journey of more than 120 kilometres. One can presume that they spent a few days at Manyeding, where Luka and his wife and sons took their leave of Olebile and other members of the wider family.

He probably called on the magistrate in Kuruman to see if anything had been done about buying him a farm. Scholtz, who had taken Luka's £115 for a farm in 1893, had been replaced as magistrate by a man called Bam and he would have had the job of telling Luka that the government had not set aside any farm for him. There does not appear to be any record of whether Luka ever got back his £115.

Luka then made his way down the Kuruman valley to Dibiaghomo to collect the advance party who had gathered there the previous year. By this time it was early July and Luka appears to have sent emissaries to *Kgosi* Toto to signal his intention to move into the Langeberg reserve.

In spite of the difficulties that Toto claimed to be having with overcrowding

---

[11] CA, NA 235, W Hall, 30 May 1896, enclosed in CC Barkly, 3 June 1896.

in the reserve, there is no sign that he showed any hesitation about welcoming Luka to the Langeberg. He probably saw it as an advantage to have such a senior and well-respected *kgosi* as an ally in the reserve. For the moment, however, Toto was fully engaged in dispute with the colonial authorities and Luka appears to have agreed to hold back his arrival for a few weeks.

Toto had been accused of evading the tax collectors and of refusing to answer a summons to Kuruman to explain himself.[12] By the end of June he had heard of the impending annexation to the Cape and of the other *dikgosi*'s petitions against it. He summoned a *pitso* of the Batlharo to discuss the matter, and on 11 July they drew up and signed a petition protesting against the proposed annexation. What they appear to have feared most was the likelihood of a general disarmament, as had happened in Griqualand West shortly before its annexation by the Cape. And as if to demonstrate their need for guns, Toto invited his people to a *letsholo* (a grand hunt) to take place the following week, on 22 July.

From his base in Kuruman, Magistrate Bam interpreted this as a show of force in preparation for rebellion, and the gunrunners of Griqualand West stepped up their export of up-to-date Martini-Henry rifles to the Batlharo in the Langeberg. Two troopers from the Bechuanaland Border Police (BBP), who made up the small police detachment at Gamagara in the reserve came into Kuruman two days later to report on the *letsholo*. Their report showed that Bam's fears had been greatly exaggerated. The police had been invited as observers to the hunt, which they were told was merely 'to kill wild dogs and jackals' that had been troubling the cattle. No more than forty men had turned up, only five of whom were armed. All was quiet at Toto's town of Puduhush[13] (*see map 16, p184*).

On 21 August 1895 *Kgosi* Luka Jantjie finally arrived in the Langeberg. Toto allocated him the valley of Twaai Kloof, near Gamasep to the north of Puduhush. A Motlharo named Twaai headed a small hamlet there, and next to Twaai's settlement, in the flat open space in front of the entrance to the valley, Luka and his people built a village of houses constructed in the traditional style. They were mostly small and simple houses, not the double-walled type typical of more established towns. In due course the village, which effectively incorporated Twaai's hamlet, became known as Gamasep. Although Luka maintained a house in this new village, in due course further houses

---

12 BCC 117, (144G), RM Bam, Kuruman, 21 July 1895.
13 *UKNA*, CO 879/43, Confidential Print 495, African (South), pp34–5, L/Cpl Bruce, Kuruman, 20 July 1895 and Gamogara, 29 July 1895.

were built within the valley itself and these collectively became known as the village of Derapedi, named after one of the side-kloofs near the head of the valley. As *kgosi*, Luka had at least one substantial house built for the privacy of himself and his family at the far, western end of the valley, some five kilometres from the entrance. Here the outline of the house foundations are still visible and nearby stands the remains of an ancient thorn tree (*see 27 in plate section*), which may well have acted as shade for the assembly of the village *kgotla*.

If Luka had hoped that his trek to the Langeberg would provide him with greater freedom from colonial oppression, he was soon to be disappointed. It was too late for that. His arrival stirred up local colonists, settlers and officials alike, torn as they were between fear of rebellion and excitement at the prospect of a final showdown with this recalcitrant 'native chief'. A few days after Luka's arrival a special patrol of the BBP was sent to investigate:

> At Gamocept [*sic*] (seven miles from Puduhush) there is a large staadt of Batlaping natives, the headman being 'Lucas Jantjie' and from all accounts this man appears to be a dangerous agitator. He arrived on the 21st instant from Taungs [*sic*], and should there be any disturbance I suspect he will be the prime mover in it.

The commanding officer of the BBP agreed with this opinion and wrote a covering minute on his subordinate's report:

> Instructions have been given for a close watch to be kept over Lucas Jantjie, who is known to be a dangerous man, but I do not anticipate any trouble from him.[14]

Clearly Luka's reputation for lack of deference towards colonial authority had gone before him, even to the furthest reaches of the Langeberg. The colonial net was tightening and the time would soon come when he would be expected, by followers and colonists alike, to live up to that reputation.

Luka himself steadfastly resisted the impulse to rebel. Yet, in spite of this, he still got dragged into a conflict that was not of his own making. In order to understand how this came about, one needs to leave Luka in the Langeberg for the time being and look firstly at the mindset of the colonists who were so determined on confrontation, and then at the actions of his fractious cousins in Phokwani. For it was they who provided the spark that land-hungry colonists so eagerly fanned into rebellion. And it was these Phokwani cousins that

---

[14] BCC 117, (No.191), Lt Drury, BBP, to Capt Walford, Adjutant BBP, Mafeking, 30 August 1895, and minute attached; also (without the minute) in Confidential Print 495, pp48–9.

brought their conflict with the colonists to Luka's refuge in the Langeberg, a refuge that was to be his last.

Rumour of rebellion was a regular feature of nineteenth-century colonial South Africa. Violence as a political tool was always available in the constant tension between ruler and ruled. Colonists took it for granted that if the colonised did not submit to them, then force could legitimately be employed. The violent seizure of Lobengula's Ndebele kingdom, in present-day western Zimbabwe, by Rhodes' British South Africa Company in December 1893 was a recent example. The deceptive ease of that campaign was an inspiration to colonists in Bechuanaland, many of whom had directly or indirectly been involved in the Company's pioneer column that had settled eastern Zimbabwe in 1890. Lobengula's Ndebele had been considered the most powerful independent African military force in southern Africa. And they had been swept aside by a small force of colonists armed with a handful of mounted Maxim machine guns.

The colonists of Bechuanaland looked to their own territory and saw plenty of good land still in African hands, and too many African leaders who had not yet bowed their heads to the whim of the white colonist. These colonists did not merely hear the rumour of rebellion: they actively sought it. 'Why are the natives in possession of the best ground in Bechuanaland?' a correspondent in the *Bechuanaland News* had asked in August 1893. Ignoring the importance of the Batswana's non-intensive grazing techniques, the writer went on to complain about the thousands of acres of good riverside land in the Kuruman reserve, hardly any of it cultivated:

> Take again the Matlaring and again the Mashowing to Madebing, splendid farms all and nearly all lying waste. Many [white] farmers would be glad of these farms and it would open out the country.[15]

Significantly these were the very places that suffered raids by white 'volunteers', supposedly acting against 'rebellious natives' following the outbreak of rebellion elsewhere in December 1896.

Even colonists in Griqualand West had their eyes on the land of the African reserves of British Bechuanaland. In September 1894 some of them had told a trooper of the border police that they had not yet heard of a planned rebellion in the Crown Colony, but they would be glad of one if it came:

---

[15] *Bechuanaland News*, Supplement, 12 August 1893.

The culling of cattle in 1896, to prevent the spread of the rinderpest epidemic, was devastating.

... as they would then be able to get hold of some valuable farms, as the natives have some of the best farms in Bechuanaland.[16]

May, shortly after harvest, was the month of the greatest expectation of rebellion. In 1894 the outgoing Magistrate Scholtz of Kuruman had heard that one was planned for May 1895. That month passed without rebellious incident while most political attention was turned towards Cape annexation, completed in November 1895.

At the same time all were aware of the encroaching crisis from the north as the highly contagious and deadly cattle disease of rinderpest made its way inexorably southwards.[17] The disease, thought to have originated in India, had entered East Africa in the 1880s in the wake of European conquest. It left devastation in its wake, especially among cattle-herding specialists like the Maasai in East Africa, many of whom succumbed to famine, their grazing lands left vulnerable to colonial encroachment. In 1895 the disease entered the Bechuanaland Protectorate (modern Botswana) and slaughtered ninety percent of the cattle in its path down the wagon road towards the south.

In April 1896 rinderpest crossed the Molopo River and entered the former Crown Colony of British Bechuanaland. Surely, thought eager colonists, this would provoke the southern Batswana to rebellion? The BBP were put on high alert as the government implemented a shooting policy of all cattle

[16] CO417/127, (Confidential of 22 September 1894) Report, Trooper Clear, 12 September 1894.
[17] C Van Onselen, 'Reactions to Rinderpest in South Africa, 1896–97', *JAH*, 1972, pp473–88.
Rinderpest was a viral cattle disease that has only recently been conquered in Africa.

Kgosi Molala meeting with his councillors and Assistant Magistrate Chalmers in Taung, 1896.

that came into contact with infected stock. This failed to halt the disease, but combined with a total restriction on the movement of cattle, it did slow its advance.

A few weeks previously the Ndebele in the new colony of Rhodesia had risen in rebellion against their oppressors, for reasons not wholly related to rinderpest. The first white settler was killed on 24 March 1896. Within a week a further 144 Rhodesian colonists were dead and the rest were holed up in defensive laagers in the main towns of the colony.

The Ndebele rising had put the Bechuanaland colonists on high alert. On 9 May the *Bechuanaland News* reported that a 'native uprising' in the colony was planned for 15 May. The white people of Vryburg district went into laager in the township, barricading the streets with wagons, and the Civil Commissioner issued them with 250 rifles and fifty carbines; but still no rebellion. According to later accounts from the Batlhaping of Phokwani, an uprising was in fact planned for May 1897, but events tipped the scales before that.

When rinderpest arrived in the Taung reserve on 31 August 1896, *Kgosi* Molala reluctantly accepted the logic of the shooting policy. Over the next month 2,000 of the Taung cattle were shot and compensation was duly paid. But by the end of the year all but 500 of the remaining 10,000 cattle belonging to Molala's people had died of the disease.[18]

[18] CA, BBNA, G19 – '97, C Brown, RM Taung, 14 January 1897.

Galeshewe, on the other hand had refused to countenance the shooting policy. He took the view that cattle had often died of disease in the past and he saw no reason to hasten the slaughter by shooting healthy cattle. In any case, Galeshewe suspected that the disease was deliberately being spread by the veterinary department in order to ruin the Batlhaping and force them into the colonial labour market. The disinfectant, Jeyes Fluid, that the vets carried with them was believed by many Batlhaping to be bottled rinderpest, such was the distrust of the colonial government. Thus Galeshewe refused to allow any colonial officials near his cattle although he resented the fact that Molala got compensation for those of his cattle that had been shot.[19] Partly because of resistance such as Galeshewe's, the shooting policy was abandoned on 8 October, although the ban on cattle movement remained in force.

About a week after the suspension of the shooting policy, the first Phokwani cattle succumbed to the disease. It spread rapidly through the herd and according to the resident Anglican missionary, Revd W H R Bevan:

> When the people saw that the loss of their cattle was imminent, they began to slaughter them freely; and for some six weeks or two months they lived upon fresh beef.

And what they could not eat they dried as *biltong* and stored in the roofs of their houses. As their cattle ran out Bevan reported that 'political disaffection … rapidly increased.'[20]

Galeshewe's cousin, Petlhu Petlhutsile, summoned a meeting at about this time and told the people that they must not allow any of their cattle to be killed by the Europeans. According to an eyewitness Petlhu said: 'If the Police shoot any of the cattle, shoot at the Police: for every ox that is shot, a policeman must be shot.'[21]

The Phokwani cattle had hitherto been free to roam within the southern part of the reserve, and that included the border farm Springbok Nek, bought by Galeshewe a few years previously. Now, with rinderpest killing more cattle every day, herdsmen kept their remaining healthy cattle on the move, intent on avoiding contact with infected animals. They had been accustomed to grazing them on some of the private border farms where normally their main concern was to avoid the cattle impounders. On 17 November a number of

---

[19] *LMS*, J Brown, 18 September 1896.
[20] *SPGA*, Annual Report 1897(B), W H R Bevan, Phokwani, 1 February 1897.
[21] *CA*, Crown Prosecutor's Office (CPO), Kimberley, No 3468, Sworn evidence of Klaas Kharebe, 23 September 1897.

Phokwani cattle, intentionally or otherwise, strayed onto the private farm called Trinidad. In straying out of the reserve they had broken the rinderpest restrictions on cattle movement, which still remained in force.

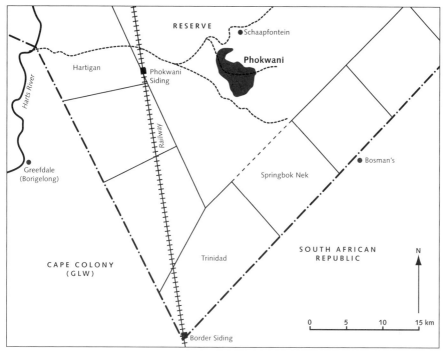

MAP 17: *The Phokwani Rebellion, December 1896.*

The trespassing cattle were rounded up by a couple of police who were stationed at Border Siding on the railway, about twenty kilometres from Phokwani, in the southern corner of the farm Trinidad. Petlhu followed them up, wanting to retrieve the cattle, though Galeshewe would not let him take armed men with him. Petlhu went on alone to the police post and protested that these animals had been exposed to the disease and had developed natural immunity – they were 'salted' – and so need not be shot. But his protest was in vain. All seventeen cattle were shot.[22]

Galeshewe complained to the magistrate in Taung who told him he only had himself to blame for not looking after his cattle. According to his own account, published a year later, Galeshewe 'let the thing remain so. I did not complain, as the law prevented me from so doing.'[23]

Petlhu, on the other hand, was not so reticent, and from this moment a

---

[22] AG 497, Statement of Gasebaatje, Kuruman, 19 February 1897, papers of Law Dept. Vryburg.
[23] *Cape Times*, 13 October 1897.

split appears to have emerged within the leadership. Petlhu (*below*) and his supporters favoured armed action to protect their cattle, while Galeshewe remained hesitant about taking any rash action that might bring the wrath of a colonial army down upon their heads. Galeshewe had already served eight years in prison for violent disorder; Petlhu (*below*) had not. Besides, the family had a history of suffering at the hands of well-armed white men. Petlhu's father, Petlhutsile, had died in the same war of 1858 that had seen the beheading of Galeshewe's grandfather, Gasebonwe.

Some of those who now sided with Petlhu took the view that he was the rightful *kgosi*, not Galeshewe. They argued that when Gasebonwe had succeeded *Kgosi* Mothibi in 1845, he had only been acting as regent for Petlhutsile, the infant son of his elder brother (*see family tree, page 16*). And it followed from this that after the death of both of them in 1858, Gasebonwe's son, Botlasitse, should have been acting as regent for Petlhutsile's son Petlhu who was then a child of less than ten. By this argument, therefore, Botlasitse was not *kgosi* in his own right.

If Botlasitse had indeed only been regent, then one would have expected Petlhu to become *kgosi* on Botlasitse's death in 1890. Petlhu, however, allowed the title to pass unchallenged to Botlasitse's son, Galeshewe, who was thus acknowledged as full *kgosi* without dispute.

The position between the two men was well known in colonial circles. Assistant Magistrate Chalmers of Taung believed that Petlhu, the 'true heir', had never been strong enough to assert his authority. Whether that was 'strong enough' in personal terms, in wealth or in popular support was not made clear.[24] But if Petlhu was indeed perceived within the *morafe* to be weak, then the succession through the descendants of Gasebonwe was in line with Batlhaping tradition. The strongest claimant succeeds, if he has clear majority support. Even now in this time of crisis in late 1896, Petlhu made no formal challenge to Galeshewe's position as *kgosi*. But he did assume the leadership of the 'war party' within Phokwani, that is, those who were prepared to take up arms in defence of their cattle. And in this he was backed by at least two

24 NA 244, Assistant RM Taungs, 15 January 1897, Report for 1896.

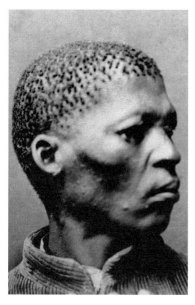

of Galeshewe's brothers, Gasebaatje (*left*) and Piet Moncho.

Since Galeshewe was not doing anything further about the cattle that had been shot, Petlhu led a group of armed men down to the Border Siding police post on 2 December and demanded compensation. He expected to get the same amount of money that Molala had received for his cattle that had been shot under the rinderpest regulations. On 6 December, rinderpest commissioner Robinson went to Phokwani to investigate; but he came to the same conclusion as that already expressed by Chalmers: the fault was Galeshewe's for failing to safeguard his cattle and no compensation would be paid. Petlhu's response to this was unrecorded, but the trader Arthur Blum, who was also the colonial field-cornet for Phokwani, reported that all was quiet within the town. Tension, however, was clearly rising, and Gasebaatje and Piet Moncho were seen to be going around with an armed body of a dozen men.[25]

A week or so later Galeshewe received a complaint from the police at Schaapfontein, five kilometres north of Phokwani, that there were a lot of diseased dead cattle around that needed burial. Galeshewe sent a group of men to bury them, but because they were not Phokwani cattle, they buried them where they had fallen, close to the Schaapfontein police station. According to Galeshewe, the police took exception to this and drove the men away:

> They sent a message to Taung saying that I was causing trouble with the police. I then saw that war was coming.[26]

On 21 December 1896, as the people of Phokwani armed themselves in anticipation of a colonial incursion, Sergeant Ward of the Schaapfontein police came into the town to remonstrate with Galeshewe. Ward reported that a hundred 'armed natives' threatened him, whereas Galeshewe recalled that it was Ward, who was armed, who did the threatening.

[25] NA 244, ARM Taungs, 15 January 1897.
[26] *Cape Times*, Galeshewe's affidavit, 13 October 1897.

Galeshewe went to seek the advice of his friend Piet Bosman, the field-cornet for Christiana in the Transvaal, who lived on a farm just across the border, about ten kilometres from Phokwani. The Anglo-Boer tension that was to lead to outright war in 1899 was already riding high in 1896. It was less than a year since the infamous Jameson Raid, part of a failed plot by Cape premier Cecil Rhodes to stage a *coup d'état* in the Transvaal's gold-mining city of Johannesburg. Bosman, therefore, as a loyal burgher (Boer citizen) of the Transvaal, urged Galeshewe to fight the British. He sold him some gunpowder and percussion caps, but would not sell him guns. When Galeshewe protested that this was not enough to fight the British, Bosman promised that once the Batlhaping had started the war, Bosman would bring plenty of Boers to their assistance.[27]

The ruined shell of a store in Phokwani in 1978, probably Arthur Blum's.

Meanwhile in Phokwani Petlhu's 'war party' was gaining strength. On 23 December they heard that a senior police officer, Inspector Elliot from Vryburg, had arrived at Schaapfontein police post, about half an hour's horse-ride north of Phokwani. Arthur Blum had gone to meet him. Petlhu and Gasebaatje and about thirty armed men barred their progress into the town. Petlhu held the inspector's horse while, according to Elliot, Gasebaatje said that the time for talking had passed. Arthur Blum, who knew the men better, recalled in his trial evidence the following September that it was Petlhu who said: 'It is too late to talk now: now it is time to fight.'[28] Whoever spoke the words, Elliot and his escort of six armed and mounted police were turned back while Blum was allowed through.

Arthur Blum recalled that as he returned to Phokwani the road was lined

27 *Cape Times*, Galeshewe's affidavit, 13 October 1897.
28 CA, CPO, Kimberley, No 3468, Sworn evidence of Arthur Blum, 23 September 1897.

with armed Africans 'who took up their position at the sound of a bugle.' Later that day Blum was allowed to put his wife, his sister-in-law and their children into a cart that was eventually allowed out of Phokwani. But a group of armed men surrounded the store and Blum, his brother Alphonse, their two white assistants Bolton and Waldt, and a Khoesan servant named John Ruisloo were effectively held prisoner.

The following day, 24 December, Petlhu, Telekela (Fred) Gasebonwe (*top left*), Matingwe (*below left*) and others came to see them. Petlhu told Arthur Blum that he was to leave and take a message to Inspector Elliot: 'Tell the Government' recalled Blum, 'that if they would take the Police away and give them their country back, they would not fire on them; but if they sent Police they would fire on them.' Blum duly left and reported to Inspector Elliot. The Batlhaping had made it clear that no other white men would be allowed in or out of Phokwani. This meant that Alphonse Blum, Bolton, Waldt and Ruisloo were effectively held as hostages against a possible colonial attack.

Phokwani Siding station in 1920, where colonial troops arrived on 24 and 25 December, 1897.

From his church on the south side of town Revd Bevan watched anxiously and prayed for peace. The colonial authorities, however, had already decided that the Batlhaping stance on 23 December amounted to an act of rebellion, one that they would crush by force, regardless of any hostages. Magistrate Chalmers got Molala and Kgantlapane to agree not to become involved while Elliot ordered police reinforcements to Schaapfontein. At the same time

201

volunteer regiments were called up in Kimberley and they arrived by rail at Phokwani Siding over the next couple of days, bringing with them two seven-pound field guns.[29]

Mounted colonial troops getting ready for the fight at Phokwani in late December, 1896.

Inspector Elliot's initial advance from Schaapfontein on the evening of the 23rd came under fire and he withdrew. Reinforced overnight, he tried again on the 24th, but this too was driven back by about a hundred Batlhaping sharpshooters hidden in the hills.[30] That evening, Elliot joined up most of his Border Police with the Kimberley volunteers down at Phokwani Siding where they all spent Christmas Day picnicking and excitedly anticipating the fight to come. The Kimberley Commissioner of Police, who was in command as the senior officer present, sent an ultimatum to Galeshewe, demanding his immediate surrender.

Galeshewe, who had been at Bosman's on the 23rd, had returned to Phokwani on the 24th. But that evening after the skirmishing at Schaapfontein he went back to Bosman, expecting him to provide the help that he had promised once the fighting had started. The following day, Christmas Day, a messenger arrived with the Commissioner's ultimatum: 'Tell Galeshewe, if he does not come tonight, tomorrow morning we shall shoot him.' Galeshewe did not give himself up that night.

While the colonial forces had been enjoying their Christmas festivities at Phokwani Siding, the Batlhaping had been organising their defences. The town of Phokwani lay about ten kilometres east of the railway siding and Petlhu, Gasebaatje and Piet Moncho set up their first line of defence about three kilometres from the railway. A number of the people positioned here possessed breech-loading rifles, some of them Martini-Henry repeaters. Other defenders, armed mostly with muzzle-loading hunting guns, spread themselves around the hills on the approach to Phokwani. They spent much

---

29 NA 244, ARM Taungs, 15 January 1897.
30 *Diamond Fields Advertiser*, 3 April 1897, evidence at trial of Phokwani prisoners, 31 March 1897.

The Diamond Field Horse parading at Phokwani. Note the journalist, Tiller, arms akimbo, on left.

of the day casting their own lead bullets in preparation for the fight the next day. In all, the Batlhaping had about two to three hundred fighting men with good hunting experience and an unknown number of others of less experience who were pressed into service. Facing them was a force of 186 BBP troops and about 300 volunteers from various Kimberley regiments, including the Diamond Fields Artillery.

About mid-morning on Saturday 26 December the colonial forces opened their attack with a short artillery barrage before making a general advance. As they approached the first line of defence, they came under heavy fire. Not wanting to suffer any casualties on their own side, they halted their advance and pounded the Phokwani hills with the artillery. The defenders stood their ground for some hours, strengthened by the arrival in the afternoon of fifty of Luka's people from Magogong, all of them mounted and well armed. But gradually they began to suffer casualties and had to pull back to the hills closer to the town. By the end of the day they had succeeding in preventing the colonists from entering the town, but at the cost of about twenty lives. Among those killed was Galeshewe's brother, Piet Moncho.

When Petlhu saw that Moncho had been killed, he rode into the town in a fury and ordered that the hostages should be executed. This seems to be the consensus of the evidence later presented in court, although Petlhu himself denied that he was even present.[31] It is possible that, having pronounced sentence, he left the immediate scene, leaving his subordinates to do the actual killing. There was some pleading and argument about the fate of the hostages and some conflicting evidence emerged as to exactly who did what; but in the end all four of the hostages, including the servant, were killed. Revd Bevan was left untouched.

[31] *Diamond Fields Advertiser*, 9 and 10 February 1898.

Galeshewe had spent Christmas night at Bosman's, trying to persuade him to help. In an affidavit sworn some eight months later he recalled:

> The next morning [the 26th] I heard shots in the direction of Phokwani. I said to Bosman, 'You hear they are firing at my people. You have already promised to help me. Do so now.' Bosman replied, 'I am ready with my people.' He at once gave me six packets of cartridges, three bags of powder and four boxes of caps. He said, 'Go home now. I will go and get my people together.'[32]

Galeshewe arrived back in Phokwani after the main fight was over, about three o'clock the following morning, Sunday 27 December. In the first light of dawn he saw the body of his brother Piet and those of the four hostages. He then summoned the people together and addressed them from horseback. He berated them for killing the hostages and looting the store. He could not understand how they dared to do this. He accused the people of getting him into trouble and ordered them to return all the stolen goods to the store. According to an eyewitness, Abraham Thebe, a man called out that the *makgowa* were approaching and Galeshewe said: 'We cannot now do otherwise: let us go to the fight.' But as Galeshewe led them forward, some of them armed, some not, they found that the *makgowa* were already in control of the surrounding hills. Realising that further resistance was hopeless, Galeshewe ordered a general retreat and evacuation of the town.[33] Galeshewe himself then takes up the story:

> My people with myself fled in the direction of Bosman's. When I arrived there I saw a number of Transvaal Burghers, I think about 200, standing on the boundary line of the Transvaal. All were armed. I said to Bosman, 'You see the war has commenced.' Bosman answered, 'If one bullet crosses the boundary we are ready to retaliate.' I was at Bosman's house when one of my people came with a message to me, saying the Englishmen wanted to know if I would make peace. Bosman at once said, 'You may make peace.'
>
> I said, 'You have got me into trouble, and now you refuse to help me.' I told my people to return to their houses. I said to Bosman, 'I myself am afraid to return to my station.' Bosman took two guns from me, two long Martini-Henry rifles, and two new saddles. He was going to take my horses, but they were over the boundary line, so he left them. I left Bosman's place and [went] direct to the Langeberg.[34]

32 *Cape Times*, 13 October 1897.
33 CPO, Kimberley, No 3468, Sworn evidence of Abraham Thebe, 23 September 1897.
34 *Cape Times*, 13 October 1897.

...arading the prisoners at Phokwani; note the journalist, E H Tiller, again, standing with hat and pipe (centre, front row).

...he burnt out stadt, Phokwani. Note the modern implements, including iron pots, zinc buckets, a plough (right) ...nd a hoe (foreground) – needed now that rinderpest had destroyed the oxen. Below, guns captured at Phokwani, ...cludes ten Enfields (c.1860), and three Martini-Henry breech-loading cavalry carbines (foreground).

Store owner and field-cornet Arthur Blum standing (centre) with the journalist E H Tiller at the graves of his brother, Alphonse, 'foully murdered' along with their assistants, Bolton and Waldt, also 'foully murdered', but not with their murdered Khoesan servant, John Ruisloo.

The graves of Alphonse Blum, Bolton and Waldt photographed in 1978.

That Sunday, 27 December 1896, the government forces entered Phokwani and finding it deserted they looted it and burnt it to the ground. All houses were destroyed except for a few that Revd Bevan had managed to save for some of his congregation.[35] The troops spent the rest of the day scouring the surrounding area for survivors and collected several hundred civilians, mainly women and children, who were sheltering in the hills.

They also rounded up all the livestock they could find in the southern quarter of the reserve. The government had already decided that punishment for rebellion should start with the complete forfeiture of the whole of the Phokwani section of the reserve, including the private farms that Galeshewe had purchased.

Charles G H Bell (*opposite*), the Civil Commissioner of Barkly West was appointed as commissioner in charge of land confiscation and sale of loot. He arrived at Schaapfontein on Thursday 31 December and straight away began organising the auction of the Phokwani loot, the proceeds of which would be shared among the Kimberley volunteers. The first sale took place

---

[35] *SPGA*, Annual Report 1897 (B), Revd Bevan, Phokwani, 1 February 1897.

GALISHIWE'S REVOLT.

ANOTHER TRADER MURDERED.

ALARMING RUMOURS.

BATTARO'S TRIBE IN REVOLT.

VRYBURG, JANUARY 5.—[Reuter's Agency.]—Alarming news reached Vryburg

on 6 January 1897, raising £835 from 2,025 sheep and goats, £122 from 33 horses, and £20 from three donkeys. Significantly, after the devastations of rinderpest, there were only fifty cattle and these raised £217. About forty wagons were sold later.[36]

The murder in the New Year of a white trader in the Mashowing reserve (*Cape Times report above*), 150 kilometres northwest of Phokwani gave eager colonists their excuse to extend the rebellion and achieve the land grab that they so much desired. And with many of the leading survivors of the Phokwani rebellion heading westwards, the focus of the drama shifted 200 kilometres due west to the Langeberg, the newly adopted home of Luka Jantjie.

Triumphant: eight white officers and two journalists (in civilian clothes and both smoking pipes) relax after the Phokwani action; the journalist E H Tiller is standing on the left.

[36] *Bechuanaland News*, 2 Jan 1897; and *CAD*, AG 478, C G H Bell, CC Barkly West, 19 Jan 1897.

CHAPTER FOURTEEN

The gathering storm
January–April, 1897

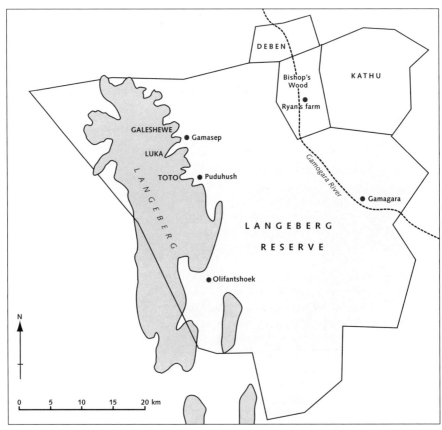

MAP 18: The Langeberg, January–February 1897, showing the location of the three dikgosi.

News of the fighting at Phokwani would have reached Kuruman within a few days. And from Kuruman it was about ten hours' horse-ride to the Langeberg, so we can assume that somebody in Kuruman would have kept Luka and Toto fully informed of events within about four days of their unfolding in the east of the country. Thus, by the beginning of January 1897 they would have learned that the surviving leaders of Phokwani were heading west, and that spelt trouble. But worse was to come, for now the colonists' blood was up, they eagerly sought an extension of the 'rebellion', and they found it in the Mashowing reserve to the east of Kuruman, still a long way from Luka's new home in the Langeberg.

The Mashowing River, like most of those north of the Vaal, is seasonal. It only flows after heavy rain; but its valley, which stretches northwest from Dithakong and away from the Ghaap plateau, is punctuated by numerous springs. Here the grass is sweet and it is good country for raising cattle. Much of the land to the north of the river had been set aside as an African reserve, while that to the south was sold to white colonists. As indicated in the previous chapter, there were plenty of colonists who cast envious eyes on the African land across the river, feeling it was wasted in 'native' hands. But there were also plenty of Africans who resented the presence of white colonists on their historic hunting and grazing lands south of the reserve.

On the evening of Sunday 3 January 1897, a group of about thirty mounted Africans came to the store of Charles Robinson at Rapwani near Kabogo in the Mashowing River reserve and demanded all the money in the house. When Robinson would not give it to them, they took him round the back, out of sight of his wife, and shot him. The next day they came back and ransacked the store. The identity of the raiders was never formally established, which suggests that Mrs Robinson, who survived the attack, did not know them.

LEFT: A photo of headman Mampe from Kabogo who took Charles Robinson's widow and child on a four-hour horse-ride to safety. Two of his sons died later, at the battle of Kabogo. Note the heavy greatcoat to keep out the cold at night, the repeating rifle and the bandolier of bullets. Typical of the better-equipped defenders in the Langeberg fighting.

Kabogo lies about thirty kilometres northwest of Dithakong (*see maps 14 and 22*) and this section of the reserve fell under the authority of the ageing Bogosin (Gert) Mahura and his son, Kgalagadi. When they heard of the attack, Kgalagadi went to Rapwani and brought Mrs Robinson and her child into Kabogo, providing a horse for the widow and carrying the child on his own horse. He then had them escorted by the local headman, Mampe, to the safety of a nearby white-owned farm.[1] In a touching report it was said that Mampe, on leaving Mrs Robinson, paid her two shillings; he said that it was what he owed her late husband for goods bought at his store.

Although the Batlhaping leadership appears not to have sanctioned the attack on Robinson, Kgalagadi probably knew who they were. He probably also guessed that, following on so closely from the Phokwani conflict, the government would treat Robinson's murder as an extension of the Phokwani rebellion; and, as in the case of Galeshewe, he and his father would be held responsible. Kgalagadi knew the indiscriminate way the government had attacked the residents of Phokwani and he may have figured that their best defence was to precipitate a wider conflict. Whatever his thinking, on 5 or 6 January Kgalagadi led a raid on a nearby farm owned by a colonist named Cullinan. They came away with about 250 mules and donkeys.

As Kgalagadi might have guessed, colonists throughout the region reacted promptly to the raid. With the Phokwani rebellion so easily crushed and the Phokwani reserve already cleared in anticipation of confiscation, there were plenty of colonists only too eager to act against further 'rebels' in Bechuanaland. Indeed, the day after the Phokwani fight, sixty local Burghers (Boer residents of the colony) had ridden into Vryburg in response to a government call for 'service against natives.' They had had to be paid off on that occasion because it looked for the moment as though there was no further fighting to be had. But, ominously, the day before the Robinson murder, the *Bechuanaland News* had returned to its earlier theme:

> There are at Takoon (Dithakong), Motito (Bothithong) and down the
> Mashowing about 2,000 huts, whereas at Phokwani there were but 800, so in
> the event of a native outbreak the southwest would require watching.[2]

When news of Robinson's murder reached Vryburg on 5 January, colonists believed that at last they had the 'native war' they had been anticipating for so long. Captain C G Dennison (*opposite*), a longstanding Vryburg resident

---

[1] *Bechuanaland News,* 9 January 1897
[2] *Bechuanaland News,* 2 January 1897

who had served in a number of volunteer regiments in 'native wars' elsewhere in South Africa, gathered a group of fifty white volunteers and led them to Dithakong where he met with *Kgosi* Gasimere and others on Friday 8 January. They could find no evidence from those at Dithakong as to exactly who had killed Robinson, but there seemed no doubt that Kgalagadi had been responsible for the raid on Cullinan's farm.[3] While Dennison waited for reinforcements, he was joined by a group of thirty-five Burghers from the nearby white settlement of Geluk. On Tuesday 12 January Dennison moved his force up to Cullinan's farm, bordering the reserve, and that night they were joined by eighty Cape Mounted Police.

On Friday 15 January the colonial force arrived on the south bank of the Mashowing, opposite Kabogo. Bogosin and Kgalagadi were poorly prepared for a fight. Fewer than a hundred men had guns and nearly all of those were muzzle-loaders. By contrast, the colonists were all mounted and armed with breech-loading rifles. Bogosin, probably aged about eighty, appears to have left Kabogo at this stage, accompanied by most of the women and children. Kgalagadi was left in charge and he positioned his men on a small hill to the north of the town.

From this position Kgalagadi and his men would have seen Dennison's messenger enter the town to demand Bogosin's immediate surrender. But the town was empty, so there was no reply. They then saw Dennison's volunteers and the Geluk Burghers circle round across the river to the north side of town, leaving the Cape Mounted Police on the south side. As the enemy came within range, some of the Batlhaping opened fire. The colonists responded by charging the hill, firing as they came. The defenders held their ground for some minutes, but when Kgalagadi and some others were killed, their resolve faltered. They beat a hasty retreat down the valley, pausing every so often to reload and fire a shot. It was a one-sided contest and no colonists were killed. Some of the victors took possession of Kabogo and started looting and burning the town while a group of Burghers continued the pursuit of the fleeing Batlhaping, riding down and killing up to forty of them, including

[3] AG 522, Minutes of meeting, 'Takoon', 8 January 1897, in RM Vryburg, 11 January 1897.

A contemporary newspaper sketch of the fight at Kabogo, at which Kgosi Kgalagadi lost his life.

several headmen. Two sons of headman Mampe were killed. It appears that Mampe was not involved in the fighting. Indeed, it was he who identified the bodies of Kgalagadi and his two sons on the battlefield, burying his *kgosi* before tending to his sons.

For the rest of that day and most of the next the Burghers and other volunteers rode on down the reserve, burning villages and firing on their residents indiscriminately.[4] In effect, they cleared the reserve, driving its residents to flee towards the Langeberg. Captain Dennison was pleased to note that when it came to fighting Africans both Boers and Britons were on the same side. He made a point of praising the actions of the Afrikaner Burghers, especially the way that they had so readily responded to the 'call to arms against our common foe.'[5]

Luka and Toto would have learned of the Robinson murder on the Mashowing within a few days of its happening. And as soon as they heard of the assembly of a colonial force at Dithakong bent on attacking Kabogo, they must have known that refugees from Mashowing would head towards the Langeberg. When that happened, they would become embroiled in the conflict, whether they liked it or not.

4 *Bechuanaland News*, 23 January 1897.
5 AG 522, Report of Capt Dennison, enclosed in CC Vryburg, 22 January 1897.

A Cape cart: the kind of vehicle Luka used to drive to Kuruman; often with two horses, sometimes with one; note the retractable hood to protect driver and passengers from sun and rain.

Toto hurried off to Batlaros to co-ordinate policy with his Batlharo cousins on the Lower Kuruman and in Huening Vlei, a remote Batlharo reserve to the north of the Mashowing (*see map 14, p163*). The Batlharo decided they would try and avoid conflict with the government, so *dikgosi* Shoeping of Tsineng and Mongale of Gamopedi escorted two colonial traders and several other white settlers into the safety of Kuruman. They received little thanks from Magistrate Bam who demanded that they immediately go out and shoot or arrest the Robinson killers. Shoeping and Mongale refused, pointing out that it would mean war, and the Batlharo did not want war.

On 14 January Toto himself went into Kuruman from Batlaros to reassure Bam of his loyalty and that of all the Batlharo. Bam was not inclined to trust him and insisted on accompanying Toto back to Batlaros to hear a general affirmation of loyalty from the Batlharo leadership who had assembled there. Even then Bam was not convinced.[6] Unable to achieve more, Toto set off on his return journey to the Langeberg, unaware that as he rode home the attack on Kabogo was taking place and several hundred refugees were being driven in his direction.

Luka too wanted to avoid war, if that was at all possible. His first imperative was to assure the colonial government of his peaceful intent. As Toto rode home on 15 January, Luka loaded up his Cape cart and set off for the two or three day round trip to Kuruman. The *kgosi* was probably accompanied by a companion and the hood would have been up to shelter them from the intense heat, for there had been very little rain that summer. But events were converging; as Luka made his way to Kuruman, Dennison was launching his attack on Kabogo.

[6] AG 522, Bam to Law Dept., Kuruman, 12 January; Letter from Bareki, Huening Vlei, enclosed in CC Vryburg, 1 February; and NA 242, Bam, Kuruman, 20 January 1897.

A late nineteenth century photo of Kuruman Mission station.

The Batlhaping *kgosi* would have arrived in Kuruman that Friday evening to find the town strangely deserted. Although it had been established in 1886 close to the 'Eye' (spring) of the Kuruman, most of the buildings were of wood and corrugated iron. These would not have offered much protection in the event of a general uprising such as the Rhodesian colonists had experienced the previous year, so as soon as he heard of Robinson's murder and the raid on Cullinan's farm, Magistrate Bam had ordered all government officials and colonial traders to move to the more secure stone-built premises of the London Missionary Society's Moffat Institute, opposite the old mission station several kilometres downstream.

For Luka Jantjie, the crowding of the white people into the Moffat Institute must have been ominously reminiscent of 1878. It would have reminded him just how dangerously volatile colonial volunteer forces could be once their blood was up. It is not clear where *Kgosi* Luka slept that Friday night, but somebody would have been only too pleased to have offered him accommodation. By the following morning the township and the mission station were abuzz with news and rumours of the attack on Kabogo; all the more reason for Luka to report to the magistrate. Bam, however, was already prejudiced against him. A few days before the *kgosi*'s visit to Kuruman, Bam had reported to the authorities in Cape Town that although he had no evidence against Luka Jantjie, 'I certainly am of opinion that he is not to be trusted.'[7] One cannot help thinking that the feeling was probably mutual.

On Saturday 16 January *Kgosi* Luka met with Magistrate Bam behind the thick walls of the Moffat Institute. According to Bam, Luka 'expressed grief at being suspected of harbouring a desire to assist his relatives against the Government.'[8] Bam clearly did not believe him and in his report to central government he urged the complete disarmament of all Africans in British Bechuanaland. Luka made his way back to the Langeberg with a heavy heart. He must have been aware that the government was already linking him to the

7 AG 522, Bam to Law Dept., Kuruman, 12 January 1897.
8 NA 242, Bam, Kuruman, 20 January 1897.

rebellious activities of his relatives. And even as he drove his cart home, those relatives were approaching the Langeberg and fulfilling the government's expectations.

≈ ≈ ≈

Initially, after the colonial occupation of Phokwani, Galeshewe and other members of the Phokwani leadership had gone to the outskirts of Taung where Molala had offered them protection. They stayed there a few days and on at least one occasion Molala met with them. He gave them food, rifles and ammunition and advised them to move on. For the sake of his own safety, after they had gone, Molala mounted an artificial attempt to 'capture' them, but their tracks had gone cold and they escaped, presumably as Molala had intended.[9]

At this point the main leaders split up. Gasebaatje, Galeshewe's brother, headed northwest, hoping to reach Namibia, but in early February he was captured somewhere near Kuruman. Galeshewe had more luck. He made his way directly west, through Luka's old *morafe* to the south of Kuruman. He and his ten companions received help on the way and no one betrayed them, despite the fact that there was a £500 bounty placed on Galeshewe, a huge sum in those days,[10] and probably intended to encourage colonial bounty hunters. It was unlikely to have been paid to any African who betrayed him. Galeshewe arrived in the Langeberg towards the end of January 1897. His party included his young uncle, Morebonoke, also known as Andries Gasebonwe. They met with Toto, who sent them up into the steep-sided mountain ravine known as Gamasep Kloof, immediately to the north of Luka's valley of Twaai Kloof.

The steep slope of Gamasep Kloof.

Petlhu, meanwhile, made his way independently to the Langeberg. He seems to have been shunned by Galeshewe, who presumably blamed him for what he saw as the unnecessary murder of the Phokwani hostages. Petlhu appears to have been hidden somewhere within Toto's part of the Langeberg.

[9] AG 497, Statement of Gasebaatje, Kuruman, 19 February 1897, papers of Law Dept. Vryburg.
[10] *Bechuanaland News*, 30 January 1897.

Gamasep village

Gamasep Kloof

View towards Galeshewe's hideout in Gamasep Kloof (centre) with Gamasep village at entrance to it.

By this time a considerable body of people had accumulated in the reserve. Some came as fighting men from the Mashowing and elsewhere, some even from Griqualand West. Others came simply to escape the vengeful violence of colonial volunteers. Most of these new arrivals looked to Luka for protection and leadership.

As Luka and Toto pondered what to do, government forces were assembling at Kuruman. Cape Town had been informed of the Robinson murder by telegram from Vryburg, and on 8 January Captain Harry V Woon of the Cape Mounted Rifles (CMR) was ordered north with a squadron of one hundred mounted men, armed with repeating rifles and a Maxim machine gun, wheel-mounted and horse-drawn for quick deployment. Their orders were to arrest Galeshewe and the alleged murderers of Blum and Robinson. They reached Vryburg by rail on 14 January and ten days later they arrived in Kuruman. Hitherto the local Cape Mounted Police had not felt they had sufficient numbers to do any more than man the defences of the Moffat Institute. But now, in Woon's CMR, Magistrate Bam considered he had a force capable of arresting Galeshewe. He sent a message to the Langeberg, summoning Luka and Toto to Kuruman.

The two *dikgosi* arrived in their separate Cape carts and met with Bam and Woon on Saturday 30 January. Once again they protested their loyalty. They also said that they knew nothing of the whereabouts of Galeshewe. They were clearly trying not to get involved, and although they would not betray Galeshewe, having seen the strength of the CMR squadron, they probably hoped that the Phokwani *kgosi* would give himself up.

On arrival back in the Langeberg, Luka and Toto summoned a general meeting to discuss the situation. On the whole the Batlharo did not want to get involved. They felt this was a Batlhaping problem and Toto probably spoke for most of his people when he said he thought they should give Galeshewe up. At least a hundred of the Batlhaping, many from the Mashowing and some from among Luka's people, felt they should fight to defend Galeshewe.

Luka appears to have fallen between the two. He hoped he would not have to fight, but there was no way that he would give up Galeshewe against his will. His experience of the colonial mentality, however, must have told him he would not have much option. He had already moved as far west as he could. There was nowhere else for him to go. If the colonists insisted on confrontation then he would have to stand and fight.

On Friday 12 February Captain Harry Woon (*above*) brought his squadron of one hundred mounted men to Bishop's Wood, a farm on the Gamogara River on the eastern edge of the reserve. He was accompanied by Bam, the Kuruman magistrate. Bishop's Wood was owned by John Ryan, a Justice of the Peace for Kuruman district. That morning Ryan had gone over to a general meeting that was being held at Luka's village of Gamasep, in the flat land in front of the mouth of Luka's valley. In the two years that Luka had been there, the population of Gamasep had grown to about four hundred people, all living in the traditional round style of house. There was just one mud-brick rectangular building with an iron roof and that was the village store, owned and run by a trader named Frank Pearce. Other members of Luka's community had built houses up the length of the Twaai valley.

Toto had come over from Puduhush for this second meeting. Galeshewe's uncle, Morebonoke, was also there. He had come down from Galeshewe's hiding place and he taunted Toto by saying that if the Batlharo wanted to give Galeshewe up, they should go up into the mountain and get him. But Toto agreed with Ryan that this was probably a trap. Anybody venturing up there would probably be shot.[11]

At this point Luka asked to have the meeting postponed for twenty-four hours. When he did not reappear at the appointed time the following morning, Ryan and Toto waited for him throughout that intensely hot day. As the sun sank behind the Langeberg and Gamasep village was cast into the cool shadow of the evening, Luka finally appeared. He looked grim. He was tired and suffering from a fever. He told Toto and Ryan that he felt as though he had 'risen from the dead!' He had been up into the mountain and had seen Galeshewe, who told him that if he had come with anyone else he would have been shot. Galeshewe had gone on to say that he was no child, and did not want any sweets; he had ten cartridges, nine of which he would fire at anyone who came for him and with the tenth he would shoot himself as he would

---

[11] AG 497, Sworn affidavit of John Ryan, Postmasberg, 17 March, 1897.

not be taken alive. He had asked Luka to tell the government that he was not responsible for the death of Blum in Phokwani for he had been at Bosman's in the Transvaal at the time. Gesturing towards the mountain behind him, Luka said to Toto: 'There is Galeshewe. Go and take him you Batlharo.'

Toto took this as an invitation to go and get himself shot! He talked it over with Ryan. They concluded that the Batlhaping would probably assist Galeshewe. And that would mean war. Toto advised Ryan to leave his farm and take all his livestock with him. That night, while Ryan reported back to Woon and Bam at Bishop's Wood, Toto went to see Luka whose fever had worsened. Toto asked him to give Galeshewe up, and Luka responded: 'I have come from death and I will not go again.'[12]

The next morning Woon and Bam and some of the CMR squadron came up to Pearce's store at Gamasep and Toto rode over from Puduhush with thirty to forty of his men. Luka sent a message to say that he was sick and could not attend; but this did not satisfy Woon. Although he had never been in this part of the country before, Woon had heard of Luka Jantjie, who was believed in colonial circles to be the most dangerous man in Bechuanaland, and he was determined to meet him. Pearce pointed out Luka's house, over near the mouth of the valley. Woon went up to the house and demanded that he come out. After a while the *kgosi* appeared and, with Pearce interpreting, he said that he was sick. Just emerged from his sickbed, this was not the elegantly-dressed man of his portrait (*4 in plate section*), but Woon's description of him clearly indicates a prejudiced mind:

> He was one of the most forbidding looking scoundrels of a native I have ever seen, and appeared to me to be more like a Hottentot than ever. I was certain he intended mischief by the insolent manner in which he answered Pearce, but the latter did not deem it advisable to interpret for my benefit, and only repeated that Luka was sick.

Elsewhere in his memoir, Woon described Luka as having 'a strain of Hottentot in his appearance, with the usual vicious, cunning look peculiar to that race.'[13]

'Hottentot' was a derogatory term in common colonial usage at the time. It referred to the indigenous Khoesan of the Cape, from whom the Korana of the Orange River region were descended. Woon was writing his memoirs a decade after the event, and considering what was to happen over the next

[12] AG 497, Ryan's affidavit.
[13] H V Woon, *Twenty-Five Years Soldiering in South Africa* (1909), pp335, 345.

A view from the road of the Gamasep mountain landscape, where the first battle was fought.

six months, it was in his interests to besmirch Luka's reputation as much as possible, in advance of the first colonial assault on the Langeberg. As for Luka's supposed 'insolent manner', this may have referred to the *kgosi's* failure to cast his eyes down and show the 'respect' that colonists assumed to be their due.

Woon withdrew to his main camp at Bishop's Wood farm and planned an assault on Galeshewe's hiding place the following day. During the night, up to a hundred of Luka's men moved over to the Gamasep mountain spur that commanded the northern approach to Gamasep Kloof, the steep and narrow valley in which Galeshewe had taken refuge (*see map 18, p208*). Luka himself commanded the slopes of the shorter, southern spur that separated his valley from Gamasep Kloof. This spur was to earn the name 'Fighting Kopje' because of its determined defence by Luka Jantjie in the months ahead. Now, during the hours of darkness, Luka's men prepared their defences. The steep slopes of these eastern-facing mountain spurs had their own natural defensive system, a series of trenches and protruding rocks that marked the natural contour lines of the mountain. The Batlhaping were able to adapt these natural defences into a multitude of stone schanzes, loose stone walls behind which one could hide and return fire through small gaps between the stones.

The following day, Monday 15 February, Woon sent forty mounted men of the CMR under the command of Lieutenant Curtis, to effect the arrest of Galeshewe. But they soon found the terrain was too rocky for their horses and they were forced to dismount before making their final approach. And as they neared the entrance to Gamasep Kloof they came under heavy fire from the mountainside. The Batlhaping were experienced hunters and the accuracy of their fire was too much for the attacking column who lost two men killed, Lieutenant Hopkins and Private Venn, and several wounded. Woon brought up the Maxim gun, and raked the mountain with machine gun fire while Hopkins was hastily buried beneath a tree at the back of Pearce's store. Venn's burial is not mentioned, but both Hopkins and Venn were later reburied in

A heroic representation of Captain Harry Woon's failure to take Gamasep Mountain, 15 February 1897.

Graveyard for European troops beneath Gamasep Kopje; (inset) Lt Hopkins killed near Pearce's store on 15 February and (right) Lt Harris who died 7 April; (below) twelve-pounder colonial guns at Bishops Wood.

a special graveyard below Gamasep Kopje (*left*) near the modern road that runs up the eastern flank of the Langeberg. That afternoon the CMR withdrew to Bishop's Wood farm, carrying their wounded and abandoning fifteen horses that had been captured by the defenders. It is not known how many of the Batlhaping were killed, but there were certainly some casualties. Woon's 'Basuto spies' informed him that Luka and Toto had joined Galeshewe and that they were planning a night attack on his Bishop's Wood base, so that evening Woon decamped and withdrew his entire force to Kuruman.

In his cabled report to Cape Town, Captain Woon claimed that he had come under attack by 600 men – probably an exaggeration – and that Luka Jantjie and all the Batlhaping of the Langeberg were in rebellion against the government. Woon's withdrawal to Kuruman and urgent request for reinforcements was to turn the simple pursuit and arrest of Galeshewe into the first, abortive stage of a major campaign. It was perhaps why Woon became the subject of rumour and criticism by fellow officers, which culminated in his dismissal from the service after the campaign was over.[14]

In the meantime, Woon's report sealed Luka's fate. It confirmed the government's assumptions. It provided them with the excuse that they wanted to clear the Langeberg as a stronghold of 'native lawlessness', to close down and confiscate the whole of the Langeberg reserve, and to initiate a final confrontation with that most defiantly obdurate and unwilling colonial subject, *Kgosi* Luka Jantjie.

Luka, on the other hand, still stuck to the view that he and his people had only been acting in self-defence. So far as he was concerned, he had still not rebelled against the government. At the same time he must have been well aware that the government would not share this view.

The Batlhaping as a whole, both within the Langeberg and beyond, hailed this first battle of Gamasep as a great victory. They had driven off a strong attack and had captured fifteen horses, Lieutenant Hopkins' horse and saddle being taken by Galeshewe. It was Luka, however, with a reputation stretching back some twenty years, who was credited with having directed the defence. Galeshewe had fewer than ten men with him, and there must have been at least a hundred involved in the defence of Gamasep Kloof. They would have been Luka's people and it is unlikely that they would have been so well organised without his direct leadership.

[14] *South Africa*, November 1897, p280, reporting dismissal of Capt Woon on 15 Sept 1897.

Although he would undoubtedly have preferred to avoid direct involvement, Luka may have taken the view that Galeshewe was technically his senior *kgosi* and he was therefore bound by duty to protect the man. He may also have felt a sense of loyalty towards Galeshewe in the face of what had now become a common enemy. There were those within his family, however, who did not take such a magnanimous view. According to a story related by Batlhaping witnesses to Corporal Paul of the government's Cape Native Contingent six weeks later, Luka's wife, Masehoro, in particular was very hostile to Galeshewe. Referring to him publicly by the Afrikaans insult *'braniekte schaap'* ('scabby sheep'), she blamed him personally for bringing all this trouble upon her family. In particular, she blamed him for the death of her eldest son, who was apparently one of the Batlhaping casualties in that 15 February battle at Gamasep.[15] The use of Afrikaans may have been a translation by Corporal Paul of a Setswana equivalent, or it is possible that Luka's wife, probably not an Afrikaans-speaker herself, knew that Galeshewe spoke Afrikaans and deliberately used this Afrikaans insult, for its power or appropriateness.

Although the row between Luka's wife and Galeshewe was reported to members of the government's troops some time after the event,[16] there is no reason to doubt the story. It should be noted that it was her eldest son who had died. Luka's eldest son, by his first marriage, Dikare (*left*), also known as Dokwe, was still alive. Indeed, he lived until 1912. But from the time of that casualty in February 1897, Galeshewe moved away from proximity to Luka's family. With his small band of close followers from Phokwani, he sought refuge among the hills and steep valleys, known as *kopjes* and *kloofs*, to the north of Gamasep.

In the days following the fight at Gamasep some of Galeshewe's men threatened to loot Frank Pearce's store. Luka prevented them, but he was not sure how long he would be able to guarantee Pearce's safety. He and Toto advised the storekeeper to move

---

[15] Intelligence from Corporal Paul, Cape Native Contingent, *Cape Argus Weekly*, 9 June 1897.
[16] *Cape Argus Weekly*, 9 June 1897.

Pearce's store near Gamasep village with Gamasep Mount behind; photo by Private Miller in 1897.

into Kuruman; and he was accompanied there by the two policemen who were normally stationed at Gamagara in the reserve. Luka then took on the responsibility of looking after Pearce's store and a couple of weeks later, in early March, he sent a man in to Pearce at Kuruman with £3 17s 6d for goods that he had sold at the store, with a detailed account of the expenditure.[17] At the same time Toto sent a message to Magistrate Bam expressing his continued loyalty to the government, but added that if attacked, he would defend himself. As an indication of his confidence, Toto sent in his gun for repair, indicating that the cost could be recovered from his monthly allowance from the government of £16, for which he also applied.[18]

It would have been clear to anyone in Kuruman at the time that the government was in no mood to listen to expressions of loyalty from the Langeberg *dikgosi*. Government preparations for a general attack on the Langeberg had gone too far for that. Lieutenant-Colonel Edmund H Dalgety was already in Kimberley, having been summoned from Natal to head a major field force of up to a thousand men, a third of them to be locally-raised volunteers and the rest to come from regular Cape volunteer regiments.[19] By the time that Luka and Toto's messengers came into Kuruman, the local volunteers had already started assembling, and they were eager to take the fight to the Langeberg, or anywhere else in the vicinity.

Barely a week later, on Sunday 14 March, Captain J W Fuller led a force of 110 Vryburg Mounted Volunteers and 55 Geluk Burghers in a raid on Gamopedi, forty kilometres down the valley, northwest from Kuruman. There is some dispute as to what prompted the attack. Captain Fuller claimed

---

[17] A pound contained 20 shillings (s) and a shilling 12 pence (d). Commonly sold items in these rural stores included coffee, sugar, tobacco and gunpowder. Wholesale prices for these items in Kimberley ranged between one and two shillings per pound weight (0.45kg) (*DFA,* market reports). Retail prices in Pearce's store may have been double that.

[18] *Bechuanaland News,* 13 March 1897. *Kgosi* Toto had received this allowance since 1890.

[19] Edmund Henry Dalgety was a regular British army officer who commanded the Cape Mounted Rifles (CMR) in the Colony. He had fought against Sigcau in Pondoland (1896).

The mounted patrol under Captain Fuller beginning their unprovoked attack on Gamopedi.

it was a punitive raid against 'rebels' who had stolen cattle from 'loyal natives'.[20] Special Commissioner Charles Bell, however, noted confidentially that it was supposed to have been 'a Burgher patrol sent down to gather green food for the horses out of Mongale's lands.'[21] Thus it appears to have been a regular patrol that ran amok. After a night-march down the valley, Fuller's men attacked Gamopedi at sunrise, killing at least forty, among them *Kgosi* Mongale. They burnt the town to the ground and drove the survivors off towards the Langeberg.[22] In summing up the exploit, Captain Woon recalled that Fuller's volunteers:

> …paid a visit to the natives living along the Kuruman River, in the hope of meeting with opposition. Catching sight of some natives, they opened fire on them; the natives, who were not armed, fled; the column returned having succeeded in driving the natives off into Langeberg and in shooting one of the Burghers in their excitement.[23]

The missionary Revd John Tom Brown was scathing in his condemnation:

> Their general idea on these occasions seems to be that they are out to shoot [natives], and that it is difficult if not pedantic, to make such distinctions as that between loyals and rebels.[24]

The Gamopedi affair indicated clearly to the people in the Langeberg that the government would no longer listen to reason. Luka sent a further £24 to

[20] *CPP*, G3 – '98, Capt. Fuller's Report, enclosed in Lt. Col. Dalgety's Report on the Bechuanaland Rebellion, 1897, pp5–6.

[21] *CA*, PMO 254, Compensatory claim No.58, unsigned pencilled note in distinctive handwriting of C G H Bell.

[22] See also *Bechuanaland News*, 20 March 1897.

[23] Woon, *Twenty-Five Years*, p356.

[24] *Cape Times*, 14 October 1897, J T Brown interview.

Pearce in Kuruman, for goods that he had sold in the store, but it was probably more an indication of his responsibility to Pearce as an individual than any attempt to persuade government of his peaceful intent.

In the weeks following the Gamopedi attack, Luka and Toto began preparing for the defence of the Langeberg and the prospects of a long-term siege. Rinderpest had not yet reached this far west and so there were still large herds of cattle to be protected from colonial looters. Milch cows were grazed close to the east-facing valleys so that they could be withdrawn to the protection of the kloofs in the event of an attack. A number of sheep and goats were slaughtered and their meat dried for storage, while the majority of the Batlhaping cattle were driven northwards, across the Molopo and into what was then the Bechuanaland Protectorate (modern Botswana).[25] Toto kept several thousand Batlharo cattle within the Puduhush region, while most of the rest of the Batlharo cattle were grazed between Puduhush and Olifantshoek, fifteen kilometres to the south.

Within the Langeberg itself, stone wall defences, known as schanzes, (*above*) were built and strengthened throughout the east facing hills. Toto, too, though not expecting to be attacked, strengthened the defences of the hills protecting Puduhush. There was some water to be had from a small number of springs within the kloofs of the Langeberg, so in the event of a siege, the defenders would have just about enough fresh water to drink.

The Langeberg defences were completed just in time, for by the end of March, Colonel Dalgety had a force of about nine hundred men assembled in Kuruman, half of them locally-recruited groups of volunteers, eager for loot and an easy fight like that at Gamopedi. The rest were from regular volunteer regiments that had come up from Cape Town and the eastern Cape.

[25] *Bechuanaland News*, 27 March 1897.

~ ~ ~

Within days of Woon's rebuff at Gamasep, rumours had reached Cape Town that Luka Jantjie was boasting of a great victory, and that the 'natives of Bechuanaland' were crowing that their *kgosi* had thrashed the CMR 'like dogs.'[26] The rumours, swiftly followed by receipt of Woon's official report on 18 February, enthused members of Cape Town's colonial volunteer regiments and prompted Sir Gordon Sprigg's government into action.

Volunteers poured into their regimental headquarters and within days a force of more than three hundred men was ready to depart for the north. They consisted of 120 Duke of Edinburgh's Own Volunteer Regiment (DEOVR), popularly known as the 'Dukes', under Lt-Colonel William A Spence; a further 80 Mounted Dukes under Captain Frank Johnson; and 60 Cape Town Highlanders (CTH) under Captain James S Searle. It was to be the CTH's first experience of real battle. These men were to be accompanied by 17 officers of the Medical Corps and 42 gunners of the Cape Field Artillery (CFA), with three brand new twelve-pounder field guns and a further Maxim gun to add to the one already at Kuruman with Woon's CMR.

On the morning of 24 February these 'gallant volunteers' were seen off from Cape Town amid much jubilation, with bands playing as they marched down Adderley Street to the newly-constructed platform of the city's railway station. Trains in those days were not very efficient – this one broke down at least once – and it took them three days to reach Kimberley. There they were joined by further volunteers from eastern Cape regiments and Johnson's Mounted Dukes who had gone on ahead.

At Kimberley, Dalgety took overall command and decided that the quickest way to get to base camp at Kuruman, was to march directly north-west via Barkly West and Daniel's Kuil, rather than take the train due north to Vryburg and march west from there. It was the first occasion of several that Dalgety was to learn that he, and his political masters, seriously underestimated the difficulty of the task ahead of them.

The marching men, their wagons and artillery – with two old seven-pounders added at Kimberley – stretched for one and a half kilometres and their journey of two hundred kilometres took them ten days instead of the six that Dalgety had estimated. Fed by rumours from Kuruman, they expected a rebel attack on their column at any moment.

---

[26] Neil Orpen, *The Cape Town Highlanders, 1885–1970*, p21; *Cape Times*, 20 February 1897.

The colonial troops: from top left, Lt Col William Spence, Capt James Searle (with the all-important water cart), Capt Frank Johnson, a tented camp at Gamasep Kopje used as a hospital, Cape Native Police (not all troops were white), Searle with his motley troop of Cape Town Highlanders.

Dalgety (*left*) finally pitched camp just north of Kuruman Mission on 14 March, the day that Fuller's Vryburg and Geluk Volunteers were carelessly spreading rebellion by their unprovoked attack on the inhabitants of Gamopedi. Dalgety then had two further weeks in Kuruman waiting for wagons, water-carts and general supplies from Vryburg. The Volunteers relieved their boredom by staging a sports day on 26 March. Dalgety finally moved out on 30 March, leaving eighty-five men and one seven-pounder to guard the camp at Kuruman.

The following day he reached Kathu, forty kilometres southwest of Kuruman, just off the modern road to Olifantshoek. Kathu was a small African reserve bordering the far larger Langeberg reserve, and Dalgety's troops easily scattered its residents, driving them in the direction of the Langeberg. Dalgety then ordered a detachment of local Burgher Volunteers to dig for water at Kathu, while he himself led his remaining force of 800 men closer to the Langeberg.

During the first few days of April, Dalgety assembled his main force at Ryan's farm, Bishop's Wood, the nearest point to the Langeberg where he could get a reliable supply of water. He was to become very dependent upon this sole source of water to fill his water-carts, for there was no other water to be had between Ryan's and the Langeberg, apart from within the mountain range itself. A major part of Dalgety's strategy, therefore, was to seize control of the water supply in one of the kloofs of the Langeberg, which loomed twenty kilometres away on the western horizon.

From their vantage points on the mountain spurs of Gamasep, Twaai Kloof and Puduhush, the Batlhaping and Batlharo of the Langeberg would have seen the columns of dust that announced the arrival of the colonial troops at Ryan's farm. It was the signal for the people of the villages of Gamasep and Puduhush to abandon their homes and withdraw into the kloofs of the mountain range. On the hills and in the valleys they watched and waited, knowing that the time for talking was long passed.

CHAPTER FIFTEEN

The battle for the Langeberg
April–May, 1897

The defenders of the Langeberg did not have long to wait. On Monday 5 April they observed Dalgety's force approach from the direction of Ryan's farm and set up a forward base camp out on the plain, several kilometres short of Gamasep village. This much would have been plainly visible from the commanding heights of the eastern Langeberg.

What may not have been clear to the defenders was the exact composition of the government force, especially the heavy artillery and Maxim machine guns. In support Dalgety had brought up eight ox-wagons loaded with supplies and seven horse-drawn water-carts. He also had a heliograph (a mirror-flashing telegraph) detachment to communicate with Kuruman, where a team of despatch riders linked him to the electronic telegraph office in Vryburg. He was thus only two days from direct communication with the Secretary of Defence in Cape Town. Urgent preparations were already underway to bring the telegraph to Kuruman, to be completed in June.

Government troops were also accompanied by correspondents from most of the major colonial newspapers; these tended to have their own riders to carry reports from the front to Kuruman where they made use of government despatch riders to get their reports to Vryburg. Reports from the Langeberg could be in the Cape newspapers in less than a week. And with volunteer regiments assembled from as far away as Cape Town and the eastern Cape, the Bechuanaland expedition was treated as a major news event. Further north, the 'Rhodesian' settlers were still struggling to overcome Mashona resistance, and newspaper editors knew that their colonial readers were keen to read of a gallant victory over their 'common foe'.[1]

---

[1] The following description of the events in the Langeberg is based partly upon Colonel Dalgety's official reports: *Cape Parliamentary Paper*, G3–'98, *The Bechuanaland Rebellion* as well as reports in contemporary newspapers: *Bechuanaland News, Diamond Fields Advertiser, Cape Times* and *Cape Argus*. The latter two often printed fuller reports in their *Weekly* editions. The Batswana viewpoint is drawn from prisoner interviews and trial evidence published in the newspapers as well as newspaper reports from Basotho auxiliaries in the Cape forces who talked to the defenders during pauses in the fighting.

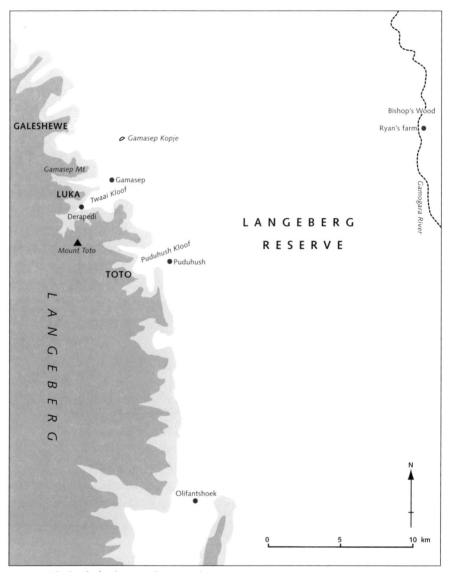

GALESHEWE

Gamasep Kopje

Gamasep Mt

● Gamasep

LUKA *Twaai Kloof*

● Derapedi

▲

Mount Toto *Puduhush Kloof*

● Puduhush

TOTO

L
A
N
G
E
B
E
R
G

Bishop's Wood

Ryan's farm ●

L A N G E B E R G

R E S E R V E

Gamogara River

● Olifantshoek

N

0   5   10 km

Map 19: The battle for the Langeberg, April–May 1897.

Dalgety had 750 fighting men under his command. He had left about fifty men, mostly local volunteers whom he did not trust with frontline work, to guard the base camp and his only source of water at Ryan's farm, and he decided he could afford to divide the remainder of his forces for the forthcoming attack. He did not have any direct experience of the Langeberg and his plan had been drawn up in Kuruman, based upon a 'mud-pie' model of the mountain range made by Captain Johnson of the Mounted Dukes.

Dalgety viewed the mountain range in front of him as a vast east-facing amphitheatre. The southern flank, led up to Toto Peak, while the northern flank stretched westwards from Gamasep Mountain to enclose the upper (western) end of Luka's Twaai Kloof and join the other at Toto Peak. Dividing the amphitheatre was a central mountain spur that separated Luka's valley from the steep ravine of Gamasep Kloof. The eastern head of this spur was in due course to become known as 'Fighting Kopje'.

Assuming that Galeshewe was still within these kloofs, Dalgety's plan was to encircle the Batlhaping by occupying the mountains of both northern and southern flanks of the Langeberg 'amphitheatre' that he saw before him. He anticipated that once he had achieved this, he would be able to gain control of at least one spring of fresh water within the kloofs. From that commanding position he could, he believed, force a defeat or surrender. Dalgety had already, on the previous day, Sunday, sent off Commandant Wessels with 130 Vryburg Volunteers to circle the north end of the Langeberg range and position themselves there, in order to cut off any attempted escape from the western side.

It is clear from this plan that the government was no longer interested in simply capturing Galeshewe. They were now out to get Luka Jantjie as well. For too long he had been a thorn in the government's side, and his repulse of Woon's attack on Gamasep in February gave the colonists the excuse they craved to ignore his protestations of loyalty and to declare him a rebel and the object of a full-scale government assault.

Dalgety kept 300 men under his direct command, ready to reinforce his attacking columns with supplies and artillery as needed. The remainder were divided for a two-pronged attack on the mountain. Captain Woon, commanding 145 men of the CMR (Cape Mounted Rifles) and First City Brigade was ordered to seize Gamasep Mountain; while Captain Johnson was to take 170 of the Dukes and Native Contingent to the southern mountain promontory that separated Luka's valley from Puduhush. Johnson's orders were to reach the mountain peaks that overlooked the head of Luka's valley and capture the fresh springs hidden within its kloofs. According to Johnson the Geluk Burghers assigned to accompany him refused to do so because they were 'too old and fat'.[2]

The two columns felt their way slowly forward during the night, reaching a point near the modern road by about 2 a.m. Now only the village of Gamasep separated them from the base of the mountain. They dismounted and linked

---

[2] Frank Johnson, *Great Days* (1940), p245.

horses and Johnson's Dukes headed south on foot while Woon's CMR waited for first light. Ahead of them the ground was covered by a network of thorn fences that protected the gardens and houses of the village and they would need a bit of light to make their way through these dense barriers.

At the first sign of the approach of the enemy from Ryan's on the Monday morning, Luka had ordered the evacuation of his village of Gamasep and the withdrawal of the people and their remaining livestock into the protection of Twaai valley and its adjoining kloofs. He anticipated a dawn attack on Gamasep Kloof (*see the panoramic view of the battlefield from Gamasep Kopje below*). This was where Galeshewe had been hiding at the time of the last attempt to 'arrest' him, in February. In fact, however, ever since the first fight at Gamasep, when he had fallen out with Luka's family, Galeshewe had been hiding out with only seven of his own men among the network of kloofs and kopjes to the north of Gamasep. He was to complain later that Luka had not provided him with enough men to defend his mountain hideout.[3]

Luka placed the majority of his men on Gamasep and the central spur, above the village and overlooking the approach to Gamasep Kloof. He had no particular defences on the southern mountain flank that was the target of Johnson's column. As the setting sun cast its shadow over the deserted village, the defenders settled down behind their mountain schanzes to keep watch through the night. Below them Gamasep village was in complete darkness and no fires were lit within the mountains that night.

About 4 a.m. on Tuesday 6 April, just as the sky was beginning to lighten in the east, the government troops were heard making their way through the village. A man who had remained in one of the houses near the foot of the mountain fired his rifle at a moving shadow in the half light and thus set off the alarm. A few minutes later a volley rang out from the mountain stronghold and the advancing troops were halted in their tracks.

Although some of the Batlhaping owned breech-loading rifles and a few, like Luka himself, owned repeating rifles, the vast majority were armed with muzzle-loading hunting guns. They were, after all, hunters, not soldiers. They were not trained in the discipline of reloading and firing in regular, alternating volleys. Thus, after that initial volley, the practice was to 'fire at will', at any target within range. Nevertheless, they were experienced hunters and the accuracy of their fire astonished their opponents.

---

[3] *Cape Argus Weekly*, 9 June 1897.

Colonial troops posing with their big gun dug in at Gamasep Kopje.

At about 6 a.m., with the sun rising into the eyes of the defenders, Woon ordered his men forward. As they approached, however, they came under such intense fire that they were forced to fling themselves into a gully about a hundred metres short of the mountain. Unable to extricate themselves, an officer was sent back to alert Colonel Dalgety who in the meantime had moved up his remaining force to establish a forward base camp where the two columns had left their horses. Dalgety moved forward to the village and ordered a Maxim gun to rake the mountain to cover the withdrawal of Woon's men from the gully. While this was happening, up to a hundred Batlhaping rode out from behind Gamasep and attacked Dalgety's relatively unguarded camp. Dalgety, however, was able to scatter them with his Maxim, and the Batlhaping rode back to the cover of the mountain.

Frustrated by the lack of success of Woon's attack on Gamasep, Dalgety ordered the twelve-pounders to destroy the village (*see above contemporary sketch of the bombardment*). The first shot blew out a window of Pearce's store. Subsequent firing flattened a number of houses. Colonel Spence was then sent in to burn and raze the village to the ground. The Batlhaping, however, kept up such an intense fire on the men in the village that they were forced to retire. Dalgety had noticed that the most intense and accurate fire had come from the central spur, earning it the name of 'Fighting Kopje', and he ordered a general advance on that position. But it too was beaten back.

The artillery pounded the mountains for most of the rest of the day (*opposite*), while various attempts were made to advance in skirmishing order towards the Batlhaping positions. The whizzing sound of incoming shells must have been frightening at first, but the defenders soon got used to them and learned to duck behind their schanzes. As some of the Batlhaping defenders later recalled:

> When we were all seated quietly we would hear a great noise and then the whizz of the big bullet as it passed over our heads.[4]

The seven-pounders were old and unreliable, their shells tended to explode while in the air and so they could not be reliably fired over the heads of advancing men. The twelve-pounders were the newest and largest field guns ever to have been deployed in warfare in South Africa, but even they were ineffective when used against opponents that were scattered across a huge expanse of mountainside. As noted already by General Wolseley, the author of *The Soldier's Pocket Book*, carried by every officer in the Bechuanaland Field Force, 'The effect of artillery … was absurdly small on an enemy not fighting in large or formed bodies.'[5] The guns were, however, good at destroying villages.

Despite the efforts of the artillery, the Batlhaping maintained a steady rate of fire across a broad front. Although the colonists kept praising the accuracy of the Batlhaping fire and a considerable number of the white volunteers were hit, they were almost all struck in the legs rather than the torso. It leads one to wonder whether the Batlhaping marksmen might have been trying to immobilise rather than to kill. Only one man died on the government side, a Lieutenant Harris of the Dukes, and he was hit by a ricochet that entered his thigh and passed up into the centre of his body.

It is impossible to estimate the extent of Batlhaping casualties. Government sources claimed they were 'very heavy', but they had no way of knowing. What is sure is that there was no serious diminution in the general rate of fire from the mountain schanzes protecting Gamasep Kloof, and this suggests that casualties may have been light.

The whereabouts of Luka throughout the fight is unknown, but he probably positioned himself on Fighting Kopje where he would have had a good view over a broad front as well as to his left across Gamasep Kloof to the Gamasep spur. At about two o'clock in the afternoon he received reports

[4] *Cape Times*, 28 September 1897, prisoners interviewed by F R Thompson.
[5] Quoted in *The Cape Town Highlanders*, p22.

from Twaai Kloof behind him that government troops – that is, Johnson's column – had been spotted on the southern mountain, across the valley to his right. They appeared to be making their way to a position that would overlook Derapedi village in the western head of the valley where the *kgosi* himself had established his private family home. Luka immediately ordered men across the valley and up the mountain to block the enemy's advance and prevent them reaching their destination.

Johnson's column of 170 men had encountered no opposition in the predawn light as they climbed the mountain spur on the south side of Twaai Kloof. But they were ill-prepared for the difficulty of the task that faced them. The mountain side was deceptively steep, there was no path to follow and the ground was covered by a mass of sharp rocks and large boulders. The compact column soon became a long straggling line. Each man carried just one water-bottle and in the heat of the morning they began to run short of water. Individuals stopped to rest and some even turned back. By early afternoon, at about the time that they were first spotted by Luka's men, Johnson was nearing a position below Mount Toto; but he had a mere twenty-six men left; and he was unable to signal back to base camp as the man who carried the heliograph had dropped out earlier. He had not even made it to the crest of the ridge.

At about this time Johnson began to come under fire from the Batlhaping who were climbing up the mountain towards him. There was no way he could get down into the kloof to collect fresh water and very soon he was in serious danger of being surrounded and cut off. He tried building a defensive wall to protect his men; but as Batlhaping sharpshooters crept ever closer, he was forced to retire up the mountain to the peak of Mount Toto behind him. From there, under cover of darkness, Johnson slowly withdrew his men in an easterly direction along the highest point of the Toto spur, with Batlhaping riflemen his constant pursuers.

As the sun began to set behind the peaks of the Langeberg, Luka must have realised that the first day's fight had gone in his favour. Even though they had suffered the loss of their village of Gamasep, his people had successfully beaten back a force that, on paper, was far superior to their own. Desultory firing could be heard from behind him as some of his more intrepid mountain fighters drove the remnant of Johnson's force back onto Mount Toto. From their positions on the mountain spurs, Luka and his fellow leaders could see Dalgety's forces being withdrawn to their new forward base camp close to Gamasep Kopje, a small steep hill that stands by the modern road, directly opposite Gamasep Kloof. And as Dalgety's men formed a laager of

wagons and artillery in the fading light, Luka sent out men to harass the laager from both north and south. They were held off by the Maxim machine guns (*left*), but throughout the night the Batlhaping patrolled within range of the laager, firing the occasional shot and hoping to capture some horses. Dalgety had sent his water-carts back to Ryan's farm so that they could re-supply the column the next morning, and these too came under attack, causing water to leak, from a contingent of Batlharo that Toto had sent out from Puduhush.

Luka's strategy throughout seems to have been firstly for his men to defend themselves from direct attack, secondly to suffer the minimum number of casualties – there was to be no reckless risk to life or limb – and thirdly to issue forth and harass the enemy wherever a weak point was observed. It is probable that in this way he hoped to make an outright colonial victory impossible, and to harass the enemy sufficiently so that they would give up and move away. Perhaps then it might be possible to negotiate a way out of this impasse. If the first day was anything to go by, the strategy, if that is what it was, seems to have been working.

A sure sign of the colonists' failure to bring their opponents to heel was their wanton destruction of defenceless villages. Commandant Wessels and his Vryburg Volunteers enjoyed several days of looting and destroying villages and burning crops around the northern and western extremities of the mountain range.

The following morning, Wednesday 7 April, Dalgety sent Colonel Spence

Dalgety's forward base camp protected by one twelve pounder and a fast-firing Maxim gun.

forward with Captain Searle of the Cape Town Highlanders and a Maxim gun to cover the descent of Johnson's bedraggled column. While they were at it, across the valley and out of range of Fighting Kopje, they burnt Twaai's homestead and up to sixty houses within the entrance to the valley. Not to be left out of the 'sport', Dalgety brought up two twelve-pounders and began firing westwards up the narrowing valley where many of the refugees were hiding. Luka's men on Fighting Kopje, however, turned a withering fire on the gun contingents, forcing them to withdraw after firing only three rounds each. The Batlhaping were scornful of the colonists' efforts:

They burned the huts, but never came to where we were. They were afraid of us.[6]

The following day Dalgety retired the bulk of his force to Ryan's farm to recuperate, leaving a small contingent with one twelve-pounder and a Maxim gun to guard the forward base camp at Gamasep Kopje. From 'Camp Ryan' Dalgety reported back to his superiors in Cape Town, remarking in his own defence of his apparent failure: 'I consider the Langeberg to be the strongest position I have ever seen.'[7]

As Dalgety wrote his report ensconced in Ryan's farm on the night of 10 April, the camp at Gamasep Kopje came under serious attack. The Maxim gun ultimately ensured that the camp was not overrun, but the attack was maintained through several hours of darkness. Clearly Luka and the Batswana of the Langeberg were not satisfied with merely holding off government attacks. They were prepared to take the fight to the enemy and hopefully drive him away from the Langeberg altogether.

A few days later, however, a more effective enemy than Dalgety's army attacked the Langeberg. Rinderpest finally arrived in the reserve, probably brought from Kuruman by Dalgety's transport oxen. The remaining cattle that the Batswana had not sent away northwards into the Protectorate were

[6] *Cape Times,* Prisoner interviews by F R Thompson.
[7] G3-'98, pp6–10, Dalgety's report, 10 April 1897.

Cattle in Twaai Kloof in 1978 drink from one of the streams that filled with the dead in 1897.

struck by the disease. Confined within the kloofs, the animals quickly succumbed. Within a couple of weeks only a handful of cattle were left alive. The ground was too hard to allow for any burials and the rotting carcasses of the dead cattle gave off a fearful stink that could be smelled for miles around. And in both Puduhush and Twaai Kloof it appears to have affected the water supply.

Having failed in his attempt to achieve a military victory at Gamasep, Dalgety decided to lay waste the country and so starve the residents of the Langeberg into submission. This would also give him the opportunity to avenge the Batlharo attack on his water convoy. Accordingly, after resting his troops for a few days at Ryan's farm, he took 568 men, a twelve-pounder and a Maxim gun on a night march in the direction of Puduhush. At daybreak on Thursday 15 April he launched an all-out attack on the town of Puduhush. The twelve-pounder had already proved its destructive ability, and over the space of one hour Dalgety's force destroyed 280 houses, including the one that was identi-fied as belonging to *Kgosi* Toto. Dalgety made no claim to have caused any casualties, so the town was probably deserted, the occupants having with-drawn into the kloof behind.

Dalgety then proceeded south for about fifteen kilometres, burning villages as he went. By the end of the day he was able to report with some satisfaction that all the villages east of the Langeberg between Gamasep and Olifantshoek had been destroyed (*see map 19 p230*). On returning to Ryan's, Dalgety sent a strong patrol to the northeastern end of the reserve to burn the deserted village of Deben. Having destroyed all houses, burnt all crops and captured all livestock in sight, Dalgety decided to work his way through

238

the mountain range, kloof by kloof, starting in the south. With this in mind he set off for Oliphant's Kloof with almost his entire force on the evening of 22 April. During the course of their night march they came under almost constant sniping from Batswana riflemen; but they appear not to have suffered any serious casualties and the next morning they established a laager close to the entrance to Olifant's Kloof. Dalgety hoped to find sufficient water for his transport animals and horses and then to make his way slowly northwards, across the mountains and thus gain access to Puduhush from the rear.

For several days Dalgety's men were engaged in digging wells, assuming that the initiative of the war was still in their favour. But by this time, as the night attack on the column had shown, the Batswana were taking the initiative themselves. As soon as it became clear what Dalgety was doing, Luka sent men south to give support to Toto's Batlharo. On the night of 28 April, Dalgety's Oliphant's Kloof laager came under serious attack. It was a well coordinated assault with a constant, steady rate of fire. In the darkness the colonists could not tell how many were attacking them, but the Batswana were able to pick their targets by the light of the cooking fires within the laager. After fifteen minutes of carefully directed fire, the Batswana withdrew, leaving two colonists dead and four severely wounded, one of whom later died. The Batswana suffered no losses of their own.

The night attack appears to have helped convince Dalgety that he no longer had the time for a slow and steady northward sweep through the mountains. He was in constant danger of repeated night attacks as long as the main northern kloofs of Puduhush, Twaai and Gamasep remained in 'rebel' hands. At the same time Dalgety was under 'urgent and repeated requests from Government [to] at once attack and conclude the war.'[8] He decided he had no option but to move up at once and attack Puduhush. The stronghold of Toto and the Batlharo was chosen in preference to its northern neighbours because Twaai and Gamasep were too well defended by the Batlhaping. And the leadership there of Luka Jantjie had proved so effective that two attacks on Gamasep had already failed. Dalgety believed that Puduhush would be easier to take. And he would then have a secure source of water at the front line, rather than depending on Ryan's farm nearly twenty kilometres away. Maintaining his supply of fresh water had proved to be a major problem for Dalgety. Johnson recalled that the Batlhaping regularly attacked the column's water carriers, shooting holes in them so that they would leak.[9]

[8] G3–'98, Dalgety's report, p51.
[9] Johnson, *Great Days*, p245.

Camping probably at Ryan's Farm in Bishop's Wood, the nearest source of water outside the kloofs.

Dalgety knew he would not have enough men both to hold Puduhush and assault Luka's stronghold, but he hoped that the taking of the former would have such a dispiriting effect that the rest might surrender. In the meantime he ordered the burning of the ripening crops of 'loyal natives' in the southern, Olifantshoek region, just to make sure there was no possibility of any of it making its way to the 'rebels' in the Langeberg.

It must have been difficult to maintain morale within the Batswana ranks in view of the recent destruction of their homes and fields of corn. But they were always on the alert to exploit any weakness they perceived within the Cape government's field force. And one such opportunity occurred in early May, a week after the successful night attack on the laager at Oliphant's Kloof.

The Batswana leadership noticed that Dalgety had so many men concentrated in the south that he had left open his supply route from Kuruman and Ryan's farm. On 7 May, three supply wagons were observed passing Puduhush en route for Olifant's Kloof with no military escort. A troop of mounted Batswana immediately sallied forth and captured the wagons. They were piled high with ammunition and food, including champagne and caviar provided for the officers, courtesy of Cecil Rhodes' De Beers Consolidated Mines. So the Batswana defenders were understandably in high spirits when news reached them the following day that Dalgety was striking camp with a view to marching on Puduhush.

That night Toto strengthened his defences, manning the schanzes throughout the cold of the night. As dawn lit up the eastern mountainside, a forewarning of the attack was announced by the booming of the twelve-pounder that was entrenched at Gamasep Kopje, three kilometres to the north of Puduhush. It kept up a steady fire from first light. The intention was to keep Luka's men in Gamasep and on Fighting Kopje fully engaged so that they could not go to the assistance of their comrades in Puduhush.

Once it became clear to Luka, however, that the infantry assault was to be directed exclusively at his Batlharo neighbours, he was able to slip away many of his best fighting men from their schanzes and send them over to reinforce Puduhush.

Probably a staged photo showing colonial troops firing at African positions some distance away.

Puduhush was a double kloof, with northern and southern wings enclosing a central mountain spur (*see map 19*). Toto had men well concealed in schanzes on the front and sides of the outer wings of the kloof, with his main force concentrated on the central spur that was set back some one thousand metres from the entrance.

Dawn on 9 May revealed a government force of 450 men, positioned near where the modern road passes Puduhush. Once again, Johnson had been sent up into the mountain, with 270 men to command the southern heights, but this was not yet apparent to the Batswana in the schanzes.

Colonel Spence had been given overall command of the attack. On his left wing he had Woon's CMR while on his right were Searle's Cape Town Highlanders and a small detachment of the Prince Alfred Guard, an eastern Cape regiment based in Port Elizabeth. For several hours nothing happened, and the defenders must have been hoping that the colonial troops were having second thoughts about an attack. Spence, however, was waiting for a signal from Johnson that his men were ready and in position.

At 11 a.m. he got the signal and from his position in the centre, with Woon on his left and Searle on his right, Spence ordered a general advance.

The defenders held their nerve and kept out of sight. The advancing column was led by a troop of mounted Basuto scouts. It was common practice for colonial forces to send African troops in ahead of colonial regiments, as 'human shields' to draw the enemy's fire. Behind them the infantry spread out in skirmishing order. But the Batswana held their fire until the white men themselves were drawn well into the kloof.

The advance troop of Basuto had almost reached the foot of the central spur when the defenders finally opened up. They poured a heavy fire into the enemy, from both sides and the centre. Spence's men were forced to ground, seeking cover behind rocks and bushes. They were unable to return fire until Spence ordered up the Maxim gun to rake the mountains from side to side. Even then the Batswana kept up a heavy fire and the Maxim was kept so busy that Spence had to send back for more ammunition. The contest went on for hour after hour. Spence was unable to advance, but he refused to withdraw even though his men could only return fire when they were protected by bursts from the Maxim gun.

All this time Johnson's men were approaching from behind and above the Batswana lines. Gradually they moved to the edge of the mountain top and began to identify their targets, hidden behind their schanzes. Coming under fire from behind and above, as well as at the front, the Batswana defenders began to feel the effect of Johnson's careful targeting.

By half past one Spence observed a slackening in the pace of Batswana firing, and he ordered Searle and Woon to advance and take the northern and southern spurs respectively. Although many Batswana had already been felled by Johnson's firing from above, few chose to leave their positions in the face of the colonists' charge with fixed bayonets. Most remained at their posts and fought 'to the very last, many of them being shot … inside the schanzes.'[10]

Once it was clear that the outer defences had been lost, the Batswana in the central spur gradually withdrew into the mountain, leaving the government troops in control of the lower reaches of the kloof. Much to their dismay, however, Spence's men found that the main stream in Puduhush had been contaminated by the rotting carcases of hundreds of rinderpest-infected cattle. The only clear spring was much further up the rocky kloof, out of reach of the force's water-carts. And without a ready supply of fresh water it would be next to impossible to hold their position in Puduhush, let alone use it as a base from which to assault the neighbouring kloofs to the north.

Dalgety had formed a laager of the wagons and the two twelve-pounders on the plain beyond the entrance to the kloof; and as the sun began to drop behind the mountains, Spence, Woon, Searle and Johnson withdrew their men towards the laager. As they did so, they came under fire once more from the Batswana, who had silently slipped back into position behind their schanzes. Only a pounding from the twelve-pounders slowed their rate of fire.

Thus although the government forces had clearly won the battle, they had failed to achieve their objective, which was to find and hold a reliable source

---

[10] G3–'98, Spence's report, p22.

Contemporary newspaper sketch of Dalgety's forward base at Gamasep with locations of the hospital (on top and behind the hill), the heliograph, the Maxim gun and the twelve-pounder.

of clean water in the kloofs of Puduhush. Consequently, the following day, Dalgety withdrew his whole force back to Ryan's farm, leaving only a small garrison to man the forward base at Gamasep Kopje.

The government had suffered what Dalgety considered to be heavy losses for a position that could not be held: three killed and seven seriously wounded. But for the first time the Batswana too had suffered, and far more heavily. Dalgety estimated that they had lost as many as seventy killed and many more wounded. The government usually made wildly exaggerated claims of 'rebel' losses, mostly to cover up for their own shortcomings, but on this occasion it seems to have been an underestimate. As reported to a member of the Native Contingent a few weeks later, the Batswana on Fighting Kopje reckoned their losses at Puduhush to have been two hundred killed outright and many more wounded.

Whatever the exact tally, losses were clearly very heavy and their impact was felt throughout the Langeberg. It is probable that from this point morale began to suffer and people began to wonder whether they should, or indeed could, go on fighting.

CHAPTER SIXTEEN

Siege and final stand
May–July 1897

Lieutenant-Colonel Dalgety, Officer Commanding the Bechuanaland Field Force, reported to Cape Town on 11 May 1897 on the impossibility of capturing and holding the fortress of the Langeberg without a doubling of the troops under his command.[1] He estimated he would need a minimum of 1,500 trained European troops and a large Native Contingent.

The local Burgher Volunteers were in his opinion worse than useless. Now that there was no more loot to be had, they were eager to disband, besides being unruly when not fighting and unreliable in battle. Indeed, the day after Dalgety wrote his report on Puduhush, Commandant Meintjes and Lieutenant Coetzee of the Geluk Burghers murdered three unarmed African men, including their leader, Jan Zulu, one woman and a young girl at Gamagara. The murdered men had worn armbands and hat insignia that indicated that they were members of the government's own Native Contingent, but Meintjes and Coetzee shot them just the same. In their trial some months later they claimed in their defence that their orders were to 'shoot natives'.[2] These were the sort of people that composed half of Dalgety's force, and he wanted them replaced.

It took a month for the government to agree to Dalgety's demands and it took a further six weeks to assemble the additional troops.

In the meantime Luka, Toto, Galeshewe and the people under their protection had to survive what was in effect a state of siege. Their livestock were nearly all dead from disease or had been stolen, their crops had been destroyed and they were desperately short of food. Nevertheless, with responsibility for thousands of refugees hiding in the kloofs with no proper shelter, the *dikgosi* in the Langeberg did not forget their responsibilities for their people further afield.

---

[1] G3–'98, Dalgety's Report, 'Camp Ryan', 11 May 1897.
[2] *Bechuanaland News*, 31 July 1897. Charges against Coetzee were dropped. Meintjes was acquitted at the trial. There were other examples of shooting unarmed Africans in the area.

Towards the end of April news had reached the ears of the Batswana leadership that several of their people had been shot dead at Dikgatlhong near the junction of the Mashowing and Kuruman Rivers, some fifty kilometres northeast of Kuruman and close to the small Batlharo reserve of Tsineng. Although this was about ninety kilometres north of the Langeberg stronghold, a small troop was sent out to investigate and take punitive action. They arrived at Tsineng on 2 May and learned that the incident involved an Afrikaner family named Drotskie who had recently begun illegally squatting on government land at nearby Dikgatlhong. In the light of recent government attacks down the Mashowing and Kuruman Rivers, the local Batlharo had done their best to steer well clear of these *maburu*.

Nervousness, however, cut both ways. One day the Drotskie son had seen some 'natives' nearby, and he had panicked and shot three of them dead. Believing they would get no justice from the government, the Batswana troop from the Langeberg took the law into their own hands. They shot both father and son, though they did not harm Drotskie's wife or children. They then loaded up the Drotskie wagon with ten bags of grain, seized three horses and herded one hundred cattle and three hundred sheep and goats in the direction of the Langeberg.[3] The troop would have had to skirt well round the western side of the Korannaberg to avoid the government's patrols and they probably arrived back in the Langeberg just after the battle at Puduhush.

By their concern and reaction to events such as this, the Batswana leadership in the Langeberg maintained the loyalty of people from as far away as Manyeding and the Kuruman valley.

There was at least one report of Luka's brother Olebile sending food to the Langeberg from Manyeding.[4] Contributions such as this, however, had little impact on the deteriorating condition of the thousands of people who were by now trapped in the mountains of the Langeberg, and through the cold winter months of May, June and July 1897 the siege began to take its toll. The people began to feel the effects of starvation and morale suffered. Psychologically, they were particularly affected by the government's policy of keeping up an irregular bombardment by the twelve-pound field-gun entrenched at Gamasep Kopje. Throughout the day and night the relentless pounding of Gamasep and Fighting Kopje was enough to wear down the resolve of even the most determined of defenders.

---

[3] *Cape Times*, 14/10/97, J T Brown interview; and *CA*, PMO (Prime Minister's Office) 254, Claim for compensation No.55, Mrs M M Drotskie.
[4] *Weekly Press*, Pretoria, 19 June 1897.

Between bouts of artillery fire, small platoons of Basuto from the Native Contingent patrolled the mountain frontage. And on one day towards the end of May one of the patrols was hailed by the defenders from behind the schanzes on the southern spur of Twaai Kloof.[5] The leader of the platoon, Corporal Paul, responded, prompting several Batswana to emerge from the schanzes and come forward unarmed. Paul's party put down their arms and the two groups met on neutral ground. Tobacco was exchanged and as Paul could speak Setswana, they communicated freely. What Paul learned from these Batswana was that they were 'utterly sick of fighting', but that they felt compelled to continue by their *dikgosi*, Luka and Toto. It was from this conversation that the Basuto learned the story of the 'scabby sheep' insult and the falling out between Galeshewe and Luka's family.

A few days later, on 30 May, the two parties met again and this time the Batswana were accompanied by Luka's chief councillor, unfortunately unnamed. He confirmed everything that had previously been said, regarding the low morale and the general desire for peace. Apparently, a few days previously Galeshewe had come into Luka's camp with only three men and complained about not receiving enough support. He asked for more troops to go with him to help defend his kopje, but Luka had refused point blank.

Then, on 31 May, Paul was unable to make contact as previously arranged because Luka had summoned a large general meeting at Derapedi in Twaai Kloof to discuss their options. That meeting, however, was delayed a day while they awaited the arrival of Toto from Puduhush, and in the meantime the correspondent from the *Cape Argus* departed to file his report without waiting to hear the result of the adjourned meeting. Nobody else seemed particularly interested in the intelligence that Corporal Paul had been collecting, and so the outcome of the meeting on 1 June was not recorded. One can surmise, however, that Luka won over any doubters and convinced them that they must not submit to ignominious defeat. Rather, they should continue the fight while hoping for an honourable peace. At best this might entail the withdrawal of all Cape government troops and the peaceable surrender of Galeshewe.

At the conclusion of the meeting Luka sent a formal protest in writing to the officer in charge of the detachment at Gamasep Kopje, in which he complained of the harassment his people were suffering from the continual firing of the big gun whenever someone was seen to move on the mountain. At the same time he reiterated his stance that he was not fighting against the

---

[5] Based on the report of Corporal Paul (Native Contingent), *Cape Argus Weekly*, 9 June 1897.

Sharpshooters practising before the final battle in the Langeberg.

government. In other words, so far as he was concerned he was only acting in self-defence, and he could not understand why 'his family' were being killed indiscriminately.[6]

It soon became clear that the colonists were not interested in a peaceful resolution. The reply to Luka's message was a continuation of firing by the twelve-pounder at Gamasep Kopje the following day, and so that night, 2 June, Luka sent out a raiding party to attack the gun detachment. There do not appear to have been any colonial casualties, but it was enough for Dalgety to refer to it as a 'serious attack'.

Over the following month, numerous foraging and raiding parties were sent out from the Langeberg, some of them reaching far beyond the mountain stronghold. Two hundred and sixty cattle were taken from a farm near the Griqualand West border and in one particularly bold raid six CMR horses were seized from the military camp at Kuruman. Much of this raided livestock was hidden in the kloofs of the Korannaberg, a day's ride north of the Langeberg. On 13 June a police patrol near Tsineng clashed with what was said to be a 'large body of Galeshewe's men' taking horses back to the Langeberg.[7] If that was so, then it was perhaps a sign of things to come.

Tension was rising within the fortress of the Langeberg, and resolve was failing. There were rumours reported in the colonial press that Toto wanted to surrender, and it was probably from about this time that Galeshewe began to consider leaving what was clearly a doomed scenario, hence the need for horses. It seems that only Luka Jantjie's resolve remained unshaken. All reports and rumours that filtered into the mass of correspondents at Kuruman confirmed that Luka remained firmly set against an ignominious surrender. Nevertheless, Luka was a realistic man and it is doubtful that he would have considered the lack of any formal assault on the Langeberg since early May as any slackening in the government's hostility.

[6] *Cape Argus Weekly*, 9 June 1897.
[7] *Bechuanaland News*, 3 July 1897.

Lt-Col Edmund H Dalgety (seated centre), Officer Commanding, Bechuanaland Field Force, relaxing at Ryan's farm: planning (perhaps) the final assault with his recent reinforcements.

By the end of June, Dalgety had his reinforcements; 1,700 of them assembled at Ryan's farm on 6 July. Over the following week, as government raiding parties harassed the Korannaberg, burning villages, killing fugitives and capturing livestock, Galeshewe decided it was time for him to leave. He was later to claim that he believed that if he made it into the Bechuanaland Protectorate, the people there would rise up and support him. But that was clearly wishful thinking. With their protectorate status so recently confirmed, the northern Batswana *dikgosi* had no reason to rebel. In reality Galeshewe was desperate for a way out of his predicament. Luka seemed no longer interested in his fate, and so far as he could see, the Langeberg as a stronghold was finished.

Sometime between the second and third weeks of July, Galeshewe and a small band of close adherents rode out of the Langeberg, bound for the border region of the Protectorate, two hundred kilometres to the north. Word quickly spread to the government troops at Ryan's and in Kuruman that Galeshewe, was no longer in the Langeberg. By now, however, the principal quarry was Luka Jantjie. He was the 'trophy' that many colonists sought.

As government forces accumulated at Ryan's farm, groups of refugees – mostly women and children – tried to escape from the Langeberg. But government patrols were being stepped up. Most of the fleeing refugees were

The view from the colonial officers' mess cave on Gamasep Kopje of the battlefield to come.

captured and escorted to Kuruman where they were held in a fenced enclosure, open to the cold winter skies.

Then on Friday 23 July a Batlharo foraging party was surprised at Tsineng by a troop of Cape Mounted Police. They lost thirty killed and many wounded. Three were captured, along with a large quantity of stock. Among the dead was one of Toto's brothers. It was a serious blow to the defenders of the Langeberg. And it was probably the last foraging party to leave the mountain stronghold, for the government net was tightening around the Langeberg.[8]

Despite attempts by some to escape, there were still four to five thousand people in the kloofs from Puduhush to Gamasep. Since the beginning of July they had been reduced to chewing on raw hide as a substitute for meat, and they were now faced with the prospect: starve or fight, or possibly both.[9]

Dalgety arrived at Ryan's farm to take command of the troops on 19 July and at about the same time one last effort was being made by the Batswana to avoid a violent confrontation. They did not trust Dalgety or his officers, so Luka's son, Dikare, sent a letter to the Kuruman missionary Revd John Tom Brown, who was believed to be a man of peace. Dikare's letter asked the missionary to intercede for them; but it took several days to reach its destination. By the time that Brown received the letter on 28 July it was too late for him to do anything. It is probable that Brown would have spoken to Special Commissioner Bell, who was in Kuruman. But Bell was waiting to supervise the confiscation of the Langeberg reserve and the distribution of the prisoners. He would not have been interested in anything other than the finality of a military solution. At the last minute too, Toto wrote to Brown in similar vein, but his letter did not arrive until 3 August, after it was all over.

On 28 July Dalgety moved his whole main force of about two thousand fighting men up to Gamasep Kopje where he established a secure laager, leaving just small detachments at Kuruman, Kathu and Ryan's. His men were fit and fresh: at least half of them now well experienced with fighting in

8 *Cape Argus Weekly*, 28 July 1897.
9 *Cape Times*, 28 September 1897, evidence of prisoners interviewed by F R Thompson.

Luka's view of Gamasep Kopje, left, in the middle distance, as he waited for the final assault.

this terrain. And this time Dalgety had with him eighteen water-carts, so there would be no shortage of water to compromise his strategy. Once more his main target was Gamasep Mountain and Kloof, Fighting Kopje and the southern spur of Mount Toto which enclosed Luka's Twaai Kloof. Toto and the Batlharo in the kloofs of Puduhush were to be dealt with later.

From the heights above Fighting Kopje, *Kgosi* Luka Jantjie viewed the approach of Dalgety's greatly enhanced force throughout that day, 28 July. In the preceding days he had ordered a barricade of wagons, thorn scrub and rocks to be erected across the upper reaches of Twaai Kloof, protecting the village of Derapedi and his royal homestead beyond.

Remains of the wall Luka had built to protect his village, Derapedi, further up Twaai Kloof.

Luka felt that this time he might not be able to hold back the colonial assault at the outer entrance to the valley by well directed fire from Fighting Kopje, as had happened on the two previous assaults. But he was a brave and stubborn man and there is no sign that there was any weakening in his resolve: he would not be humiliated by ignominious surrender, imprisonment and possible hanging; he would fight to the end.[10]

---

[10] Luka's position was recalled some eighty years later by his surviving nephew, Molehabangwe Jantjie, who was a teenager in Manyeding at the time. The story was told to him by Luka's wife. Interviewed by the author at Manyeding, in March 1978, Molehabangwe, then in his late

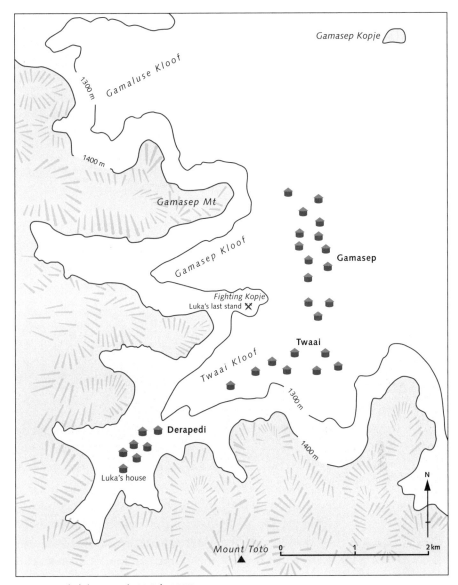

MAP 20: Luka's last stand, 30 July 1897.

On the following day, 29 July, Luka would have seen the enemy divide its forces into five columns of about four hundred men each. By contrast, the total number under Luka's command had been seriously weakened by injury, illness, death and desertion and Luka may have had less than five hundred men who were fit to fight in the schanzes in this final confrontation.

nineties, was probably the last man alive to have personally known *Kgosi* Luka Jantjie.

Dalgety's strategy must have become apparent to the Batlhaping as he deployed his forces throughout the course of that day. His aim once more was to command the mountain heights to the north and south of Luka's central position (*see map 20*). One column assembled opposite Gamaluse Kloof on the northern flank of Gamasep Mountain, and a second opposite the Gamasep spur itself. The third and fourth columns faced Gamasep Kloof and Fighting Kopje while the final column was positioned to mount the southern spur that separated Twaai Kloof from Puduhush.

The Batlhaping rather than the Batlharo were clearly the primary object of this coming assault and Luka could not expect any assistance from Toto's men, for Puduhush would be next in Dalgety's sights. With a shortage of men under his command, Luka made the decision to concentrate his forces in the centre, on Fighting Kopje; but he waited for the failing light of evening before calling in his men from the outer spurs of Gamasep and Puduhush.

The Twaai Kloof side of Fighting Kopje showing the rocky boulder-strewn nature of the terrain.

It was a bitterly cold night, with temperatures below freezing and one can imagine the men shivering on Fighting Kopje while with frozen fingers they strengthened their schanzes and checked their ammunition. It is doubtful that Luka got any sleep that night. He probably checked his defences and encouraged his men before going up the valley, beyond the barricade to Derapedi. There he would have spoken with his family, whom he left in the care of his eldest son, Dikare (*left*). We know from later reports that he reiterated his determination to die fighting rather than surrender and he told Dikare that, if it

252

The view down Twaai Kloof from the entrance to Darepedi towards Fighting Kopje (centre left).

should come to it and he failed to hold the enemy at Fighting Kopje, then he was to surrender rather than endanger the family at Derapedi.[11] It would have been a hard parting as Luka made his way back down the valley to meet his fate the following day.

Before dawn on Friday 30 July the Kaffrarian Rifles of the northern columns of the colonial force began their assault on the northern Gamaluse Kloof and Gamasep Mountain.[12] They were surprised to find their advance unopposed and by late morning they had secured the whole of the northern mountain spur. Dalgety had originally expected them to spend the day securing the mountain heights before he launched his own attack from the front the following morning. But with the Gamasep Mountain already secure by late morning, he ordered the Kaffrarian Rifles back down the mountain to join his own central column which he brought forward from Gamasep Kopje to Pearce's store. At this point they came within range of Luka's sharpshooters on Fighting Kopje and the battle commenced.

The unofficial photographer with the colonial force, Private Miller of the Prince Alfred Guard, mounted his tripod and camera on the tin roof of Pearce's store (*p223*). Miller was a professional photographer in civilian life and he hoped to get a good view of the battle for Fighting Kopje, but he was peppered by Batlhaping rifle-fire and he quickly scrambled down to safety behind the store. Meanwhile, as the fifth column secured the Puduhush spur which formed the southern side of Twaai Kloof, the fourth column entered the valley, keeping as close as possible to the southern side, but still just within range of Fighting Kopje. Luka, who was commanding the southern edge of the Fighting Kopje promontory, urged his men to hold their fire until

[11] *Cape Times*, 14 October 1897, J T Brown interview.
[12] University of Cape Town (UCT) Archives, typescript copy of a letter from Trooper Greenwood to his mother, East London, 18 September 1897.

Fighting Kopje

Pearce's store

*Derapedi at head
of Twaai Kloof*

A view towards Fighting Kopje and where the final battle was fought on July 30 1897.

they had drawn more of the colonial troops further into the valley, a tactic that had been used to advantage before. Dalgety, meanwhile, had fanned out his central and northern columns into skirmishing order, and he decided to rest his men before the coming fight, while his artillery pounded the Batlhaping defences on Fighting Kopje.

Dalgety had placed the 160 men of the Transkeian Native Contingent and forty Cape Native Police in the front firing line, ahead of his white volunteer regiments. No sooner, however, had Dalgety's white volunteers settled down to rest and consume some of their generous ration of a gallon of water a day, than they realised that the Native Contingents, impatient for battle, had already started their advance on Fighting Kopje. The resting men were quickly ordered to their feet and sent in pursuit of their advance guard. And as the colonial force came under fire from the kopje, the Native Contingents turned the general advance into a full-scale charge.

From his position on the southern flank of the kopje, Luka and his men had begun firing on the southern column that was entering Twaai valley; but it was the northern flank that took the full brunt of that initial charge from Dalgety's column. As the Native Contingents neared the base of the kopje they fired a volley from their breech-loading rifles and charged up the steep slope in full cry with fixed bayonets.

Until this moment Luka's fighting men seem to have retained a certain level of confidence in their ability to hold their own in the forthcoming battle. Twice, in February and April, they had held off colonial attacks. But as some of the Batlhaping survivors later admitted, the soldiers whom they now faced were of a different calibre:

The first lot were young men who had come up to learn to fight, and we did not mind them, for they were children. [But] the men who conquered us were the soldiers [Kaffrarian Rifles] who came at the eleventh hour from the [Transkei] and the [Xhosa] they brought with them. These were men who came to fight.[13]

The charge came so quickly that most of the Batlhaping, who were armed with muzzle-loading hunting guns, would have had time for only one or two reloads: that is, no more than two or three shots fired at the charging enemy before hand-to-hand fighting for their lives. The defenders stood little chance of holding off such an assault. Many died in the schanzes – twenty-five to thirty '...bayoneted and shot at close quarters', according to one account;[14] others withdrew up the mountain spur, escaping to Derapedi or over the mountain to Puduhush.

Within fifteen minutes the head of Fighting Kopje and its northern flank had been occupied by cheering colonial troops. This encouraged their southern column to drive up the centre of Twaai Kloof, burning houses as they went. They brought their artillery up to the mouth of the kloof and, from behind the protection of hastily-built stone semi-circles (*below*), they fired into the barricaded Derapedi at the head of the kloof. They then decided to consolidate their position before attempting to take the barricade.

The stone semi-circles today at the mouth of Twaai Kloof probably used to protect the artillery.

13 *Cape Times*, 28 September 1897, prisoner interviews.
14 *Weekly Press*, Pretoria, 7 August 1897.

A Winchester repeating rifle (1892 model) similar to the one used by Luka (cf. gun on p38).

Meanwhile, Luka and those Batlhaping in the schanzes on the southern flank of Fighting Kopje had been firing at the advancing colonial troops as they passed up the Twaai valley. Those troops in the valley seem to have assumed that the southern schanzes would be taken care of by the colonists who now commanded the top of the mountain spur. But this southern flank is very steep and those on top do not seem to have been aware of the dangers lurking below. This left Luka and five of his closest adherents unmolested in their schanzes. Realising that the battle was lost, they held their fire as they observed the wanton destruction and looting of their homes within the valley.

Soon after noon a troop of the eastern Cape's Prince Alfred Guard and Kaffrarian Rifles passed back down the valley, close to the southern schanzes. They came within fifteen metres of Luka's position. At this point Luka made the fateful decision. He and several of his companions stood up waist-high in their schanze and began firing at close range into the men of the Kaffrarian Rifles. They felled two before the repeating mechanism on Luka's Winchester repeating rifle appears to have jammed and for a moment he lowered his gun. Most of the colonial troops, surprised by the sudden assault, had flung themselves to the ground. But Surgeon-Lieutenant Temple Smyth of the Medical Staff seized the opportunity of the pause in Luka's firing. He drew his revolver and rushed forward across the rocky terrain to within a few metres of Luka's position. Then, at close range, he shot the *kgosi* in the chest, killing him instantly. Three of Luka's companions were also killed in the ensuing skirmish and the remaining two were taken prisoner, alive but badly wounded. Sergeant Bruce of the local Cape Mounted Police, who was with Surgeon Smyth, knew Luka personally and was able instantly to identify the man whom Smyth had killed.

As news spread among the Batlhaping of the death of their *kgosi*, the last remnants of resistance on the mountain collapsed and those who could not escape to Derapedi or Puduhush surrendered.

The colonists were in high spirits over the killing of their 'notorious' opponent. Medical staff were not in fact supposed to take any active part in hostile military action. The surgeon's pistol was intended purely for personal

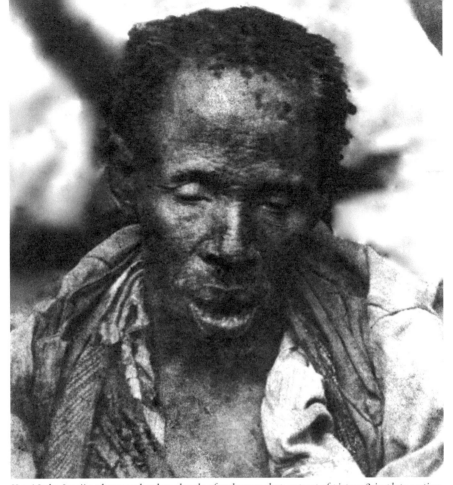

Kgosi Luka Jantjie: photograph taken shortly after he was shot; extract of picture 3 in plate section.

self-defence and that of patients in his care. Dr Smyth, however, had been pretty close to the front line all day, tending to casualties as they were hit. He had been directly shot at on several occasions and it could reasonably be argued that in shooting Luka he had been acting in self-defence.

> We have had a terrible time of thirst fatigue & pain The latter due to the way the sharp rocks knock about our feet about We charged one hill (the strongest position in the Langberg) with the bayonet We stormed the place finally under our awful fire I was up amongst the leaders & saw a fellow drop beside me. I saw 2 him (he was dead, Shot thro the head)

Smyth's own account, written in a private letter to his family in Ireland (*see above extract*), confirms other newspaper accounts and gives a graphic feel for what may have happened:

257

Three of the enemy jumped up within 10 yards of me on the side of the hill above me. The leader aimed at a young Kaffrarian [Rifles man] beside me & I dashed up straight at them. The chief (it was Luka Jantjie's) rifle bullet passed over my shoulder & he turned to get the rifle (a Winchester repeater) up again to fire when I shot him thro the heart with my revolver.

I turned to find the second man almost on me when I shot him thro the liver & again thro the arm. But he still came on so I had to club him with my revolver on the head. Then my greatest danger for about 15 Kaffrarians fired a volley into us hoping to save me. Providence was kind to me for my third enemy was bowled over & I was not hit. Then the whole column began cheering & everyone came up to shake hands with me.[15]

Surgeon Smyth (*left*) was feted as a hero for killing the man whom the colonists called 'the Paramount Chief'. Private Miller brought up his camera and Luka's prone body had to suffer the indignity of being propped up in a sitting position and photographed surrounded by triumphant colonists, in the manner of a hunting trophy: for to many of them, that is what he was. After a while, a shallow grave was dug by eight men from the Kaffrarian Rifles led by Lt. J W McLean fifty metres from the entrance to Twaai Kloof in the hard rocky ground at the foot of the kopje where he had died, and there *Kgosi* Luka Jantjie was laid to rest, for the time being.

That afternoon Dalgety decided to leave his troops to bivouac for the night in the positions they had captured. The next morning on 31 July he brought two twelve-pounders further into the valley and began his advance up Twaai Kloof towards the Derapedi barricade. At once a man emerged bearing a white flag with the message that Dikare, son of Luka Jantjie, now *kgosi* of the Batlhaping, was offering his surrender.

---

[15] http://dustymuffin.wordpress.com/2007/07/01/luka-jantje-pieces-of-the-puzzle/, see blog, from David Fayle, 16 November 2009.

Two Batlharo messengers bring the white flag of surrender from Puduhush to colonial troops, 2 August 1897. Capt. Searle of the Cape Town Highlanders kneels (right); note the woollen mittens on his hands to keep warm; (centre left) a soldier from the Native Contingent wears a bandolier.

Colonial troops pose with their 'loot' after their victory.

The messenger was taken to where his late *kgosi* was buried and Luka's body was dug up for him to identify. The body was then reburied, but carelessly. There were said to be toes and hands protruding.

259

Prisoners: (top) male prisoners, some wearing the coats that helped keep out the intense night cold; (right) child prisoners looking distressed, some wearing karosses; (below) some of the female prisoners with their young children and cooking pots; (bottom) more male prisoners and armed guards lined up for the 'traditional' victor's photograph.

Kgosi Toto of the Batlharo after his surrender on 2 August; still able to project his status as kgosi.

Dalgety was under orders to clear the Langeberg completely, so he decided to ignore the white flag and press on to Derapedi. With troops on the mountains and the artillery firing at the barricade, the defence of Derapedi quickly collapsed. After at least twenty further Batlhaping were killed, the colonists were finally persuaded to stop firing. Dikare and the remaining defenders laid down their arms and were taken prisoner.

The following day, Sunday 1 August, Toto sent in a message offering surrender. Dalgety refused to accept it unless the entire population of Puduhush emerged from the kloofs and surrendered their arms. Toto himself emerged with his people on 2 August and the surrender was accepted. The will to resist had died with its hero, *Kgosi* Luka Jantjie.

CHAPTER SEVENTEEN

The aftermath

The photographing of the body of *Kgosi* Luka Jantjie immediately after death, in the manner of a hunting trophy, was the first physical record of a mentality that showed contempt for the man's dignity. (*see plate 3 in colour section*)

Throughout his life *Kgosi* Luka of the Batlhaping had striven to live as a man of honour. He respected and valued his culture and his people's traditional way of life. And he had respected elements of the European culture that he and his people were exposed to during his formative years. He valued the literacy that Anne Helmore had taught him and he accepted the religious tenets of Christianity that he learned from his father and from the missionaries Holloway Helmore and William Ross. He accepted and valued too, many of the material goods of European culture that came with the emergence of a cash economy: the cloth garments, the domestic utensils, the wagons, horseback riding and guns for hunting. With the latter he became a hunter of some renown, gaining modest wealth from the ivory and ostrich-feather trade.

Luka Jantjie would have seen himself as both a traditional Motlhaping *kgosi* and a modern Christian entrepreneur, and as such he assumed that he was due respect from all men, irrespective of colour or creed. He had been given that respect, willingly, by the Helmores; he demanded it, as of right, from the white colonists who pushed their way into his world from the late 1860s. But this was where he met his nemesis.

The aggressive colonialism that accompanied Kimberley's mining revolution pushed men like Luka aside. In the colonial mindset, an African was by definition 'a native' and 'a labourer': a second-class citizen. But Luka Jantjie refused to bow his head to colonial self-proclaimed superiority. From his flogging of a white man on the river diggings in 1869, to his rejection of surrender in the Langeberg in 1897, *Kgosi* Luka was an indigenous leader who stood out against this personal and political denigration. Consequently, he quickly earned a reputation among colonists as 'the greatest living scoundrel', 'a mischievous and cunning fellow', 'a wild fellow who hates the English', 'a dangerous agitator' and, finally and fatally, 'a rebel'.

To his own people *Kgosi* Luka Jantjie was a beacon of hope: a great leader, a protector and a war hero. It was that reputation which the colonists who set out to conquer him were most determined to destroy.

After a lifetime of refusing to accept the indignities of colonial subjugation, the sixty-two-year-old *kgosi* of the Phuduhutŝwana Batlhaping had sought dignity in an honourable death on the field of battle. However, the strength of his persistent defiance of his would-be colonial masters, in civilian as well as in his final military life, had built Luka Jantjie up into an anti-colonial symbol of such proportions that he had become a trophy that every colonial soldier hoped to 'bag'. And there was worse to come.

The initial colonial reaction to the manner of Luka's death was one of grudging admiration for his bravery, though even that was tainted by insult. Describing Luka Jantjie's last stand as 'not an un-heroic one', the *Cape Times* opined:

> Nothing in his life became this worthy so well as his leaving of it. Luka Jantjie has been painted in many diverse colours. He has been represented in turn as a great general, and as a miserable craven, who was conspiring to betray Galeshewe and get the blood-money set upon his head. Luka Jantjie's end shows that he was libelled. As our correspondent pithily puts it, 'He lived like a dog and a rebel, but died like a man', shot down at fifteen paces by the gallant Surgeon Smyth.[1]

Even this grudging respect for the manner of his death, however, did not mean any respect for the sanctity of his person. Thus, the man who had hoped to find dignity in death was denied even this by his conquerors as, in the aftermath of his defeat, a shameful atrocity was committed on his body.

Within forty-eight hours of his death Luka Jantjie's body had been dug up and mutilated – his head cut off[2] as a trophy on the orders of the senior officer of one of the volunteer regiments.

There were several witnesses to the mutilation that was committed on the morning of Sunday 1 August, and gossip and rumour ensured that by the

---

[1] *Cape Times*, 31 July 1897. Similar sentiments were expressed in *Cape Argus Weekly*, 4 August 1897 and *Bechuanaland News*, 7 August 1897.

[2] Severed with some difficulty 'by a private in one of the Cape Town corps ... [with] no proper scientific appliance ... the reader may be spared the details how he devoted himself to the task.' *Glasgow Herald*, 22 September 1897.

end of the day notoriety of the deed had spread throughout the camps of the victorious colonial troops. But no official word of condemnation was uttered, even from the commanding officer, Lt-Colonel Dalgety. The only comment that Dalgety made was to deny the persistent rumour that a medical man had been involved. Dalgety does not appear to have based this assertion upon any detailed enquiry. Perhaps, being unable to deny the deed, he merely wished to quash the distasteful notion that it could have been carried out by so respectable a person as a medical officer. For the time being, the newspapers did not pursue the subject.

At the time of the mutilation of Luka's body there were still several thousand Batswana hidden within the kloofs of Puduhush and elsewhere, pondering their coming fate at the hands of the conquering colonial troops. One can be sure that news of *Kgosi* Luka's decapitation would have spread like wildfire through their hideouts. Their horror and sense of humiliation can only be imagined; but, so too, their fear of similar deeds being perpetrated on them. This was a time when white flags of surrender were still being brushed aside and Batswana survivors were being expected to put down their arms and trust in the integrity of Dalgety's field force. It was not until the following day, 2 August, that Toto's surrender was accepted.

Although no further Batswana corpses were mutilated, many were left unburied. Dalgety's priority seems to have been to bury the hundreds of dead cattle in the kloofs that had succumbed to rinderpest and were rotting in the water courses. Having found little to loot within the kloofs, the volunteer troops were mainly concerned with getting home as quickly as possible to what they expected to be a heroes' welcome.

Colonial troops return to rapturous reception from white society.

His last engagement!,
The finish of the Langbers Campaign.

In due course, towards the end of August, a lavish welcome was laid on in Cape Town to welcome back the Dukes and Highlanders. In the Drill Hall a common topic of gossip among the celebrating troops was the decapitation of Luka Jantjie. The newspapers at the time had chosen not to publicise the shameful deed; but when the *Cape Times* correspondent, who had been with the troops in the Langeberg, heard the story doing the rounds in the Cape Town Drill Hall, he persuaded the paper that the time was right to publish the story before it appeared in their rival paper, the *Cape Argus*. The story was duly published in the *Cape Times* on 30 August 1897.

The deed had attracted little criticism from among the colonial troops in the field, but here in Cape Town, at the heart of British South African colonial power, and in London where the news reached the British imperial government by telegraph within the hour, it was considered a major embarrassment. It flew in the face of the entire European colonial project that was supposedly bringing 'civilisation' to the continent of Africa.

The Cape government needed no urging from London and that same day they appointed a Court of Enquiry to look into the allegations. A member of the enquiry team was Colonel Walter E Stanford (*left*), recently appointed as Special Commissioner for Bechuanaland to oversee the disposal of prisoners and confiscation of land. Stanford had recently arrived in Kimberley and he immediately began his enquiries into the affair while the President of the Court, Lt-Colonel Richard Southey, interviewed witnesses in Cape Town.[3]

Stanford despatched the Kuruman magistrate to the Langeberg to confirm the allegation by exhuming the body. He was accompanied by the Inspector of Native Locations, J P McCarthy, who knew Luka well, and Sergeant Bruce

---

[3] In the absence of any report from the Court of Enquiry, the most reliable source of evidence in the affair is Stanford's confidential Telegram Book, housed in the Cape Archives, file NA 253.

of the Cape Mounted Police who had been with Surgeon Smyth at the time that Luka was shot and knew where to find the body. Expecting to have to dig up bodies, they would have taken some servants with them. They reached the spot on 1 September and found several bodies lying there, still unburied and in a state of advanced decomposition. Among them was one that was missing its head as well as one hand, some fingers of the other hand and some toes. Identified by the old bullet wound in his lower left leg, there was no doubting that this was the body of Luka Jantjie and that it had been mutilated.[4] Although it is not mentioned in the record, one can assume that Bruce and McCarthy ordered the burial of the bodies, where they lay, at the foot of Fighting Kopje.

Arriving back in Kuruman on 2 September, they informed Stanford by telegram what they had found. By this time Stanford in Kimberley and Southey in Cape Town had all the evidence that they needed. One witness said he had heard Dr Saunders of Grahamstown's First City Volunteers offer Dawson, the cook for the officer's mess, £5 to cut off Luka's head, explaining to him that he would then need to boil the head to remove the flesh and hair.

Two volunteers claimed they had actually seen Dawson cutting off the head and that he had admitted that it had been on the orders of Captain James Searle (*left*) of the Cape Town Highlanders, with no mention of Dr Saunders. Stanford was convinced that Saunders was implicated, so it seems likely that Searle, determined to have his trophy, consulted Saunders, a medical man who would know how to 'clean up' the skull, and Saunders then explained to Dawson what to do. But there was no doubting that it was Searle who was the instigator of the mutilation. He reportedly slept in the Langeberg that night with the stripped-down skull in a blood-stained sack next to him.

The Court of Enquiry, having discovered what it believed to be the truth, decided not to publish its findings. The commanding officer of First City was asked to 'speak to' Dr Saunders while Searle, who had brought the skull to Cape Town, was confronted with his deed at a regimental meeting of the Cape Town Highlanders. Told that he was a disgrace to the regiment, he was forced

---

[4] According to a report in the *Diamond Fields Advertiser* (28 August 1897) Luka's fingers and toes were also cut off 'and preserved in bottles of brandy as momentoes [mementos].'

Cartoon published in the Cape Times Weekly expressing the consternation of some in Cape society.

to resign his commission. Unabashed, Searle admitted his responsibility to the *Cape Times*. In his opinion he had merely been 'indiscreet'. He claimed that he had intended to present the skull to the South African Museum 'for the benefit of students of physiology.'[5]

Exactly what became of Luka's skull remains unclear. According to one account, as an embarrassing artefact it may initially have been hidden in Cape Town's General Post Office before being sent to Grahamstown.[6] According to another source it was believed to have been housed in the wing of the Grahamstown museum that was subsequently burnt down, reducing Luka's earthly remains to ashes.[7] A third, more recent, story claims that the skull was rescued by Private James Joseph Cooke and kept in a drawer in the man's study for many years before being 'buried in the rose garden.'[8] The whole story is in need of further investigation.

The story of Luka Jantjie's decapitation has modern resonances in South Africa with the publication of a book about a Xhosa king named Hintsa whose head was allegedly hacked off following his treacherous killing by colonists in 1835.[9] The case became an issue at South Africa's Truth and

---

[5] *Cape Times*, 29 September 1897.

[6] 'Look Backward' by 'Johannes', *The Cape* (magazine), 4 December 1908.

[7] 'The True Story of Luka Jantjie's Head' by D R Forsyth, typescript, 10 February 1974.

[8] http://dustymuffin.wordpress.com/2007/07/01/luka-jantjie-pieces-of-the-puzzle/

[9] Premesh Lalu, *The Deaths of Hintsa* (Cape Town 2009).

Reconciliation Commission in the 1990s. Bambatha, a Zulu chief who led resistance to tax collectors in Natal in 1906 was similarly mutilated by colonial troops. But there were more mutilations of prominent indigenous men in nineteenth- and early twentieth-century South Africa who had dared to defy the colonial will. Indeed, not only in South Africa, but elsewhere in the continent of Africa, particularly in the decades of initial colonial conquest, between 1885 and 1914.

∼ ∼ ∼

Galeshewe (*left, photographed in prison*), whose grandfather had been decapitated by the Transvaal Boers in 1858, was perhaps lucky to have escaped from the Langeberg before the final colonial assault of 30–31 July 1897. Although at the time of the Batlhaping surrender, prisoners claimed that Galeshewe had just that day fled over the mountain into the neighbouring kloofs, this was clearly an attempt to mislead the colonial troops, thus providing Galeshewe with more time to make good his escape. Dalgety had initially acted on these reports and sent out mounted patrols to scour the northern kloofs, just in case Galeshewe was still there, or had returned, following reports of his earlier escape. Perhaps Dalgety hoped to vindicate his long campaign by being the man to capture Galeshewe; but on 5 August he was obliged to cable Cape Town that all reports about Galeshewe still being in the Langeberg were 'unreliable'.

The truth was that Galeshewe and about two dozen companions had left the Langeberg during the third week of July. They were making their way north on horseback through the Korannaberg on Wednesday 21 July when they were spotted by a patrol of the Cape Mounted Police. In the ensuing fight, Galeshewe lost five men killed and ten more wounded and captured. Galeshewe himself and the remainder of his band made their escape northwards. The wounded prisoners confirmed to the police that their troop had been led by Galeshewe.[10]

10 *Cape Argus Weekly*, 28 July 1897.

The news of Galeshewe's escape was heliographed from the Korannaberg to Kuruman on Thursday 22 July from where it was dispatched by telegraph to the Defence Department in Cape Town. Confident of the truth of the report, the government acted with haste. Captain Dennison, who was in Vryburg and had not taken any part in the military campaign following the January attack on Kabogo, was asked to raise a special force to capture Galeshewe. He was to proceed at once to Khuis on the Molopo River border with the Bechuanaland Protectorate (modern Botswana). Here he was to intercept Galeshewe before he managed to cross the border and lose himself in the sparsely populated thirstlands of the western Kalahari. According to Dennison's memoirs it took a day for him to consider the commission and a further day for the Defence Department to agree to his proposals for the force's composition.

As a long-standing resident of Vryburg from the old Stellaland days of 1884, George Dennison (*below*) was able to assemble the pick of the colonists from the Vryburg district. Over the following week he gathered together 120 mounted men. They called themselves the 'Stellaland Horse' and wore on their hats the old Stellaland insignia of a white star on a green band. They were accompanied by twenty 'Basuto' trackers, six of them mounted. Dennison was taking no chances and he assembled a convoy of twenty wagons and water carts with supplies for two and a half months.[11] He was ready to leave Vryburg on 31 July, the day that Dikare, Luka's son, and now *kgosi*, surrendered in the Langeberg and prisoners were assuring Dalgety that Galeshewe was still in the Langeberg. Three weeks later Dennison's convoy reached Khuis in the valley of the Molopo where they dug wells to water the horses in the dry riverbed.

The few Batswana they had encountered in the valleys of the Mashowing and the Lower Kuruman had fled at their approach; but as they neared their destination Dennison managed to capture and cajole some local people into revealing where Galeshewe might be hiding. Thus at dawn on Thursday 26 August, Galeshewe and his few remaining companions were surrounded and captured among the sand dunes that characterise that border region between the Molopo and the Lower Kuruman. Those captured with Galeshewe were his young uncle Morebonoke (Andries Gasebonwe), his brothers Mootametsi

[11] *Cape Argus Weekly*, 4 August 1897.

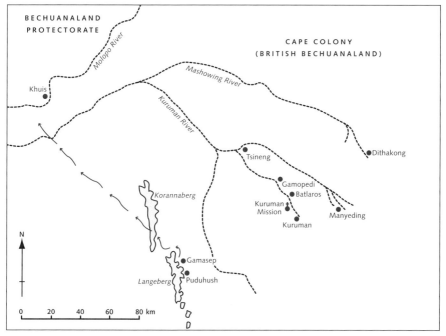

Map 21: Galeshewe's escape and capture, July–August 1897.

(Paul Gasebonwe) and Telekela (Fred Gasebonwe), a man named Magodi and two others, unnamed. They appear to have been taken by surprise and though well armed they offered no resistance. According to Dennison's memoirs, written some years later, Galeshewe told him:

> I wanted to get help and fight again, and I should have got away from here if you had not caught me. Dennison, you are like a dog on a spoor... Still I am glad you have come. If it had been the police they might have shot me.[12]

It is perhaps a rather fanciful account of Galeshewe's words, considering that it was troops under Dennison's command that had shot people so indiscriminately at Kabogo in January that year.

The following day Dennison questioned Galeshewe in Afrikaans, a language with which they were both familiar. Dennison made a contemporaneous record of the *kgosi*'s evidence in English, an account which was subsequently confirmed by Galeshewe to be an accurate record. It was mostly to do with the original outbreak of conflict in Phokwani: Galeshewe's

[12] Major C George Dennison *Zulu Frontiersman* ed R Lock & P Quantrill (2008) p124, and his *A History of Stellaland* (1928). He later served with the South African Mounted Irregular Forces during the Anglo-Boer War, and died in Plumtree (Rhodesia) in 1932 aged 88.

Kgosi Galeshewe with colleagues who were captured with him; (from top left) Andries Gasebonwe, Paul Gasebonwe, (seated from left) Fred Gasebonwe, Galeshewe, Maholi (or Magodi).

relationship with the Transvaal field-cornet, Bosman, and his innocence of any involvement in the murder of the Phokwani traders. This document was later presented as a statement of Galeshewe's evidence at the preliminary hearing for his trial in Kimberley in October 1897.[13]

Galeshewe and his companions were despatched to Vryburg which they reached at dawn on Thursday 9 September. At 9 a.m. they were marched down the high street to the courthouse, shackled in pairs, Galeshewe leading the way. Galeshewe himself, limping from a bullet wound in his ankle, received some mockery from the crowd of colonists who had gathered to see the sight. The town's photographer, William Klisser, got a good portrait of Galeshewe and took 'some splendid pictures of the prisoners' which he offered for sale as 'interesting mementoes … at low rates'.[14] The prisoners were bound over to remain in prison on charges of sedition.

[13] *CA*, Kimberley Criminal Records, 1/KIM, vol 1/1/1/66.
[14] *Bechuanaland News*, 11 September 1897.

At some stage soon after his arrival in Vryburg, Galeshewe was allowed to speak to the press, who questioned him about Luka Jantjie. The enquiry into his mutilation was still ongoing, the scandal was very much a current topic in the colonial press and journalists were eager to learn Galeshewe's views on the subject of his late cousin and comrade-in-arms. According to *South Africa* magazine, Galeshewe 'spoke very feelingly of the indignity done to the body of his old comrade, Luka Jantjie, but said he had no opinion to offer. No doubt it was done without thought.' He clearly did not wish to antagonise his colonial captors, before whom he would soon have to appear on trial, perhaps for his life. He did, however, express an opinion on the significance of Luka in the Langeberg. Galeshewe confirmed earlier reports that had come out of the mountain stronghold during the war:

> he bore strong testimony to the value of Luka, and said that he was the back-bone of the Langeberg Resistance.[15]

In due course Galeshewe and his companions joined other Phokwani prisoners in Kimberley gaol, some of whom, like Petlhu, had been taken in the Langeberg; others had been captured earlier in the year. They appeared for preliminary hearings before the Kimberley magistrate in September and October 1897, some charged with murder, others with rebellion and high treason.

The hearings focussed mainly on the murder of the white traders in Phokwani in December 1896. Nine men were charged with murder, the principal defendant being Petlhu. They all pleaded not guilty, but none of them had legal representation in court. The accused made statements in their own defence, each claiming that they were not present at the time of the murders, alibis that were mostly contradicted by other witnesses. The local Kimberley newspaper, the *Diamond Fields Advertiser*, praised the orderly nature of the magistrate's court proceedings, which had more of the military precision of a court martial than an ordinary police court. The paper admired the 'quiet and sedate bearing of the prisoners,' observing that one of the accused, Mootametsi (Paul Gasebonwe), 'spoke deliberately and with emphasis, using his right arm with the freedom of a practised orator.'[16] The defendants were bound over to remain in gaol, pending a decision concerning their appearance before the High Court for a formal trial.

In the meantime a lesser charge of 'seditiously taking up weapons and resisting the lawful authority of the Queen's Government' was brought

[15] *South Africa*, October 1897, p231.
[16] *Diamond Fields Advertiser*, 24 September 1897.

against a large number of Langeberg residents, and they appeared for trial at the High Court in Kimberley on 8 November 1897.[17] Originally more than a hundred men had been charged with this offence; but having suffered near-starvation through a prolonged siege in the Langeberg, they were in such poor physical condition at the time of their arrest that some died within days of their capture, others on the journey which they were obliged to walk, first to Kuruman and then on to Vryburg. Even then they do not appear to have received any medical attention because many more died during their imprisonment in Vryburg. By 8 November 1897 only fifty-eight were left alive to face trial.

When the judge, Mr Justice Laurence, asked why so many of the men listed in the indictment were not present in court, the Crown Prosecutor had to admit to the high mortality rate. When the prisoners had been brought into Vryburg, he told the court, they were in such a poor state that 'inquests were held almost daily.' The judge formally recorded that 'the large mortality was very regrettable.' He did not make clear whether he regretted that they had not been better looked after, or that they were no longer available for trial and punishment.

The principal accused on this charge of sedition were *Kgosi* Toto, his son, Robinyana, and Luka's son, Dikare. None of the fifty-eight defendants had legal representation in court. When asked to plead, Toto said: 'I am guilty because I did not put down my arms.'

Father and son: Toto and his eldest, Robinyana; both said to have been sent to Robben Island.

When asked whether this meant he was guilty of 'resisting the authority of the Queen', Toto responded: 'We were not resisting the authority of the Queen but were trying to escape.'

Justice Lawrence was not satisfied with this response. He told Toto that the charge was one of 'defying' and that he must either plead guilty or not

17 *Bechuanaland News*, 13 November 1897.

guilty. At this point Toto felt he had no choice and replied: 'I plead guilty. I don't deny it. I fired some shots.'

Robinyana, Dikare and all but two of the remaining fifty-five prisoners followed the lead of *Kgosi* Toto and pleaded guilty. Of the two who pleaded not guilty, one claimed that he had taken no part in the fighting; and the other said that he was blind and could not and did not take part in the rebellion. On looking through the case notes from the preliminary hearings, the judge could find no specific evidence against either of these men. So charges against them were withdrawn and they were discharged. Considering the dearth of detailed evidence against any of the accused, one cannot help wondering whether, if they had had proper legal representation, many more might have been discharged. Toto and the other accused, however, had all been persuaded to plead guilty and so the court proceeded on that assumption.

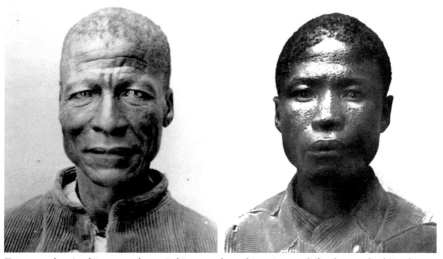

Toto, now showing his age, and son, Robinyana: dressed in prison garb for the standard ID photo.

In passing sentence the judge said that Toto would be dealt with severely because in receiving an annual allowance from the government, he was a paid servant of the Crown. As such, it was his duty to preserve peace and promote lawful conduct. Instead he had defied the Crown and led others into rebellion. On this basis, and in spite of Toto's estimated age of at least sixty-five, Justice Laurence sentenced him to six years' imprisonment with hard labour. Robinyana and Dikare, being considered responsible leaders among their people, were sentenced to four years each with hard labour, while all the remaining fifty-three prisoners were each sentenced to two years' hard labour.

Robinyana and Dikare in due course returned to the northern Cape to live among the remnants of their people. There is a belief among the Batlharo that Toto served time in the notorious Robben Island prison; but what exactly happened to him, either there or later, is not known for sure and should be a topic for future research.

According to the records of the resident magistrate in Kuruman,[18] Robinyana was at some stage committed to the mental asylum on Robben Island. His incarceration seems to have been linked to his refusal to accept the authority of the government or his eviction from the Langeberg. Time spent on Robben Island does not appear to have 'cured' Robinyana of his 'insanity'. On his conditional discharge from the asylum in 1906, he refused to live in Batlaros as assigned by the Kuruman magistrate. Asserting that, since he was a *kgosi*, he recognised no government authority, he defiantly returned to the Langeberg and built a house for himself and his wife at Gamasep. His presence there caused consternation among local white farmers who had bought land in the former Langeberg reserve. In January 1908 Robinyana was arrested, forcibly restrained and handcuffed, all the while shouting defiance of the authorities. He insisted that the Langeberg was the land of his grandfather and his father and that he had a right to die there and 'be buried near his father.' This latter point suggests that his father Toto had indeed returned home from prison in Cape Town to die in the Langeberg.

Back in 1897, a few weeks after the sentencing of Toto and his companions, Galeshewe, Petlhu (*below*) and the other Phokwani prisoners were brought before the magistrate again. This time they were committed for trial at the High Court of Griqualand West at the time of its next Criminal Session which was to be held in Kimberley in February 1898.

No fresh evidence was presented to the High Court that February. The purpose of the trial appears to have been merely to make a decision on the basis of the evidence that had already been collected at the magistrate's court. Accordingly, on the first charge of murder, the jury of nine white men found three of the accused – Jacob Manzana, Dibetswe and Raputsane – not guilty. The rest – Petlhu, Jacob Ramasabeta, Manone, Ramakulahadi, Radapeetsi and Paredi – were all found guilty of murder and sentenced to death. They were not offered any chance of appeal and all six were executed by hanging on 4 April 1898.[19]

---

[18] *CA*, AG 1808 (14071), Kuruman, papers re. Robinyana Toto
[19] *CA*, High Court Griqualand West, Criminal Session 1898/645.

hokwani prisoners awaiting trial, Kimberley gaol: (back row, from left) Andries Gasebonwe, Paul Gasebonwe, red Gasebonwe, Dibetchwe, Jacob Ramasabeta*, Paredi*, Magodi; (seated) Ramakulahadi*, Manone*, Galeshewe, etlhu*, Matingwe; (front) Maruping Pitsane, Jacob Manzana, Radapeetsi*. Marked* executed 4 April 1898.

The second charge, that of rebellion and high treason, was aimed mainly at those leading men within Phokwani who could be blamed for rebellion, but could not be convicted of murder. Telekela (Fred Gasebonwe) had died in prison, and charges against Petlhu and Manone were dropped because they were already under sentence of death. That left Galeshewe, Tyabu, Mootametsi (Paul Gasebonwe) and Matingwe.[20] Only Galeshewe was defended by a lawyer, E C Ward, and he argued his client's innocence on the grounds that Galeshewe had been at Bosman's on 26 December 1896 and so was not present in Phokwani at the time of the disturbances. He also appealed for leniency, as all Galeshewe's property had already been confiscated. The prosecutor argued that he was guilty because he did not give himself up; but Ward responded that Galeshewe did not give himself up because he could not trust the British.[21] All four men were found guilty, though the jury asked that leniency be shown to Tyabu because he was 'a common man'.

Despite his lawyer's plea, Galeshewe was sentenced to ten years imprisonment, with hard labour. Mootametsi got five years, Matinwe four and

[20] CA, 1/KIM, 1/2/1/1/1/17. Criminal Record Book, Kimberley, No.3468.
[21] Diamond Fields Advertiser, 12 February 1898.

Tyabu two years, all to be served 'with hard labour'. How long Mootametsi, Matingwe and Tyabu served is not known, but Galeshewe served five years in the Breakwater Prison in Cape Town before being released in 1903. He returned home to the Taung reserve, though not to Phokwani. That whole southern part of the reserve had been confiscated in 1897 and divided up into twenty-six farms for sale to white colonists.

Galeshewe was allowed to settle at the village of Modutung, near Taung. Having stripped him of his chieftaincy and having seized all his property and livestock, the government intended that he should live out his life in quiet retirement. In his annual report for 1904 Magistrate Bradshaw of Taung reported that 'ex-chief' Galeshewe had 'settled well to ordinary peasant life', adding that he had offered 'great assistance at the Census.'[22] Two years later, however, Inspector Davey of the local Taung police was reporting that Galeshewe was doing his best to 're-assert himself'. According to Davey the former *kgosi* had been cautioned three times by the resident magistrate during 1905, but he 'still has a large following.'[23] It appears that no amount of official government demotion affected the people's continuing respect for their true *kgosi*. But the government need not have worried. Galeshewe's days of open confrontation were behind him. He lived out his remaining days quietly in relative poverty. He died in his eighties in 1927 and was buried at Modutung in an unmarked grave.

To some extent the trials of 1897–98 for rebellion, treason and sedition were a colonial justification for the huge effort and expense of the six-month-long campaign waged against the residents and refugees of the Langeberg between February and August 1897. Aside from the conviction of the leading prisoners, however, the 'Bechuanaland Rebellion' was seen by South African colonists as a great opportunity: both to boost white settlement on confiscated land; and to reduce the Batswana of the northern Cape to a more subservient role within the colonial economy.

The relatively extensive native reserves of the original British Bechuanaland Land Settlement had allowed Africans to retain a certain level of economic independence, at least for a few more years. This had been influenced by the fact that as a Crown Colony it had come under the authority of the British imperial government rather than that of the local colonists of the Cape.

---

[22] G12 – 1904, *Blue Book of Native Affairs*, p51, R M Bradshaw, Taung.
[23] G46 – 1906, p31, Inspector Davey, Taung. Ironically, F R Thompson met Galeshewe in 1920 on a train to Kimberley on his way to give evidence to the Native Reserves Commission.

Under pressure from humanitarian lobbyists such as Revd Mackenzie and General Warren, the British had felt obliged, at least nominally, to protect the interests of the 'native' inhabitants from the more obvious depredations of land-hungry colonists. Thus for a while longer the Africans of British Bechuanaland had been able to engage with the cash economy on their own terms and on the whole avoid acceptance of the meagre wages offered by white farmers or the hardship of working in the mines. Following the transfer of the Crown Colony to the Cape in 1895, however, local colonists were eager to bring the region into line with the far more severe 'native policy' of the Cape Colony. The rebellion that started at Phokwani in 1896 provided all the excuse that they needed. The extent of the reserves could be greatly reduced, thus destroying at a stroke any lingering African hope of economic autonomy. The southern Batswana as a whole would be reduced to the position of second-class citizens whose economic purpose was to serve the labour interests of the colonial settlers – that very thing which Luka Jantjie had spent much of his adult life resisting.

The decision to pursue a policy of collective land confiscation for acts of rebellion in Bechuanaland was taken virtually the moment that the Phokwani reserve was declared to be 'in rebellion' in late December 1896. Collective land confiscation was in fact against colonial law, according to the legal opinion expressed by James Rose-Innes, Under Secretary for Native Affairs, in 1882.[24] In the light of the government's desire to confiscate land in Bechuanaland, therefore, the law was changed by a special Confiscation Act, signed into law on 25 June 1897. The legality, however, was six months behind the practice.

Within a day of the military occupation of Phokwani, Charles Bell had been appointed Special Commissioner with the authority to proceed immediately to Phokwani to supervise the clearance of the reserve. The estimated population of the Phokwani section of the Taung reserve before the rebellion was four thousand men, women and children, and those residents who could not obviously be arrested for murder, rebellion or sedition were 'apprenticed' out to work on white-owned farms in the Vryburg district. As the conflict spread to the Mashowing and finally to the Langeberg, Commissioner Charles Bell moved to Kuruman where he expected to carry out a similar role in those regions. Continued resistance in the Langeberg, however, had delayed the process and by the time of Toto's surrender on 2 August 1897 Bell had been replaced by Walter E Stanford, the Cape's Superintendent of

---

[24] G4 – '83, *Cape Native Laws and Customs (Tembuland) Commission*, Vol I, evidence of J Rose-Innes, 6 May 1882.

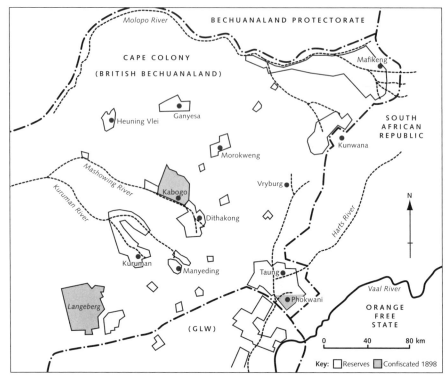

MAP 22: *Land confiscation, 1898: compare with maps 14 and 16 on pages 162 and 184.*

Native Affairs (later Sir Walter Stanford). Under-Secretary Rose-Innes took over Stanford's role in Cape Town as Acting Superintendent of Native Affairs.

Stanford's brief was to supervise the removal of all Batswana from the Langeberg region, 'loyals' as well as 'rebels'. The former were to be packed into the lower Kuruman reserve at Gamopedi – temporarily depopulated since the government's raid on the town in March 1897. The latter, the 'rebels' and their families, were declared prisoners of war and as such were to be collectively apprenticed out to white settlers as indentured labourers. The government's intent was 'to place them as far as we can from their country so as to make their return to it difficult if not impossible.'[25]

The prisoners of war amounted to approximately 3,850 men, women and children. According to Trooper Greenwood of the Kaffrarian Rifles who had been camped in the Langeberg for a week after the final battle 'Some of the men…had legs just like drum sticks and as for the women and children they were like skeletons, a great number had partly healed wounds.'[26] Revd

[25] NA 253, Native Affairs to Stanford, 18 August 1897, Stanford Telegram Book.
[26] UCT Archives, Trooper Greenwood typescript, 18 September 1897.

Prisoners captured in the Langeberg suffering in a crowd in Kuruman waiting to walk to Vryburg.

John Tom Brown reported that they arrived in Kuruman in a terrible state, many having died during their long walk from the Langeberg and all having a 'very starved look.'[27] Nevertheless, some remained defiant. Interviewed by F R Thompson, they spoke contemptuously of the fearfulness of the colonial troops who had confronted them in the early months of the campaign before starvation had weakened their ability to continue the fight. Asked by Thompson, 'Will you fight again?' one man replied: 'As I feel now, no; but perhaps when I get fat again I might feel differently.'[28] For most, however, fighting would have been furthest from their minds as they suffered from the winter cold with no protection in the fenced enclosure on the outskirts of the town.

With many dying in Kuruman (31 by the end of August), the children especially suffering from dysentery and some children allegedly being stolen from the camp, Stanford recognised that the scale of the task was too great for the resources immediately available. He proposed the release of those considered unfit for work and was eventually given authority to do so. Between 16 and 19 August 1897 Stanford released 1,763 prisoners. Among those released was Luka's widow, Masehoro, who was sent to Manyeding where she was made the responsibility of her late husband's brother, Olebile Devolk Jantjie.[29] Most of the remainder of those released were children with relatives to go to and adults considered too old or too infirm for work.

It was proposed that the remaining 2,000 prisoners would become indentured farm labourers in the Cape Town region of the colony where they would be far from their homes. But the government was sensitive to the fact that compulsory indentured labour had been internationally classified as a form of slavery, so to avoid this inconvenience Stanford was instructed:

[27] *LMS*, J T Brown, Kuruman, 9 August 1897.
[28] *Cape Times*, 28 September 1897.
[29] Evidence of Molehabangwe Jantjie, interviewed by the author at Manyeding, March 1978.

Prisoners at prayer in their Cape Town prison camp awaiting selection as indentured labourers.

> You must put to every man the question whether he will come and take employ-
> ment in the Western Province at wages and food under Government supervision
> or stand his trial as a rebel so as to make the legal position assured.[30]

The threat of trial was clearly a bluff as the government had already arrested
the one hundred men whom it considered it had most chance of prosecuting
for rebellion. The choice was thus a fiction, but for the sake of legal niceties
the government wished to establish the notion that the prisoners had willingly accepted their indenture to the western Cape.

The terms of service, Stanford was told, 'will be five years, but if they
object but not otherwise you may make it three years. ... You will endeavour
to make the period of service five years if possible.'[31]

Stanford appears to have experienced little difficulty in cajoling the prisoners into 'volunteering' for five years' service. A numbered brass tag was
placed around each man and woman's neck and between 19 and 26 August
more than 2,000 men, women and children were despatched on foot to
Vryburg in groups of 300. Fourteen died during the 200 kilometre walk to
Vryburg and seventy-seven died in the Vryburg camp, awaiting transporta-
tion to Cape Town.

While many white colonists had no sympathy for the prisoners and some
were eager to benefit from their cheap labour, the Aborigines' Protection
Society in Britain expressed outrage at the Cape government's policy towards
the prisoners of the Langeberg. In particular they objected to their being
forced into indentured labour which was 'akin to slavery'. On 7 September
a group of fifteen white women of Cape Town, led by the missionary wives
Mrs John Moffat and Mrs Elisabeth Hepburn (*see pp288–9*), managed to have
a meeting with Acting Prime Minister Sir James Sivewright. They presented
him with a formal petition objecting to the Cape government's policy and
calling for its immediate abandonment. Their reasons were so eloquently
argued that they are worth quoting at some length:

---

[30] NA 253, Native Affairs Dept. to Stanford, 12 August 1897.
[31] NA 253, NA Dept. to Stanford, 13 August 1897.

Farmer selecting indentured labourers to work on his farm; see official advertisement below.

1. That this summary method of punishing a whole community confuses all distinctions of degrees of guilt, and is contrary to all principles of even-handed justice. …

2. That the proposed punishment seems scarcely justified by law, to say nothing of the principles of equity. It has been stated that the alternative was offered the prisoners of accepting compulsory apprenticeship, or standing their trial for high treason. Not to speak of the hollow mockery of such a proposal, where unknown terrors were held up on one side, and practically no choice was left save the other, it seems a strange method of legal arraignment to settle a penalty without a fair trial.

3. That it is contrary to all civilised precedent to treat conquered people in this fashion. The hardships caused by defeat, the devastation of homes and lands, and the bloodshed of the war itself, may well be regarded as sufficient punishment for the mass of the people. To these has been added in the present case, the further severe penalty of confiscation of territory, so that the punishment might well satisfy the most exacting without further measures.

White women, probably including Mrs Moffat and Mrs Hepburn, visit the camp to provide succour.

4. That the proposed punishment differs in no essential point from the enslavement of the people, and is therefore contrary to the most deep-rooted instincts and dearest principles of our race. It seems scarcely credible that the very measures which caused such outcry and indignation when they were attempted or carried out in recent times, in neighbouring countries, should now be sanctioned in our own Colony. ... We have refused in the past to recognise any real distinction between compulsory apprenticeship and slavery, and we cannot uphold any such difference now.[32]

This delegation of liberal-minded white women was an early foreshadowing of the Black Sash movement that joined the struggle against apartheid half a century later. Despite their eloquence, however, the Moffat and Hepburn delegation received little satisfaction from the Acting Prime Minister. Sivewright insisted that the contracts were being entered into voluntarily and considering the state in which these people were at the end of the war, the government's policy of employment was one of 'humanitarian concern'.

The government pushed ahead with its chosen form of collective punishment and over the following week 1,896 men women and children were transported by train to Cape Town where twelve more died before they could begin their contracts.

Mrs Moffat's husband, J S Moffat (*above*), challenged the validity of the government's supposed choice between signing up or standing trial, and at his instigation two men were returned from Cape Town to Kimberley in

32 *Cape Argus Weekly*, 8 September 1897.

November to stand trial. The Crown Prosecutor declined to prosecute as there was no evidence to bring against them and the two men were set free.[33]

Following the controversy and disgrace that had characterised the Langeberg campaign and its aftermath, the population removals of 1897 can be seen as a deliberate attempt to erase the existence of these Batswana communities.

The colonial establishment was helped in this regard by the looming South African War that was to engulf the whole region in 1899. That war's larger scale of horrors immediately pushed the Bechuanaland story into obscurity. And during the reconstruction of South Africa that followed the restitution of peace in 1902, the story of *Kgosi* Luka Jantjie and the resistance of the Batlhaping and Batlharo faded rapidly from the general South African consciousness.

This process was aided by the massive Batlhaping and Batlharo loss of homes and land and the huge displacement of people to far-off farms in the western Cape or the mining compounds of Kimberley and Johannesburg. With whole communities dispersed, chiefly authorities destroyed, demoted or humiliated, the communities' links with their history and culture were weakened or lost altogether.

The story of how Robinyana Toto was labelled a lunatic because of his unrelenting defiance perhaps symbolises the fate of the whole community. While it is true that two of the farms in the Langeberg area still bear the names of Luka and Toto, many more are named after the white officers who fought against them – Dalgety, Spence, Woon, Hopkins, Harris, Lukin, Fuller, Smyth(e) and even Searle.[34]

It is interesting to note that the name of Luka's cousin, Galeshewe, against whom no shameful atrocities were committed, has been allowed to live on, and has recently been raised to new heights. Even in the apartheid era the main African township of Kimberley was named after Galeshewe. In recent years a greater effort has been made to raise his profile in the public consciousness. A South African naval ship has been named in his honour and a gravestone was erected over his unmarked grave in Modutung in 2007. In 2010 the South African state awarded Galeshewe a high posthumous

---

[33] AG 523 (245/97), Kimberley, 23 November 1897.

[34] Harris and Hopkins died in the Langeberg campaign, but Dalgety, Spence, Lukin, Temple Smyth and Woon all went on to fight for the British in the Anglo-Boer War. Dalgety served with distinction at the siege of Wepener in April 1900, and Spence was mentioned in dispatches on being killed in action at Douglas on 30 May 1900.

honour for his bravery in fighting the colonialists at Phokwani. In April 2010 *Kgosi* Kgosiemang Mothibi of the Phuduhutŝwana Batlhaping, received from President Jacob Zuma the Order of Mendi for Bravery (Gold) on behalf of the late *Kgosi* Galeshewe-a-Botlasitse of Phokwani.[35]

There can be no dispute that leaders of early African resistance to colonialism in South Africa deserve posthumous honour in this way. Unfortunately, however, the recent elevation of Galeshewe has been at the expense of his cousin, Luka Jantjie. In raising the profile of the brief Phokwani resistance of December 1896, the far more significant Langeberg resistance, partially in defence, ironically, of Galeshewe, but undisputedly led by Luka Jantjie, has once more been relegated in the country's historical memory. Even Galeshewe himself had acknowledged that Luka was 'the backbone of the Langeberg Resistance.'[36] Thus, surely the greatest hero of Batlhaping resistance in the late nineteenth century, the leader who throughout his life had refused to accept colonial subjugation and who stood firm to the last was *Kgosi* Luka Jantjie.

Luka Jantjie deserves a higher profile in the annals of southern African history and it is hoped that this book has done something to rectify that omission. Here was a traditional African leader who sought through his life and leadership to demonstrate an alternative to the racism that confronted him.

Luka Jantjie did not hark back to some ancient pre-colonial ideal that European culture was destroying. He embraced many aspects of the economic and cultural changes that the European presence had introduced to South Africa, not least its Christianity and its literacy. But unlike some of his near-contemporaries who wholeheartedly accepted the new Christian literate culture, Luka Jantjie did not seek to distance himself from his traditional cultural roots. He sought to marry the two: the old and the new. It is not too fanciful to think that he sought a modern African way to live in a non-racial South Africa. It was the racist aggression inherent in colonialism itself that denied him that right and cast him in the role of rebel and resistance fighter.

35 *Diamond Fields Advertiser*, 26 April 2010.
36 *South Africa*, October 1897, p231.

KEY CHARACTERS

Batlhaping
Luka Jantjie's family
Mohalabangwe (great grandfather)
Mothibi (grandfather)
Kegogile (grandmother)
Jantjie (father)
Kegipeling (mother)
Gasiikangwe, Masehoro (wives)
Dikare (eldest son)
Kaelo, Olebile, Peter (brothers)

Galeshewe's family
Mothibi (great grandfather)
Mahuto (great grandmother)
Gasebonwe (grandfather)
Botlasitse (father)
Morebonoke (uncle) (Andries
  Gasebonwe)
Gasebaatje, Mootametsi (Paul
  Gasebonwe), Piet Moncho, Telekela
  (Fred Gasebonwe) (brothers)
Petlhu (cousin)

Mankurwane's family
Mohalabangwe (grandfather)
Mahura (uncle & regent)
Molala (son)
Bogosin, Maswe, Kgalagadi (cousins)

Batlharo
Toto's family
Makgolokwe (father)
Robinyana (eldest son)
Seimpe (brother)
Morwe & Bareki (cousins)

Other African leaders
Montshiwa (*Barolong*)
Nicholas Waterboer (*Griqua*)
David Mosweu, Taaibosch &
  Jan Bloem (*Korana*)
Mampe (*headman, Kabogo*)
Khama (*Bangwato*)

Missionaries
LMS: Robert Moffat (*Kuruman*),
Holloway & Anne Helmore
(*Dikgatlhong*), William Ross, William
Ashton (*Barkly West*) , Alfred J Wookey,
John Brown (*Taung*), John Tom Brown,
John Mackenzie (*also administrator*),
John S Moffat (*also administrator*)
Anglican, Phokwani: W Henry R Bevan

Local colonial administrators
Richard Southey, Sidney Shippard,
William Lanyon (*also military*), John
Ford (*Kho*)), Sam Edwards, Charles Bell,
C Bam (*Kuruman*)

Traders, law agents and landowners
A W Greef, W H Phillipson (*Hopetown*),
Stafford Parker (*Klipdrift*), David Bebell,
John & Willie Chapman, Arthur &
Alphonse Blum (*Phokwani*), Charles
Robinson (*Kabogo*), Frank Pearce
(*Langeberg*); John Donovan, David Arnot,
Theodore Doms; Francis Thompson &
son, F R 'Matabele' (*Cornforth Hill*)

Colonial military officers
Charles Warren (*Bechuanaland
Expedition 1885*), George Dennison
(*Kabogo & Khuis*); *Langeberg soldiers 1897*:
Edmund Dalgety (*in command*), Frank
Johnson, James Searle, Temple Smyth,
William Spence, Harry Woon

Cape politicians
Governors: Philip Wodehouse, Henry
Barkly, Bartle Frere, Hercules Robinson;
mining magnate & PM of Cape: Cecil
Rhodes; Gordon Sprigg (*PM*)

Boers
M W Pretorius (*President, South African
Republic*), G J van Niekerk (*Stellaland*),
Piet Bosman (*Transvaal border farmer*)

INDENTURED: A PERSONAL PERSPECTIVE

Extracts from 'Jottings', a memoir by Elizabeth Hepburn, 1928
Elizabeth Hepburn, widow of LMS missionary, James
D Hepburn, spent twenty years among the Batswana of
present-day Botswana living first among Khama's Bangwato
and then among the Batawana near Lake Ngami. Elizabeth
recorded her memories thirty years after the events of the
Langeberg, but she had kept letters, notes and press cuttings
from the period. Together they provide us with a vivid
contemporaneous description of the desperate state that
Luka and Toto's people found themselves in.

By this time [1897], I had, with my children, settled at Wynberg, Cape Town,
believing that my active participation in work among the Bechuana people was
ended. I was mistaken. A tragic door was opened for me to minister to hundreds of
men, women and children, who had been suddenly exiled from their country and
home.

There is no doubt that the natives of the Langeberg district were harshly treated,
and harassed in many respects. One part of the country was desirable for White
settlers – the natives when subdued would afford labour for the Western Province
farmers, who required servants.

A number of prominent ladies in Cape Town and suburbs joined me in
addressing a strong protest to Sir James Sivewright, and when Sir Gordon Sprigg
returned, a protest was made to him regarding the cruel treatment meted out to the
indentured women prisoners. On both occasions we were courteously received but
we did not feel that any impression was made on either gentleman.

Several of the ladies went with me to see the first company of the Bechuana
prisoners. There are over a hundred youths and boys – most of the latter were the
herd boys of the tribe and had nothing to do with the fighting. Many of them had
never even handled a gun.

We spoke to them, at first they seemed too surprised to reply when they were
addressed in their language by a stranger, but when they realised that I was a
missionary who had lived among Khama's people, they completely changed and
became friendly and communicative.

Saw the new arrival of prisoners today – some of them had left children behind
– separated from them in an attack. One woman distressed about her little child
lost in a crowd during a rush.

Was refused entry today as I had interpreted for a gentleman whose questions
were calculated to 'make mischief'.

Represented to the Inspector that it was necessary for me to be allowed to visit
the prisoners as I was the only one who could appeal to them in their language,
and give them a little comfort and sympathy in their peculiarly distressing
circumstances.

Some of the Langberg " rebels." The father died on the journey south, *(original caption)*

Have received permission to visit them. Hear that Mr Moffat and Mr Garrett [Cape Times editor] had been turned back from the gate and had to get permits from the Native Affairs Office.

This morning saw a man and woman being indentured – the baby on the woman's back had a strange look. It was cold – dead. I took them back to the prison. In her gaze was the look of a hunted animal.

Another company today – one young mother gave birth to a stillborn babe on the train journey. Such heartbreaking tales of little ones left behind, several babies dying in their mother's arms on the terrible journey from Langeberg.

How can I write what I saw today? A woman, indentured to a farmer, her face bruised and swollen. Her master, because she was unable to perform the heavy task put upon her, felled her senseless with his crutch.

Many questions were asked me today by the women. Shall we be treated in the same way? Are all white masters alike? The Government has prosecuted the farmer. £10 fine.

The last company arrived today. The depot is crowded with farmers, scanning and examining men, women and children. A man sitting on the ground, holding a puny baby, another tiny mite sitting beside him. The mother died on the journey.

Constant cases of cruelty are occurring – heartsickening cases. Many farmers have been, and are being tried in the courts.

The indenturing is over – some parents are waiting for sick children to recover or die – then they go to their masters.

The curtain is being slowly rolled down on the closing scene of this soul-harrowing drama.

The scene staged shows me captive fathers and mothers weeping over little ones dead or dying, shows me my dark skinned sisters with features swollen and disfigured by the blows of white men.

Instead of music I hear the tap-tap of the hammer as the nails are being driven into tiny coffin lids, the sighing of the prisoners and the moans of suffering women and children, and this is our Queen's Jubilee Year.

289

SELECT BIBLIOGRAPHY

Research on the history of the people involved in this story is ongoing. There has been a recent revival of interest in the history of the Batlhaping and Batlharo in the late-nineteenth century and there is much work still to be done and other stories to be researched and written about the people mentioned in this book. In particular descendants and relatives of some of those involved in the Langeberg war of 1897, on both sides of the conflict, have been investigating and bringing to light stories, letters and photographs of their ancestors and relatives.

My primary focus in this book has been on the story of Luka Jantjie, and so the sources listed in this bibliography concern matters pertaining to his life. A more detailed bibliography for the period and people covered by this book can be found in: Kevin Shillington, *The Colonisation of the Southern Tswana, 1870–1900* (Ravan Press, Johannesburg, 1985), pp267–99. But research for a book like this is a never-ending project and even as the book has been going to press, further snippets of information, anecdotes and illustrations have come to light: as much of these as possible have been included, but there comes a time when the printing press must finally roll.

The principal sources from which I have drawn this story of the life and times of Luka Jantjie are:

Manuscript collections:
Cape Archives (CA): Griqualand West, 1871–80 (GLW 1-184); British Bechuanaland Land Commission, original claims and minutes of evidence, 1885–86 (BBLC 8-12 & 31); Bechuanaland Crown Colony, 1883–95 (BCC 1-117); Native Affairs Department (Cape Colony), 1880–1900 (NA 184-253); Prime Minister's Office (Cape Colony), 1895, 1897 (PMO 132, 254); Attorney-General's Department (Cape Colony), 1897 (AG 497 & 522-3); High Court, Griqualand West – Criminal Sessions, 1879 (619, 620), 1898 (645); Resident Magistrate, Kimberley, 1897–98

London Missionary Society (LMS): The archives of the LMS, housed in the library of the School of Oriental and African Studies (SOAS) in London, are a major source of primary evidence for the Batlhaping in the nineteenth century. The missionaries' regular 'Incoming' letters to their London headquarters – at least once a year, sometimes more – are housed under Africa (South), Bechuanaland and are listed and stored chronologically. For the period 1820–99 see principally Dithakong (Lattakoo/Letako), Kuruman (New Lattakoo), Griquatown (Klaarwater), Dikgatlhong (Likatlong), Bothithong (Motito), Taung (Taungs) and Barkly West.

Society for the Propagation of the Gospel (SPGA, London): Reports and correspondence from the Bloemfontein Mission to the Bechuana, Phokwani, 1877–99

United Kingdom National Archives NA(UK) [formerly Public Records Office (PRO)]: Griqualand West, Original Correspondence, 1875–80 (CO 107/1-9)

University of Cape Town (UCT) Archives

Private papers (unpublished):
J D Barry, High Court Judge and Recorder, Griqualand West, and Acting
Administrator (1878) (*Jagger Library,* University of Cape Town); Holloway and Anne
Helmore, private correspondence, 1840–59 (*Transvaal Archives* A928); W O Lanyon,
private correspondence, 1876–9 (*Transvaal Archives,* A596); J Mackenzie, private
correspondence, 1855–90 (*University of Witwatersrand,* A75); R Southey, private
correspondence, 1866–72 (*Cape Archives,* A611); James Wykeham letter-books,
Hopetown, 1868–70 (*De Beers Archives,* Kimberley, NAD68)

Official published papers:
British Parliamentary Papers (GBPP): various correspondence, 1871–98, re. *Affairs
of South Africa, Transvaal, Bechuanaland and Adjacent Territories; Cape Parliamentary
Papers*: A14 – '77. *Census of Griqualand West* (1877); A23, 30, 35, 52 – '78, *Papers re.
Native Disturbances, Griqualand West*; A80 – '81, *Return of Farms and Lands granted
in Griqualand West* (1880); A58 – '83, *Petition by Mankoroane and Councillors for
annexation of Tlhaping Territory by the Cape Government (25 May 1883)*; G13 – '91,
*Report of Commission to select land in British Bechuanaland, under Railway Agreement
of 23rd January 1890*; A7 – '93, *Return of Revenue from Native Locations*; G33 – '97,
Special Report on Rinderpest in South Africa (1896–97); G78 – '97, *Rinderpest: Report
of Native Representatives, Bechuanaland*; G3 – '98, *Lt Colonel Dalgety's Report on
Bechuanaland Rebellion* (1897); G4 – '98, *Reports by W E Stanford and J Rose Innes on
disposal of Bechuanaland Rebels*; G10 – '98, *Bechuanaland Rising, War Losses*; G57 – '98,
*Bechuanaland Natives Reserves Commission; Blue Books of Native Affairs, annual reports,
1880-98*

Occasional Publications: *Bloemhof Blue Book. Evidence taken at Bloemhof ...* (Cape
Town 1871); *Evidence taken before Judge Stockenstrom (1875–1876) in the matter of
certain Land Claims* (Cape Town 1877); *Report on the Land Question in Griqualand
West by Lt Col Warren* (Colonial Office, London, 1880)

Contemporary Newspapers and periodicals:
Bechuanaland News, 1888–98; *Cape Argus (& Cape Argus Weekly)*, 1878, 1897–98;
Cape Times (& Cape Times Weekly), 1897–98; *Diamond Field*, 1870–77; *Diamond Fields
Advertiser*, 1878–98; *Diamond News*, 1870–80; *Eastern Province Herald*, 1868–70;
South African Telegraph Bi-Weekly, 1896–7; *The Weekly Press* (Pretoria) 1895–1898; *The
Cape*, 1897–1908; The *Cape Illustrated Magazine*, 1899; *South Africa* (London, UK);
The Graphic (UK), 1870–1900; *Illustrated London News* (UK), 1860–1900

Contemporary publications, and private papers subsequently published:
F ALGAR, *The Diamond Fields, with notes on the Cape Colony and Natal* (London 1872)
J L BABE, *The South African Diamond Fields* (New York 1872, facsimile reprint
   Kimberley 1976)
J BARROW, *A Voyage to Cochin China ... to which is annexed an account of a journey
   made in the years 1801 and 1802 to the residence of the chief of the Booshuana nation*
   (London 1830)

J T BROWN, *Among the Bantu Nomads* (London 1926)

W J BURCHELL, *Travels in the Interior of Southern Africa*, 2 vols (London 1822–24, 2nd edition (ed. I Schapera) 1953)

J CAMPBELL, *Travels in South Africa, Second Journey*, 2 vols (London 1822)

J CHAPMAN, *Travels in the Interior of South Africa*, 2 vols (London 1868)

R GORDON CUMMING, *The Lion Hunter of South Africa. Five Years Adventures in the far interior of South Africa, with Notices of the Native Tribes and Savage Animals* (London 1850)

C G DENNISON, *A History of Stellaland* (Vryburg 1928)

C G DENNISON, *Zulu Frontiersman* (ed. R Lock & P Quantrill, Barnsley 2008)

H R FOX BOURNE. 'The Case for "The Bechuana Rebels"', *Fortnightly Review*, LXII, 371 (1 November 1897), New Series, pp708–17

E HEPBURN, *Jottings: by Khama's friend* (London 1928)

E HOLUB, *Seven Years in South Africa*, 2 vols (2nd edition (trsl. E E Frewer) London 1881)

F JOHNSON, *Great Days, the autobiography of an empire pioneer* (London 1940)

W H C LICHTENSTEIN, *Travels in Southern Africa*, 2 vols (London 1814, VRS edition Cape Town 1930)

W H C LICHTENSTEIN, *Foundation of the Cape. About the Bechuanas* (1807, trsl. & ed. O H Spohr, Cape Town 1973)

J MACKENZIE, *Austral Africa, Losing it or Ruling it, being incidents and experiences in Bechuanaland, Cape Colony and England*, 2 vols (London 1887)

J MACKENZIE, *Papers of John Mackenzie* (ed. A J Dachs, Johannesburg 1975)

J W MACQUARRIE, *The Reminiscences of Walter Stanford*, 2 vols (Cape Town 1962)

F MACNAB, *On Veldt and Farm* (London 1897)

J S MOFFAT, *The Lives of Robert and Mary Moffat* (London 1886)

R MOFFAT, *Missionary Labours and Scenes in Southern Africa* (London 1842)

R MOFFAT, *Apprenticeship at Kuruman, being the journals and letters of Robert and Mary Moffat, 1820–28* (ed. I Schapera, London 1951)

R MOFFAT, *The Matabele Journals of Robert Moffat, 1829–60*, 2 vols (ed. J P R Wallis, London 1945)

R U MOFFAT, *John Smith Moffat, CMG, Missionary. A Memoir* (London 1921)

F C SELOUS, *A Hunter's Wanderings in Africa* (London 1881)

A SMITH, *The Diary of Dr Andrew Smith*, 2 vols (VRS edition Cape Town 1939)

A SMITH, *Andrew Smith's Journal of his Expedition into the Interior of South Africa, 1834–36* (ed. W F Lye, Cape Town 1975)

F R THOMPSON, *The Autobiography of Matabele Thompson* (ed. N Rouillard, London 1936)

C WARREN, *On the Veldt in the Seventies* (London 1902)

R WILLIAMS, *The British Lion in Bechuanaland* (London 1885)

R WILLIAMS, *How I Became a Governor* (London 1913)

H V WOON, *Twenty-Five Years Soldiering in South Africa* (London 1909)

Published Secondary Sources:

P-L BREUTZ, *The Tribes of Kuruman and Postmasburg* (Pretoria 1963)

P-L BREUTZ, *History of the Batswana* (Margate, Natal 1989)

M DICKSON, *Beloved Partner: Mary Moffat of Kuruman* (London 1976)

E ELBOURNE, *Blood Ground: Colonialism, Missions, and the Contest for Christianity in the Cape Colony and Britain, 1799–1853* (Montreal 2002)

N ETHERINGTON, *The Great Treks: The Transformation of Southern Africa, 1815–1854* (Harlow 2001)

C HAMILTON (ed.), *The Mfecane Aftermath: Reconstructive Debates in Southern African History* (Johannesburg 1995)

N J JACOBS, *Environment, Power and Injustice. A South African History* (Cambridge 2003)

M KOBOEKAE, *Taung Wells* (Cape Town, 2004); [a historical novel set in Batlhaping society in 19th century, published by Kwela Books]

P LALU, *The Deaths of Hintsa: Post-apartheid South Africa and the Shape of Recurring Pasts* (Cape Town 2009)

P S LANDAU, *Popular Politics in the History of South Africa, 1400–1948* (Cambridge 2010)

M C LEGASSICK, *The Politics of a South African Frontier: The Griqua, the Sotho-Tswana and the Missionaries, 1780–1840;* his 1969 thesis, introduced by R Ross (Basel 2010)

P T MGADLA AND S VOLZ (translated and edited), *Words of Batswana: Letters to Mahoko a Becwana* 1883–1896 (Cape Town 2006)

S M MOLEMA, *Montshiwa, Barolong Chief and Patriot, 1814–1896* (Cape Town 1966)

N ORPEN, *The Cape Town Highlanders 1885–1970* (Cape Town 1970)

N PARSONS, *King Khama, Emperor Joe and the Great White Queen* (Chicago 1998)

N PARSONS, *Clicko: The Wild Dancing Bushman* (Johannesburg 2009; Chicago 2010)

M ROBERTSON, *Diamond Fever. South African Diamond History, 1866–69, from Primary Sources* (Cape Town 1974)

R ROSS, 'The Kora Wars on the Orange River, 1830–80,' *Journal of African History,* XVI, 4 (1975), pp561–76

R J L SABATINI, K DUMINY, *Fifty years on the diamond fields, 1870–1920* (Kimberley 2007)

H SAKER & J ALDRIDGE, 'The Origins of the Langeberg Rebellion,' *Journal of African History,* XII, 2 (1971), pp299–317

I SCHAPERA, *The Tswana* (London 1953)

I SCHAPERA, *Tribal Innovators: Tswana Chiefs and Social Change, 1745–1940* (London 1970)

K SHILLINGTON, *The Colonisation of the Southern Tswana, 1870–1900* (Johannesburg 1985)

K SHILLINGTON, 'Irrigation, Agriculture and the State: The Harts Valley in Historical Perspective', in W BEINART, P DELIUS & S TRAPIDO (eds.), *Putting a Plough to the Ground: Accumulation and Dispossession in Rural South Africa, 1850–1930* (Johannesburg 1986), pp311–35

A SILLERY, *Founding a Protectorate* (London 1965)

A SILLERY, *John Mackenzie of Bechuanaland, 1835–99. A study in humanitarian imperialism* (Cape Town 1971)

E C TABLER, *The Far Interior* (Cape Town 1955)

C VAN ONSELEN, 'Reactions to Rinderpest in South Africa, 1896–97,' *Journal of African History (JAH)*, XIII, 3 (1972), pp473–88

W W WILLIAMS, *The Life of General Sir Charles Warren* (Oxford 1941)

Unpublished theses and dissertations:

J D ALDRIDGE, 'The Langeberg Rebellion, 1896–7: a study of an African Society under the Pressures of Colonialism' (MA dissertation, SOAS, University of London 1968)

A J DACHS, 'Missionary Imperialism in Bechuanaland, 1813–1896' (PhD thesis, University of Cambridge 1968)

I B SUTTON. 'The 1878 Rebellion in Griqualand West and Adjacent Territories' (PhD thesis, University of London 1975)

Oral informants *(interviewed February–March 1978)*:

Manyeding: Molehabangwe Jantjie, Olebile Jantjie, Mpete Bodunele, Prince Setungwane, Sianang Moseki, Galeleywe Galeleywe, Titus Museke; *Batlaros*: Frans Kgokong, Kaborone Sebeco, Jonas Sekobe; *Bothithong*: Jimson Mukime, Sengalboy Ejang, June Basiani, Wilson Basiani, Mrs Monchu, George Motlaro; *Dithakong*: Kgosi Motshwarakgolwe, Neogaborone, Peter Sebati; *Cassel*: Kgosi Thaganyane, Marubis, Joseph Tong; *Taung*: Cecil John Matolo, James Bantobetsi, John Olivant; *Magogong*: John O'Reilly; *Hartigan* (*Phokwani*): W H 'Willie' White; *Manthe*: Kgosi Matlhabani; *Vlakfontein* (*Geysdorp*): Izaak Barnard

ACKNOWLEDGEMENTS

Although much of the writing and production of this book has taken place over the past three years, it had been simmering on the back burner for more than thirty years before that. Those people who so generously helped me during the original research in the late 1970s, and from which this project arose, were acknowledged in my *Colonisation of the Southern Tswana* (1985).

Foremost among those who have helped me since then has been my wife, Pippa, who has shared with me all the travels and tribulations of 'never-ending' research and without whose unstinting support and faith in the project it may never have come to fruition.

I am grateful, too, to Fiona Barbour formerly of the McGregor Museum in Kimberley who over the years has willingly provided hospitality as well as references for illustrations, obscure articles and snippets of information that have been invaluable in keeping 'Project Luka' on track. I am particularly grateful to her for organising and accompanying Pippa and me on a trip to the Langeberg where I was able to track down the site of Luka's 'last stand'. In a similar vein the late Revd Alan Butler, who did so much to restore the Kuruman mission station, was a constant source of encouragement and inspiration.

For their more recent help, I am grateful to the staff of the McGregor Museum: Robert Hart, Sephai Mngqolo, David Morris and Sunet Swanepoel for their keen and continuing support of the project and to the Director Colin Fortune who kindly gave permission to use their illustrations. Also extremely helpful were the staff of the University of Cape Town Archive, the Cape Archives and the South African Public Library in Cape Town, the Cullen Library, University of Witwatersrand and the Kimberley Africana Library.

My thanks, too, to artists and illustrators Judy Seidman, Kevin Ancient and Doug Hewitt.

Recently, too, through Dusty Muffin's internet blog on Luka Jantjie, descendants from the Langeberg campaign of 1897 – Siobhan Dawson, David Fayle, Wendy Goddard, Tumo Dikare Jantjie, Barbara Keitumetse Mashope, Robin Scott, the late Michael Searle and the late Professor Greenwood among many others – have brought to light valuable family insights, letters and pictures from the period.

I have indeed been fortunate in having John Aldridge and Charlotte Rolfe of Aldridge Press as my publisher and editor respectively. As publishers they have far exceeded my hopes and expectations. John, who has a personal academic interest in the Langeberg part of the story, has displayed enormous enthusiasm for the project, in particular in the research, selection and presentation of the illustrations in the book. Charlotte's perceptive reading of the manuscript through all its stages has been invaluable in tightening up the narrative and helping to ensure clarity. To both of them I am forever grateful.

Aldridge Press in turn gratefully acknowledge the advice and assistance of Cath

Bruzzone, Richard Balkwill, Imogen Dawson, Christine Hogg, Tim Horsler, Rupert Jones Parry, Peter Kallaway, Geoffrey Kay, Russell Martin, Jennifer Pegg, Nicolas Ridley, Geoff Wadsley, David Way, Richard Whiting of Robben Island Museum, Jane Wightwick, Brian Willan, Mark Wray and Langeberg residents Fanie van Vuuren and family and Ivan van der Walt.

I thank Veronica Klipp and Julie Miller of Wits University Press, Johannesburg and Chris Chappell of Palgrave Macmillan, New York for their contributions to the book's publication in South Africa and the United States respectively.

Finally, I am especially grateful to Nancy Jacobs, Shula Marks and Neil Parsons, who willingly set aside many hours to read early drafts of the manuscript. They provided invaluable comments and encouragement to proceed with revisions and get the book published. In the final analysis, however, the responsibility for any shortcomings in text or interpretation in this book is mine alone.

KEVIN SHILLINGTON

INDEX